THE COMPLETE GUIDE TO

Strength Training

A former British Natural Bodybuilding Champion, and one of the country's most respected sports nutritionists, **Anita Bean** is the award-winning author of newly published *Kids' Food for Fitness* and bestsellers *The Complete Guide to Sports Nutrition* and *Food for Fitness*

Also available from A & C Black
The Complete Guide to Sports Nutrition
(THIRD EDITION)
Anita Bean

Food for Fitness
(SECOND EDITION)
Anita Bean

Kids' Food for Fitness
Anita Bean

The Complete Guide to Circuit Training
Fiona Hayes

The Complete Guide to Endurance Training
Jon Ackland

The Complete Guide to Stretching
Christopher M. Norris

THE COMPLETE GUIDE TO

Strength Training

SECOND EDITION

Anita Bean

A & C Black • London

Published in 2001 by A & C Black Publishers Ltd
37 Soho Square, London W1D 3QZ

Second Edition 2001; reprinted 2002
First Edition 1997; reprinted 1998, 1999 and 2000

Copyright © 1997, 2001 by Anita Bean

ISBN 0 7136 6040 6

A & C Black uses paper produced with elemental chlorine-free pulp, harvested from managed sustainable forests.

Anita Bean has asserted her right under the Copyright, Designs and Patents Act, 1988, to be identified as the author of this work.

A CIP catalogue record for this book is available from the British Library.

Acknowledgements
I would like to thank my husband, Simon, for his enormous patience and understanding during the writing of this book. He did an excellent job of cooking and looking after our children at weekends while I was writing. My thanks also go to my editor Penny Clarke without whose vision and expertise this book would not have been written.

Cover photograph courtesy of Jump, Hamburg.

Photography by Grant Pritchard, copyright © 2001 by A & C Black Publishers Ltd.

Illustrations by Jean Ashley.

The author and publisher would like to thank London Central YMCA and Leatherhead Leisure Centre for the use of their facilities for the photo shoot. Enormous thanks also to Robin Gargrave, Nick Pettett and Dave Fanthorpe for modelling the exercises.

Typeset in $10^{1}/_{2}$ on 12pt Palatino

Printed and bound in Great Britain by Biddles Ltd, Guildford and King's Lynn

Contents

List of Abbreviations

For ease of reference, this list includes abbreviations that are used throughout the book.

1RM	One-rep max	GTOs	Golgi tendon organs
ATP	Adenosine Triphosphate	GH	Growth hormone
BPM	Beats per minute	IAAs	Indispensable amino acids
BV	Biological value	MHR	Maximum heart rate
BCAAs	Branched chained amino acids	MRP	Meal replacement product
DAAs	Dispensable amino acids	ORAC	Oxygen Radical Absorbance Capacity
DHA	Docosahexaoic acid	PC	Phosphocreatine
DPA	Docosapentanoic acid	ROM	Range of Movement
EPA	Eicosapentanoic acid	RPE	Rating of perceived exertion
EPOC	Excess post-exercise oxygen consumption	RDA	Recommended daily amount
FT	Fast twitch	RMR	Resting metabolic rate
GLA	Gamma-linolenic acid	Reps	Repetitions
GI	Glycaemic index	ST	Slow twitch
		THR	Training heart rate

List of Exercises

Legs:
Barbell squat
Dead lift
Leg press
Leg extension
Front lunge
Reverse lunge
Lying leg curl
Straight-leg dead lift
Standing calf raise
One-leg dumbbell calf raise
Leg press machine calf press

Back:
Lat pull-down
Chin (pull-up)
One-arm row
Seated cable row
Bent-over barbell row
Straight-arm pull-down
Dumbbell shrug
Back extension
Back extension with exercise (Swiss) ball

Chest:
Barbell bench press
Dumbbell bench press
Incline barbell bench press
Incline dumbbell bench press
Dumbbell flye
Pec dec flye
Cable cross-over

Shoulders:
Dumbbell press
Lateral raise

Upright row
Bent-over lateral raise

Arms:
Barbell curl
Preacher curl
Dumbbell curl
Incline dumbbell curl
Concentration curl
Triceps push-down
Bench dips
Lying triceps extension
Triceps kickback

Abdominals:
Crunch
Crunch with exercise ball
Reverse crunch
Oblique crunch
Oblique crunch with exercise ball
Side crunch
Hanging leg raise

Stretches:
Quadriceps
Adductors
Hamstrings
Hip flexors
Hips/gluteals
Calves
Lower back
Neck
Upper back
Shoulders
Chest/biceps
Triceps

Foreword by Bob Smith

I first met Anita a number of years ago when we lectured on the YMCA's fitness training courses. I noticed then how she was very interested in the education behind fitness and nutrition. Today this book represents the fulfilment of that interest and I was delighted when asked to write the Foreword, not only because I know Anita, but because the second edition of *The Complete Guide to Strength Training* is written with considerable expertise and I am certain it will go a long way to helping people achieve their goals.

Strength training is probably the most eclectic form of fitness training, meaning that many techniques and systems work for a variety of different people. No one approach is necessarily better than another, but a full understanding of a number of approaches is very helpful. A book about strength training therefore needs to be both comprehensive and varied. It requires a large number of ideas and strategies to cater for individual requirements, goals, body types and personalities.

Anita has successfully combined all of these ingredients resulting in a book that is comprehensive, accurate and written in an easy to follow style. Additional information is provided about surrounding issues such as diet, fat loss and muscle physiology, which is both helpful and necessary. In *The Complete Guide to Strength Training* the reader will discover an invaluable resource suitable for any professional involved in fitness training as well as the individual wishing to gain more from their time at the gym.
Enjoy!

Bob Smith M.A. (dist) B.Ed (Hons);
Cert Ed (dist);
Lecturer in Applied Sports Science,
Loughborough University

Preface to the Second Edition

Strength training is not simply about sculpting the body beautiful. It's about building inner strength and achieving goals.

I wrote the original edition of this book in 1997 as a tribute to my success as a natural bodybuilding champion (EFBB British Lightweight Champion, 1991) and to encapsulate the fulfilment that I had experienced from strength training. As a qualified sports nutritionist and fitness trainer, I wanted to share my knowledge and first-hand experience of the subject with you. I am passionate about strength training and believe everyone can benefit from it, both physically and mentally.

The Complete Guide to Strength Training translates the science of training and nutrition into practical advice, detailed training programmes and authoritative nutrition plans. In this Second Edition I have expanded and updated all of the information, as well as adding a lot of new material. I have developed goal-specific programmes to help beginners, intermediate and advanced strength trainers improve muscle size,

maximum strength, muscular endurance and sports performance. New fat-burning workouts are featured, as well as powerful advice on achieving better definition, and the nutrition material has been expanded and now includes eating plans for fat loss and weight gain. Throughout the text I have also included references to the original sources of information, giving you the opportunity to delve further into particular topics if you wish. And the book has undoubtedly benefited enormously from a new design and inspiring new photographs of every exercise.

I no longer compete but continue to strength train three times a week following all the advice in this book to the letter, as well as looking after my two very healthy young children, Chloe and Lucy.

I wish you every success in achieving your goals, and hope you experience the same pleasure from strength training that I do.

Good training!

Anita Bean
September 2001

Introduction

Would you like a physique that you can feel truly proud of, that makes you feel confident and gives you a great sense of accomplishment? A stronger, leaner, fitter body is within your grasp. By making that commitment to change and picking up this book, you've made a significant step towards it. The following pages provide you with an integrated plan of action to achieve your personal goals. They draw together scientifically proven training methods and cutting-edge nutritional advice to provide you with the tools to devise a comprehensive training programme for yourself.

Whether you want to develop strength or simply a more symmetrical physique, this book helps you to set your goals and focus your mind on reaching them. Part One unravels the science of muscle growth. It gives you the straight facts so that you can achieve your maximum potential for growth and get the best results.

Part Two provides an illustrated, step by step guide to the exercises that form the basis of the training programmes described in Part Three. It provides six chapters, each focusing on a different part of the body: legs, back, chest, shoulders, arms and abdominals. Each gives you practical training tips to help you perfect your technique and get the very most from each exercise. Part Two also provides a stretching programme to enhance your gains.

Part Three takes you right to the heart of programme design and shows you, step by step, how to plan your sessions to meet your goals. It explains how to train for muscle size, strength, overall tone and fat loss, and provides detailed goal-specific training programmes suitable for beginners, intermediate and advanced trainers. These programmes incorporate scientifically researched training methods and the principles of periodisation. Each workout details the aims, exercises, sets, repetitions, workout frequency, training tempo and workout duration.

Part Three also shows you how to improve your body symmetry and develop your physique to its best potential. There are 'smart' training rules for different body types and specific routines for correcting symmetry problems. If previous training attempts have resulted in painstakingly slow gains, this part also provides a troubleshooting guide and puts you back in control of your progress.

What you eat and drink is vital to your success in the gym and underpins any strength-training programme. Part Four focuses on nutrition, covering seven key topics:

- carbohydrate
- protein
- fat
- fluid
- vitamins and minerals
- antioxidants
- supplements.

It emphasises the issues most relevant to strength trainers and brings you the most current nutritional advice at the time of going to print. For those who struggle to put on muscle mass, this part helps you set realistic weight-gain goals and gives you practical weight-gain strategies. For those trying to shed body fat, there is authoritative advice on fat loss, and step-by-step guidance to calculate your calorie, carbohydrate, protein and fat requirements. Part Four then goes on to detail six eating plans to cut body fat and gain muscle.

Armed with the best training methods and nutrition strategies, you will achieve your goals and enjoy your success. Good training and good luck!

PART ONE

Planning a Strength-training Programme

Chapter 1

Get Started

Making that initial decision to start training is the most important step to achieving the physique you desire. This chapter explains why strength training is so good for you – not just for the sake of your appearance but also for your health – and in case you had any doubts about the benefits of this type of exercise, it sets the record straight on some popular myths and misconceptions. This chapter also deals with the practicalities of whether to train at home or at a gym, and gives you a useful checklist on choosing a gym to suit your needs. If you are wondering whether to use free weights or machines, this chapter weighs up the pros and cons and give you the scientifically proven facts on each method of training. Finally, it gives you practical pointers on workout accessories, such as belts and straps.

♦ Reasons to strength train ♦

Strength training is not only about getting physically stronger so that you can lift more weight. Here are some of the many benefits that a well-planned and well-executed programme can bring.

Increased muscle mass and strength

A well-planned weight-training programme that trains all muscle groups leads to increases in muscle size and strength. In contrast, endurance activities do not produce significant changes in strength or muscle mass. Research has shown that a basic weight-training programme lasting just 25 minutes followed three times a week can increase muscle mass by about 1 kg over an eight-week period[1], while lean mass gains of 20% of your starting body weight are common after the first year of training.

Strengthened tendons and ligaments

Weight training increases the strength of the tendons and ligaments and therefore improves joint stability. It stimulates the production of collagen proteins in the tendons and ligaments,[1] thus causing an increase in their structural strength.

Avoiding age-related muscle loss

Muscle mass and strength tend to decrease with age. Without strength training, adults typically lose 2.3–3.2 kg muscle every decade.[2,3] Muscle loss occurs mainly in the fast twitch (FT) muscle fibres, which are involved in strength and explosive activities (*see* p. 21). This cannot be prevented by cardio-vascular exercise – only strength training maintains muscle mass and strength as you get older.

Increased bone density

Strength training improves bone strength and increases bone protein and mineral content.[4] Studies show that the bones under the most stress from weight training have the highest bone mineral content.[5] For example, it has been shown that there are significant increases in the bone mineral content of the upper femur (thigh) after four months of strength training.[7] A US study found that women who followed a weight-training programme twice a week for one year developed 76% more bone strength than those who did no strength training. These findings therefore suggest that weight training reduces the risk of osteoporosis and bone fractures.

Increased metabolic rate

Strength training increases the resting metabolic rate (RMR) – the energy required for tissue maintenance and essential functions. This is due to the fact that strength training increases muscle tissue, which has a higher energy requirement than fat tissue – i.e. muscle tissue is metabolically active. People who strength train therefore use more calories throughout the day. Research has shown that adding 1.4 kg muscle increases the RMR by 7% and our daily calorie requirement by 15%.[2] Strength training also increases exercise metabolism. At rest, 0.45 kg muscle tissue requires 35 kcal/day. During exercise, energy expenditure rises dramatically – five to ten times above the resting level. Thus, the more muscle tissue you have, the greater the number of calories expended both during exercise and at rest.

The reduction in metabolic rate experienced by most people as they get older is due largely to a loss of muscle tissue. This loss accounts for the 2–5% decrease in RMR/decade experienced by non-exercising adults,[3,7] which may translate into unwanted body fat gain. Therefore, strength training is an excellent way of preserving muscle mass, preventing a reduction of metabolic rate and avoiding fat gain with age.

Reduced body fat

Without exercise, adults gain on average 7 kg of fat every decade. Strength training can help reduce body fat by increasing RMR (*see* above) and therefore daily calorie expenditure. One study found that strength training produced a loss of 1.8 kg fat after three months of training, despite a 15% increase in calorie intake.[1] Another study of 282 adult beginners found that after eight weeks of strength training and aerobic exercise, they lost almost 4 kg fat and gained 1.4 kg muscle – a significant improvement in body composition.

Reduced blood pressure

Strength training has been shown to lower both systolic and diastolic blood pressure. The effect is even greater if strength training is combined with aerobic training. An American study found that a combination of two months of strength training and aerobic exercise resulted in a decrease in systolic blood pressure of 5 mm Hg, and diastolic blood pressure of 3 mm Hg.[8]

Reduced blood cholesterol and blood fats

Studies have demonstrated improvements in blood cholesterol and blood triglycerides (fats) as a result of several weeks of strength training.[4, 9]

Improved posture

Strength training greatly improves overall posture, as well as correcting specific postural faults. A number of factors influence our posture, including skeletal structure, basic body type, strength and flexibility. Obviously, the first and second factors are controlled by our genetic make-up and cannot be altered. However, strength and flexibility can be changed through training or disuse (i.e. increased or decreased demand). Imbalances in these two components lead to postural faults, but these may be corrected through specific strength-training exercises and stretches.

Reduced injuries

A well-conditioned and well-balanced musculo-skeletal system has a much smaller chance of sustaining injury. A stronger body is better able to avoid or resist impact injuries from falls and activities such as running or jumping. Muscular imbalances are a common cause of injury: for example, under developed hamstrings (back of the thighs) relative to the quadriceps (front of the thighs) can make the knee joint unstable, thus increasing injury risk.

The majority of lower-back problems are due to weakness or imbalance of the deep muscles close to the spine and pelvis, which contribute to core stability (*see* p. 82). A well-designed strength-training programme will improve the strength of deep muscles in the the lower back and other muscles involved in posture, thus reducing the likelihood of injury. One study found that patients suffering lower-back pain had significantly less pain after ten weeks of specific strength exercises.[10]

Improved psychological well-being

Consistent strength training helps to reduce stress, anxiety and depression; uplift your mood; and promote more restful sleep. It may help decrease muscle tension due to the intensity of the muscular contractions. It also improves body image, which has a major effect on psychological well-being. Participants report that they have more energy, greater confidence and that they are prouder of their appearance.

Improved appearance

Personal appearance is greatly improved by strength training due to increased muscle tone, strength, function and improved posture. Changes in body composition mean an increase in lean mass and decrease in fat mass, both of which greatly enhance the way you look.

♦ The myths of strength ♦ training

Despite these well-recognised benefits of strength training, there are many myths that still exist. Here are some of the most popular misconceptions, along with the scientific facts.

Myth 1: strength training makes women look too bulky

Some women avoid strength training for fear that they will look too masculine. On the contrary, strength training actually enhances a woman's femininity. It improves the tone and definition of the muscles, creating a firmer and more shapely appearance. Increases in muscle mass can be made, but women can never achieve the muscle bulk of men. This is due to the fact that men have ten times as much of the muscle-building hormone, testosterone, in their systems. Women are, therefore, genetically programmed not to achieve the muscle bulk of men.

Myth 2: if you stop training, muscle turns to fat

It is impossible for muscle to turn to fat, as it is a completely different type of body tissue. Muscle mass and strength will gradually decrease if you stop training (some physiologists believe that a muscle will never quite return to its pre-training state), and fat stores will increase if you eat more calories than you need over a period of time. However, one will not turn into the other! Once a certain muscle mass has been achieved through regular strength training, this can be maintained by training less frequently (once or twice a week).

Myth 3: strength training makes you muscle-bound and decreases flexibility

Increasing your muscle mass does not make you muscle-bound, reduce your flexibility or reduce your speed in athletic activities. On the contrary, if you train correctly – performing each exercise in strict form through a full range of motion (ROM) that gives your muscles and joints a full stretch – you can maintain and even improve flexibility. Your ROM may decrease when you lift heavy weights, so compensate for this by doing full ROM stretches between sets and especially at the end of your workout (see Chapter 10).

Continued use of heavier weights, partial repetitions and performing exercises with an incomplete ROM ('cheating reps') usually results in reduced flexibility. Also, if you have one muscle group (e.g. the quadriceps) that is over-developed in comparison with the opposing group (e.g. the hamstrings), this can cause reduced flexibility in that opposing muscle group. This is common in cyclists and footballers due to the larger volume of work performed by the quadriceps. In any case, stretching the relevant muscles after training will help prevent them shortening and increase their flexibility.

It has been demonstrated that a strong muscle can contract more quickly and generate more power than a weak one. In fact, the physiques of world-class sprinters are very muscular, which goes to prove that increased muscle mass does not hinder your speed or your flexibility.

Myth 4: strength training harms the joints

When properly and safely performed, strength training improves the strength of the ligaments that hold a joint together (*see* p. 00), thus making the joint more stable and less prone to injury. Impact movements such as running and jumping can unduly stress the ligaments and make the joints more susceptible to injury. The controlled, no-impact movements used in strength training, however, place far less stress on the joints than most other forms of exercise, and are therefore a good way of strengthening them.

♦ Where should you train? ♦

As Table 1.1 shows, home and gym environments offer both advantages and disadvantages for training.

Table 1.1 *The pros and cons of training at home and at the gym*

GYM		HOME	
Advantages	*Disadvantages*	*Advantages*	*Disadvantages*
• Greater variety of equipment, including free weights, machines and cardiovascular equipment • Instructors on hand to ensure that you are training correctly, offering advice and helping you develop your training programme • More motivating to train with other people and in a sociable club atmosphere • Spotter or training partners allow you to train harder and reduce the risk of injury or accidents • You may have access to other fitness facilities that would complement your strength training, such as a swimming pool and fitness classes	• Membership fees can be expensive, although once you've paid you may be more motivated to stick to your programme and less likely to skip workouts • Overcrowding, particularly during peak times, may be a problem • More time-consuming to travel to a gym	• You are training in the privacy of your own home • You can train when you like • You don't have to travel to the gym, so it can save time	• Initial outlay for home gym equipment can be expensive • Your budget and available space will probably limit you to only the basics • Your initial enthusiasm may wear off fast and, unless you set aside specific times to work out, you can always find other things to do instead • Unless you train with a partner or personal trainer, it can be difficult to motivate yourself and push yourself hard enough in a home environment to achieve significant gains • Greater risk of accident or injury unless training with a partner or personal trainer

Checklist for finding a good gym

Travelling distance and time

Decide how far you are prepared to travel. If the journey takes you more than 15–20 minutes you are unlikely to visit the gym regularly in the long term once the initial novelty has worn off.

Type of equipment

Is there a good range of equipment to suit your needs? If you want to build mass, you will need plenty of free weights (*see* below), benches and racks. If you are more interested in general fitness and toning, you may prefer a greater range of machines and lighter free weights.

Standard and safety of equipment

Good equipment does not need to be state-of-the-art shiny machinery. Check that the equipment is well maintained with no broken or loose attachments, and is regularly cleaned and tested.

Gym layout

The gym should be well ventilated and well laid out, with enough space between equipment to prevent accidents and overcrowding.

Atmosphere and motivation

The gym environment should be motivating for you as an individual. Some gyms are very busy and noisy, others are quieter; it is important to train in an atmosphere that suits your temperament. Try to get an idea of the type of members who train there – are they serious bodybuilders or general fitness trainers, sociable or quiet?

Instruction

Check that the instructors are professionally qualified. Most instructors in the UK will have a certificate (minimum NVQ Level 2) in fitness training or weight training, or hold a degree in sports science or a related subject.

Arrange a trial workout

Most gyms will be happy to arrange a trial workout. Arrange to visit at the same time as you plan to exercise so you can see whether the gym becomes overcrowded and you need to queue for equipment.

Cost

Make sure you find out the true cost of joining a gym. Some require an initial non-refundable joining fee, plus an annual or monthly membership subscription. Others may allow you to pay for each workout: multiply this by the number of times you intend to train per year. Also make sure you are clear about what the membership buys you, whether you need to pay extra for other facilities, and ask about different payment methods. Find out whether any discounts are available (e.g. off-peak membership).

Note: Whether you decide to train at home or at a gym, you should seek the advice of a professional instructor to demonstrate the exercises, at least for your initial workouts.

♦ Free weights or machines ♦

A key question for most weight trainers is: should I use free weights or machines? The issues you need to consider before finalising your training programme are as follows:

Plane of movement

Lifting free weights develops greater balance and motor skills than using machines. Barbells and dumbbells allow the limbs to move in their natural arcs. This helps develop greater co-ordination skills and facilitates greater strength development.

More muscle fibres and nerve inputs (motor units) (*see* pp. 18–19) are activated to balance the weight throughout the ROM. Accessory muscles (those which are not responsible for the movement but which assist indirectly) are also developed as they must work synergistically with the prime movers (the main muscles involved in the movement) (*see* also p. 20).

Since machines lock you into a fixed plane of movement, they reduce the contribution of the accessory muscles and so require less balance and skill to perform an exercise. This may be advantageous for beginners with poor motor skills and poor muscle and postural awareness, but as muscles receive less stimulation so strength and size gains will be smaller.

Biomechanics

Free weights accommodate the natural leverage of the body and the changes in force generated through the ROM. Most machines, on the other hand, place an increasing load on the muscle during each part of the movement, which means the muscle will not receive maximum stimulus in its biomechanically favourable position. A lower weight usually has to be selected in order to complete the movement correctly. Result: slower gains in strength and size.

Leverage

Another problem with machines is that they do not accommodate the natural leverage of the body. Everyone has a unique set of levers, which will not exactly fit a machine. The resistance cams are set to match the strength curves of the average person, which means that for everyone else the heaviest resistance occurs at inappropriate angles. Thus, a lighter weight has to be selected in order to complete the motion, reducing the intensity of the exercise and the training effect.

Variability

Several different variations of the same exercise may be performed with free weights – e.g. bench presses with different grip widths or with the bench adjusted to different angles – thus making many different exercises possible. Machines offer a finite number of exercises, thus potentially compromising overall development.

Safety

Machines are generally safer than free weights, particularly when training without a partner or spotter: they usually allow the weight stack to be returned to the starting position if you fail to complete a full repetition. Dumbbells and barbells can be dropped and plates can become unsecured. When training with free weights to the point of failure, it is therefore essential to have a spotter.

Beginners should start out with machines while they are developing the basic motor skills and body awareness needed to control a movement. Once they have acquired this confidence, they can include more free-weight exercises in their routine.

Aesthetic appeal

Some beginners, especially women, find free weights intimidating. Machines generally have a greater aesthetic appeal and may encourage beginners to commence training. Free weights have a more macho image, which may appeal to some weight trainers. They can encourage greater competitiveness and motivation and therefore may increase strength and mass gains.

♦ Workout accessories ♦

Although you probably don't want to invest in your own weight-training equipment, other accessories might be worthwhile considering.

Training gloves

Training gloves give your palms just enough padding to improve your grip of the bar or dumbbells and prevent calluses and blisters forming on your hands. They are useful for any pressing, pulling or curling movement.

Using gloves is also more hygienic than using bare hands – weight-training apparatus can be sweaty and dirty, and an ideal breeding place for germs. However, do make sure you wash your gloves regularly.

Training belt

A training belt is thought to provide extra support for the lower back. However, it is only advantageous when using maximal weights, and then only for certain exercises performed vertically which place considerable stress on the vertebrae, such as heavy squats and dead lifts. It helps under these circumstances by increasing abdominal wall pressure. The tighter the belt, the greater the abdominal pressure against the spine, which thereby helps to protect the discs and other vulnerable structures. The abdominal wall should be drawn in towards the spine when lifting with a belt rather than being pushed out against it.

Do not use a belt for lighter exercises or if you have a lower-back injury or weakness. Using a belt for any other exercises in your workout can stimulate incorrect movement of the abdominal wall, leading to a weakening of the abdominal muscles.

Straps

Grip failure can be a limiting factor in pulling movements such as chins, seated rows and lat pull-downs. Up to a point, training without straps will help to develop the forearm muscles and strengthen your grip. However, once your grip strength starts to limit the amount of weight you can use or reduce the number of reps you can do, you should use straps. They will help you to focus on the muscle you are training and reduce the involvement of the limiting muscles. Straps are therefore advantageous for most back exercises and pulling movements performed with heavy weights such as chins, one-arm dumbbell rows, and lat pull-downs.

Knee wraps

Knee wraps can help support the knee joint during heavy leg exercises such as dead lifts and squats because they assist the ligaments in stabilising the joint. As with training belts, do not rely on wraps if you have a knee injury or to help you lift heavier weights than your strength allows. They are best used for maximal weights (e.g. twice your body weight) rather than as a crutch for lighter sets.

♦ Summary of key points ♦

- Strength training causes a favourable change in body composition, increased muscle, tendon and ligament strength, better posture and a higher metabolic rate.
- The health benefits include increased bone strength and density, reduced blood cholesterol, reduced blood pressure and improved psychological well-being.
- Strength training can help prevent or delay the age-related decline in lean tissue mass, strength, bone density and resting metabolic rate.
- It is a myth that strength training reduces flexibility, harms the joints or gives women bulky muscles. Muscle does not turn to fat.
- The benefits of training in a commercial gym include access to a wider range of equipment, professional instruction, greater motivation and social contact.
- A home gym offers greater privacy and convenience.
- Free weights develop better balance and co-ordination than machines, accommodate the natural leverage of the body and allow a more natural plane of movement, all facilitating greater strength development.
- Machines are safer and easier for beginners.
- Training gloves are useful for all weight trainers. Training belts should only be used for vertical exercises such as the squat when using maximal weights, and knee wraps for heavy leg exercises. Straps help to reduce the involvement of limiting muscles in certain pulling and back exercises.

Chapter 2

Get Motivated

This chapter gets you started on your path to success. It shows you how to set your goals and focus your mind on reaching them, and gives you practical motivational strategies to keep you on track. Before you start training, you need to assess your goals. What do you want out of your strength-training programme? Bigger muscles? A leaner, more toned physique? Improved performance in other sports? Whatever you are looking for, your goals should be SMART:

S = specific
M = measurable
A = agreed
R = realistic
T = timescaled

♦ 1. Set SMART goals ♦

Specific

Write down exactly what you want to achieve from your training programme. Don't write vague statements such as 'To tone up' or 'To get stronger' as these will not focus your mind on achieving a particular result. Your goals could include details of how much lean weight (i.e. muscle) you wish to gain and how much fat you wish to lose. For example, you could write down 'To lose 5 kg fat and gain 3 kg muscle'. You could also write down your desired body measurements, or how much weight you wish to lift on specific exercises such as the bench press, squat and dead lift.

To help you crystallise your goals, write down the reasons *why* you want to improve – whether it is increased muscle size, a more symmetrical physique, better sports performance or more energy. Go beyond the superficial reasons and find the inner motivations that are driving your goals. Research shows that it is the internal motivators that really drive us to success.[1]

Measurable

You need to be able to *measure* your progress. Long-term goals can be broader in scope, but short-term goals must be quite specific. Indeed, the specific goals above could be in terms of your body weight, body fat measurements, girth measurements or the amount of weight lifted are clearly measurable too. For example, you may wish to set a goal of 60 kg for your maximal bench press, or as a man reduce your body fat to 12%. To help monitor your progress, photocopy the training log in Figure 2.1 to record the exact weight lifted, the number of repetitions and the number of sets completed at each workout and use them to check what you have achieved each week against your long-term goal. Keep your training records for future reference as well. In the example given in Figure 2.2 for the bench press, 40/15 means 15 repetitions (reps) with 40 kg. (See also pp. 15–16.)

Figure 2.1 Training log to be photocopied and used in your training programme

Exercise	Date	Date	Date	Date	Date	Date	Date
	Set	Set	Set	Set	Set	Set	Set
	(kg/reps)	(kg/reps)	(kg/reps)	(kg/reps)	(kg/reps)	(kg/reps)	(kg/reps)

Figure 2.2 Sample training log for a bench press

	Date	Date	Date	Date	Date
	17/4	17/4	17/4	17/4	17/4
	Set	Set	Set	Set	Set
	1 (warm-up)	2	3	4	5*
Bench press	40 / 15	60 / 10	70 / 8	75 / 7	80 / 6

*Note: only advanced weight trainers should include five sets of any given exercise in their programme.

Agreed

Ideally, discuss and *agree* your goals with someone – a qualified instructor, your partner, or a friend. The most important thing is *committing your goals to paper*; this signals a commitment to change. Write them in the form of a personal mission statement; then sign and date what you have written. Better still, ask someone else to sign the document as a witness, as you would with a contract. Then place a copy somewhere you can see it each day, such as on your desk or on a bulletin board. The goals will constantly remind you that they are waiting to be achieved. If you do not commit your goals to paper, then it is unlikely that you'll be able to commit to the work necessary to make them come true. Like a legal contract, this technique will keep your mind focused.

Realistic

The goals should be realistic – attainable for your body size, natural shape, and lifestyle. There's nothing wrong with aiming for the top but, at the same time, be realistic. If it's a gold medal you seek, study the path others have taken to achieve that goal and check it against where you are starting from and how much time and energy you have to follow a similar path.

Timescaled

Set a clear timescale for reaching your goals. Decide on a deadline – this prompts action and sets your plan in motion. Without a clear deadline, it's easy to put off starting your programme and you end up never achieving your goals.

Once you have fixed your major goals, set mini-goals, which can be reached in a relatively short period of time (such as 12 weeks) and long-term goals, which can be reached over, say, a year. You may even find it helpful to break up each 12-week goal into distinct segments and focus on the progress you make each week. For example, if your goal is to reduce your body fat percentage from 30% to 20% (*see* pp. 00–00), break it down into smaller goals spread out over the course of several weeks. You could aim to achieve 24% body fat within 12 weeks, but aim to reduce your body fat by 1% every two weeks. Then aim to achieve 20% within the next 12 weeks by reducing your body fat by 1% every 3 weeks.

Set out a programme of activities or steps that you need to complete in order to reach each goal. These steps may include weight training three times a week, eating six balanced meals a day (*see* Chapter 16), and doing a cardio workout three times a week first thing in the morning (*see* Chapter 13). The key is to make sure each step is specific, realistic and achievable.

♦ 2. Visualise success ♦

The ability to visualise success is one of the most effective tools of high-achievers. Use imagery to help you stick to your programme. Have a clear mental picture of how you will look or how you will perform at the end. Role models can help to motivate you. Pick one with a similar natural body type, shape and size as you – that way, you know you can achieve your goals and won't lose heart if you don't look similar to or perform like them after a period of training. You may find it helpful to cut out pictures from a magazine and keep these with your training log.

If you are finding it difficult to motivate yourself for a workout, visualise yourself successfully completing it. Use as many senses as possible – the sight of the gym, the sounds around you. See yourself loading the weights on the bar, see yourself completing each repetition and hear the sound of voices or music in the gym.

♦ 3. Create a motivating ♦ environment

Training should give you a buzz and make you feel good about yourself. If you have to force yourself to work out when your heart is not in it, you will not train hard enough to make sufficient gains, and you are more likely to give up. So make sure you choose the right training environment (*see* also p. 7) and consider enlisting the help of a training partner (*see* below). That way, training will become a satisfying and empowering experience that you look forward to rather than dread.

♦ 4. Work out with a ♦ partner

Training with someone else will increase your motivation, make training more enjoyable, allow you to train harder, decrease the chances of you skipping workouts, and help you to stick to your training programme. Choose someone with similar goals to your own but not necessarily the same ability. The important thing is that you can motivate each other.

♦ 5. Monitor your progress ♦

Keep a training *and* nutrition diary to record your progress. Remember, achieving your goals will not happen overnight. It comes after weeks or months of committed effort. Monitor your progress on a regular basis so you can check that your actions are producing the results you want. If they are not, you need to take the necessary steps to get you back on track. Training and nutrition diaries can be great motivators during workouts. Look back over your notes at the end of each week. If your performance matches your goals, reward yourself.

Buy a notebook so that you can record the following details:

- details of each exercise, sets, reps and how much weight you used (*see* Figure 2.1)

- how you felt before and after each workout
- what and how much you ate each day
- details of any other exercise you took
- your body measurements, e.g. percentage body fat, waist, chest, hip, leg and arm circumference measurements; or just how snugly your clothes fit.

Photographs taken before you start your new programme and then at intervals throughout your training will help to give you feedback on your progress. This is more objective than simply looking in the mirror.

Measuring your body-fat percentage

Skinfold testing and bioelectrical impedance are the easiest and most accessible methods for estimating body fat.

- **Skinfold callipers**: calibrated callipers measure the layer of fat beneath the skin at a number of specific sites on the body, usually the biceps, triceps, below the shoulder blades and above the hip bone. The sum of the skinfolds is used in a simple equation to estimate your body-fat percentage. The accuracy of this method depends almost entirely on the skill of the tester, as well as the precision of the callipers.
- **Bioelectrical impedance**: an electrode is placed on two specific points on the body – usually on one hand and the opposite foot – and an electric current is passed through them. Body fat creates an impedance, or resistance, to the current while fat-free mass permits a greater current flow. Thus, the impedance is used to measure the percentage of fat-free mass and the percentage of body fat. The accuracy depends on hydration, skin temperature and alcohol and food consumption. It is less accurate for very lean or obese individuals.

♦ 6. Maintain variety ♦

Change your workout periodically to keep boredom at bay and increase the likelihood of continual improvement. When you start a strength-training programme, gains are rapid but then slow down or reach a plateau. If you follow the same workout week after week, you will soon lose interest, your workout intensity will drop, training gains will slow down and you will give up. Instead you could change the following aspects, all of which are re-discussed in Chapter 11:

- the exercises for each body part
- the split of your programme
- the order of exercises
- the weights used.

Also take a complete rest from weight training every few months and spend a week or two doing a completely different activity.

♦ 7. Use a personal trainer ♦

If you do not have a training partner or you need extra motivation, consider using a personal trainer either on an occasional or regular basis. A personal trainer will not only design your programme but will help keep you motivated. They will make sure that you are on track with your goals and that you don't skip any workouts, give you advice on a whole range of subjects, help you get more out of your workout, and also allow you to train at a time that is convenient for you.

To find a personal trainer ask friends for recommendations or check with your gym for trainers who are qualified to NVQ Level 3 and have a qualification in personal training. Also check out their references and make sure that they are insured. The National

Register of Personal Trainers (020 7751 0719 or www.nrpt.co.uk) lists fully qualified and insured trainers in the UK. You can also contact the Association of Personal Trainers for advice (020 8692 4023).

♦ 8. Reward yourself ♦

Give yourself rewards when you have reached a goal, no matter how small. This could be something as simple as a star for reaching your weekly target, or a new training outfit, a trip to the theatre, a meal out, new clothes, or a sports massage appointment for reaching the bigger goals.

♦ Summary of key points ♦

- Motivation is a fundamental part of any training programme. You should set specific, measurable, agreed and realistic goals within a clear timescale.

- Motivation can be increased by visualisation techniques, training with a partner, keeping a training log, varying your routines, using a personal trainer, and rewarding your progress.

Chapter 3

Muscle Science

Central to your training goal is a good understanding of muscle structure and function. Once you know how your muscles are made up and how they work and respond to strength training, you can develop a programme to suit your needs. This chapter demystifies the topic of muscle physiology. It tells you what you need to know to achieve your maximum potential for growth. It gives you a better understanding of why and how your muscles grow, and what type of training produces the greatest strength increases and how. In short, this chapter empowers you with knowledge you can then apply to your own training programme. After all, knowledge is power.

♦ How are muscles made up? ♦

A muscle is made up of cylindrical fibres (sometimes called muscle cells) which are about 50–100 micrometres in diameter (or the width of a human hair). They range from a few centimetres in length to 1 m, and can run the entire length of the muscle. These fibres are grouped in bundles called 'fasciculi', each separately wrapped in a sheath (perimysium) that holds them together.

Each muscle fibre comprises thread-like strands called myofibrils, each of which is about 1 micrometer in diameter, or $\frac{1}{100}$th the diameter of a human hair. These hold myofilaments containing the contractile proteins myosin (thick filaments) and actin (thin filaments), whose actions are responsible for muscle contraction (*see* Figure 3.1). To a large extent, your muscle's cross-sectional area, together with the number and length of its fibres, determine its strength. You cannot change the number of fibres in your muscle, but you can increase both its *cross-sectional* areas through strength training, as well as the *number* of muscle fibres recruited when executing any given movement (*see* pp. 21–2).

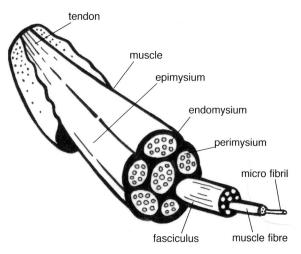

Figure 3.1 The structure of skeletal muscle

How do muscles fire?

Your muscles are connected to your nervous system. Muscle fibres are fired, or activated, by motor nerves, and a single motor nerve may stimulate anywhere between one and several hundred muscle fibres. A nerve cell and a muscle fibre is called a 'motor unit' and, when a motor nerve is stimulated, it causes *all* of the muscle fibres to which it connects to contract with a maximal force – the so-called 'all or nothing' law. The number of motor units involved in a contraction depends on the load imposed on the muscle. For example, if you lift a very light weight, only a few motor units will be involved. As you increase the weight lifted, progressively more motor units will be recruited. If you lift a very heavy weight, all or almost all of the motor units will be recruited so that you generate your maximal force. In other words, to train the whole muscle, you have to subject it to maximal stress.

Why do some people gain strength and muscle size more easily than others?

One explanation is that they have a greater number of muscle fibres in each motor unit. The number of fibres per motor unit is genetically determined and varies between 20 and 500, but averages around 200. So, if you have above-average fibre numbers in each motor unit, you can generate a greater force output compared to the average person. This creates a bigger stimulus for muscle growth. So, your gains in strength and size will be faster.

How do muscles contract?

Muscle contraction is explained by the 'sliding filament theory', and involves the two contractile proteins, actin and myosin (*see* opposite). When an impulse from a motor nerve reaches the muscle fibre, it creates chemical changes that cause the actin filaments to slide inwards on the myosin filaments. The myosin filaments contain cross-bridges – which are tiny extensions that reach towards the actin filaments. The myosin binds to the actin via these cross-bridges, causing them to swivel and pull the myosin filaments over the actin filaments (*see* Figure 3.2). This sliding is what causes the muscle to shorten and thicken – or contract. Once the stimulation stops, the actin and myosin filaments move apart and the muscle returns to its resting length and thickness.

The force generated by the muscle depends on the weight lifted and its original length before contraction. If it is in its normal resting length, or slightly longer (slightly stretched), all of the cross-bridges on the myosin can connect with the actin filaments, creating greater force. For example, during a biceps curl, you will generate maximal force in the biceps muscle by starting with your arms in the fully straightened position. Starting with your arms slightly flexed will reduce the force developed and therefore the training stimulus, irrespective of the weight lifted.

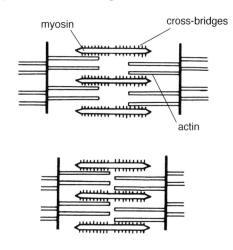

Figure 3.2 Contraction of skeletal muscle

Which muscles help me lift weights?

The muscle that brings about a movement is called the 'prime mover', or 'agonist'. For example, during a biceps curl, the prime mover is the biceps muscle.

The muscle that acts in opposition to the prime mover, that may slow it down or stop the movement, is called the 'antagonist'. This helps to keep the joint stable, and during most movements it is relaxed, allowing the movement to be performed efficiently. For example, during a biceps curl the triceps acts as the antagonist and needs to be relaxed to allow the arm to be flexed smoothly.

A muscle that assists indirectly in a movement is called a 'synergist'. For example, in a biceps curl the muscles of the forearm act as synergists because they cross the elbow joint and help to bring about the movement.

Are all types of muscle action the same?

There are three types of muscle actions:

- **Concentric** muscle actions occur when a muscle shortens during contraction. Examples of concentric actions include the upwards phase of a biceps curl, and the upwards phase of a bench press.
- **Eccentric** muscle actions are the reverse of a concentric action – they return the muscle to its original starting point. The muscle lengthens as the joint angle increases, releasing under controlled tension. Examples of eccentric actions include the downwards phase of a biceps curl, and the lowering phase of a bench press.
- **Isometric** muscle actions occur when the muscle develops tension without changing its length. For example, an isometric contraction develops during a biceps curl if you cannot continue the movement beyond

the mid-point – the tension in your biceps equals the resistance of the barbell.

♦ What is the difference ♦ between muscular strength, endurance and power?

Muscular strength is the amount of force a muscle can produce – for example, the amount of weight that can be lifted. This is developed by heavy weight training. Generally, the larger the muscle, the stronger it is, although other factors such as neuromuscular adaptation (the number of fibres controlled and recruited by your nervous system) affect your strength as well (*see* p. 23).

Muscular endurance is the ability of a muscle to continue contracting against a resistance. This is developed by maintaining a constant workload for increasing periods of time – lifting a weight for 12 or more repetitions then building up to, say, 15, 20 and so on as endurance improves. Long-distance cycling will develop muscle endurance in the thigh muscles, for example.

Muscular power is the ability to produce both strength and speed. It involves generating a great force as rapidly as possible and is therefore characterised by explosive movements. It is developed by lifting near maximal weights (a weight heavy enough to allow 1–5 repetitions) very rapidly (*see* p. 100), and it is an important aspect of performance for most sports.

Strength training will develop all three components, but the amount of weight lifted, the speed of movement and the number of repetitions will determine which aspect is developed most. In general, using heavy weights for lower repetitions (less than 12) develops strength and size; using lighter weights for more repetitions develops endurance; explosive movements develop power.

◆ Muscle fibre types ◆

Your muscles are made up of two basic fibre types:

- slow twitch (ST), or type I fibres
- fast twitch (FT), or type II fibres.

ST fibres contract relatively slowly, produce less tension and prefer to use oxygen to produce energy (i.e. aerobic metabolism). They have a high endurance capacity and do not tire easily. ST fibres are used mainly in low-intensity, long-duration aerobic activities such as jogging. They have many capillaries and mitochondria (the power houses of cells) and can easily make use of both fat and carbohydrate for fuel.

FT fibres are essentially the opposite. They are best suited to anaerobic activities and have a low aerobic power. These fibres generate the most tension, contract very rapidly but have poor endurance.

FT fibres can be further subdivided into FTa (type IIa) and FTb (type IIb) fibres, based on their ability to produce energy under aerobic conditions. FTa fibres have more capillaries surrounding them, more mitochondria and a greater number of aerobic enzymes than FTb fibres and, therefore, are more resistant to fatigue. The FTb fibres have the highest anaerobic capacity but the lowest endurance capacity of all fibre types. They tire very quickly and are used almost exclusively for explosive power activities such as sprinting and jumping.

Put simply, a top sprinter or weightlifter would probably have a high percentage of explosive FT fibres and fewer ST fibres, while an endurance athlete is more likely to have a high percentage of ST fibres and fewer FT fibres.

Which fibres do I use during strength training?

When you lift light weights – for example, during your warm-up sets or during a weight-training circuit, most of the work is carried out by your ST fibres. As you increase the weight lifted, an increasing number of FTa and FTb fibres are also recruited. When you lift very heavy or maximal weights, both ST and FTa fibres and virtually all of the FTb fibres are recruited. The recruitment of different fibre types as the intensity of exercise (i.e. weight lifted) increases is shown in Figure 3.3.

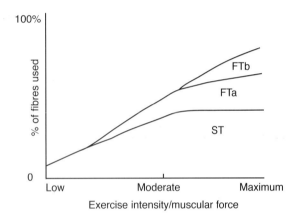

Figure 3.3 The recruitment of ST and FT muscle fibres

Note: even during maximum intensity exercise not all of the available fibres are recruited. This prevents damage to the muscles and tendons.

So, if you perform mostly light, high-repetition training, you will stimulate mostly ST fibres and develop good muscular endurance but limited strength and size. If you incorporate both medium- and low-repetition training (i.e. using moderate and heavy weights) into your programme (bodybuilding), you will stimulate all three fibre types and therefore develop good strength, size and muscular endurance. If you perform only heavy, low-repetition training (maximal strength training), you will mainly stimulate the FTb fibres and develop good strength, moderate size but poor muscular endurance.

Will my mix of fibre types affect my strength gains?

Your mix of FT and ST fibres dictates how readily your muscles will gain strength and size. People with a high proportion of ST fibres will develop strength less readily than those with more FT fibres (*see* pp. 195–6). They tend to achieve smaller, slower increases.

However, it is not necessarily a straightforward relationship since there are other variables affecting strength and endurance, such as your quality of training and your diet. Someone with a high proportion of ST fibres can still be stronger than someone with a high proportion of FT fibres if they have plenty of motivation and follow the correct training and nutrition programme. Regardless of your genetically determined fibre-type distribution, you can still improve your muscle size and strength through intensive training and good nutrition.

Can you change your muscle fibre mix?

The distribution of the different fibre types is largely genetically determined. Whether a muscle fibre is FT or ST is determined before birth and in the first few years of life. After this time there is nothing you can do to change the number or structure of your muscle fibres.

It is possible, however, to change the *function* of certain muscle fibre types through specific kinds of training. With aerobic training, FTa fibres can learn to use more oxygen and so assume some of the characteristics of ST fibres – i.e. they become more aerobic – while FTb fibres begin to assume some of the characteristics of FTa fibres and gain greater endurance. So, endurance training does not change the fibre type but will increase the muscles' aerobic capacity. It is not, however, possible for changes to occur in the opposite direction – i.e. for ST fibres to assume the characteristics of FT fibres.

◆ How does strength training ◆ make you stronger ?

Increases in strength are the combined result of developing bigger muscles (hypertrophy) and changes in the way nerve pathways serve the motor units (neuromuscular adaptations).

What is hypertrophy?

Training forces your muscles to do extra work than normal to overcome the load. This process is called 'overloading' and leads to increases in muscle strength and size through a process called *hypertrophy*.

When the muscle contracts against a resistance, it stimulates a breakdown of the muscle proteins (actin and myosin) and the formation of very small (micro) tears in the muscle fibres and connective tissue. This occurs primarily during the eccentric phase of the motion (*see* p. 20). During the rest period between workouts, new proteins are built up, the connective tissue is repaired, the muscle fibres enlarge and the muscle increases in diameter and strength.

The increase in muscle size is due to an increase in the *cross-sectional area* of the individual fibres, rather than an increase in the number of fibres.[1,2,3] This is the result of an increase in actin and myosin[4] and an increase in the number of filaments within the fibres.[5] The new filaments are added in layers to the outside of the existing bundles of filaments. Thus each muscle fibre becomes denser and bigger, enlarging the whole muscle, and increasing its strength.

It is the FT fibres that are largely responsible for moving the muscle during heavy strength training. As a result, FT fibres increase in size more readily and at a faster rate than ST fibres.[6] Therefore, it is the growth of FT fibres that results in an increase in muscle mass and strength.[7] However, strength gains are not due solely to increases in muscle size but also to changes in the way nerve pathways serve the motor units – 'neuromuscular adaptation'.

How do muscles 'tone up'?

Toning is a non-technical term that really refers to a relative increase in strength. When you start strength training, most of the strength gains come from the nerves controlling the muscle firing pattern becoming more efficient (*see* below). Next, come changes in the density or 'tone' of the muscle as new muscle proteins are added to your muscle cells. Again, there is little or no increase in the overall size of the muscle, rather an increase in the packing density of the filaments. The muscle becomes stronger and firmer to the touch in the relaxed state. This is what is commonly called 'good muscle tone'. If you don't increase your training level but maintain the same volume, the muscles do not continue to adapt so you will simply stay toned and will not increase in size. If you were to increase your training level (i.e. training volume and intensity), your muscles will increase in size as well as density.

What is a 'pump'?

The 'pump' that you get during heavy training is not the same as muscle growth. This temporary increase in muscle size is largely the result of water accumulating inside the muscle fibres making it look larger. The majority of this water returns to the blood a few hours after training and so the pump disappears.

What is neuromuscular adaptation?

The nervous system adapts to a progressive overload by improving its ability to recruit additional muscle fibres and generate more force. The more motor units involved, the greater the force of contraction. In fact, your strength gains during the first 6–8 weeks of starting a strength-training programme are due mostly to neuromuscular adaptation. Don't be put off if you don't get bigger muscles after the first couple of months of training. Your nervous system adapts to the new stimulus first, allowing you to maximise your strength with the muscle you already have. After this initial period, your muscles start to grow in size and this contributes to your strength gains.

What else happens when strength training?

Strength training causes an increase in the number of blood vessels in the muscle (capillarisation). This means that more oxygen, fuel and nutrients can be delivered to the muscles and metabolic waste products can be removed more readily. The overall result is one of increased efficiency, strength and size.

The attached tendons, ligaments and bones also increase in strength and so the whole surrounding structural framework becomes stronger.

Another key factor in muscle growth is improved co-ordination. The ability to co-ordinate specific movements can only be learned through practice. To perform an efficient lift, you need to relax the antagonistic muscles, so that unnecessary movement does not affect the force of the prime movers (*see* p. 20). A well-co-ordinated group of muscles will be able to achieve a greater training effect and, therefore, better strength gains.

♦ Summary of key points ♦

- Muscles are made up of cylindrical fibres, which comprise bundles of filaments that hold the muscle proteins.
- A single motor nerve together with the muscle fibres it activates is called a motor unit. The more motor units recruited during a contraction, the greater will be the stimulation for muscle growth. This is achieved by lifting heavy weights.
- A muscle that brings about a movement is called an agonist; the muscle that acts in opposition to this is called the antagonist; the muscles that help the agonist are called synergists.
- When a muscle contracts, the two contractile proteins, actin and myosin, slide across each other to shorten the muscle.
- Your proportion of FT and ST muscle fibres influences your ability to develop strength, muscle mass and endurance. Individuals with a high percentage of FT fibres develop mass and strength most readily.
- Strength is the combined result of hypertrophy (increase in muscle size) and neuromuscular adaptation.
- Muscles increase in strength and mass when they are subjected to progressive overload.
- An increase in muscle size is due to an increase in muscle fibre size and density rather than an increase in the number of fibres.
- It is the growth of FT fibres that results in an increase in muscle mass and strength.
- Strength gains during the first 6–8 weeks of starting a strength-training programme are due mostly to neuromuscular adaptation.

PART TWO

The Exercise Directory

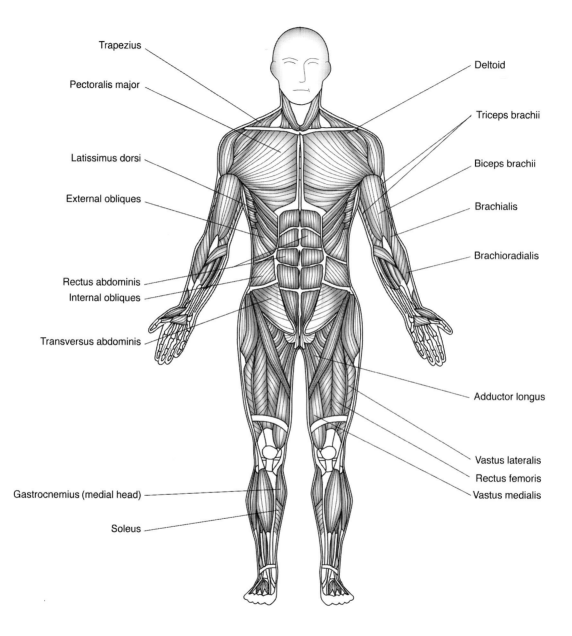

Trapezius

Pectoralis major

Latissimus dorsi

External obliques

Rectus abdominis

Internal obliques

Transversus abdominis

Gastrocnemius (medial head)

Soleus

Deltoid

Triceps brachii

Biceps brachii

Brachialis

Brachioradialis

Adductor longus

Vastus lateralis

Rectus femoris

Vastus medialis

Figure 4.1(a) Muscles of the human body (front view)

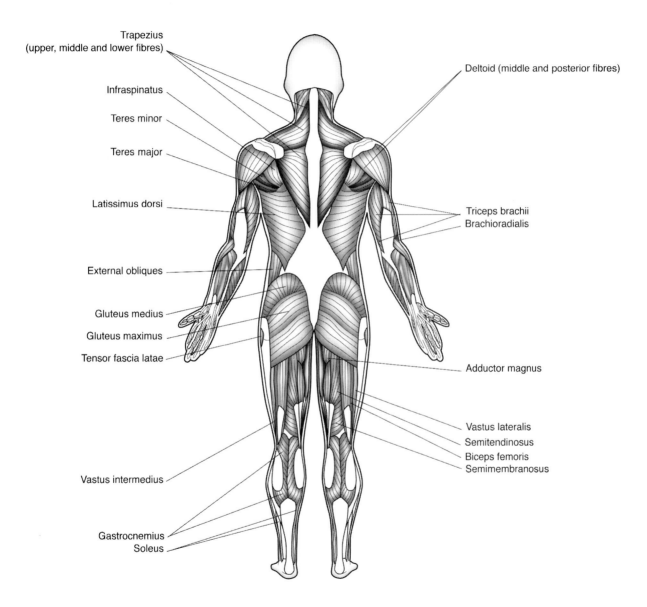

Trapezius
(upper, middle and lower fibres)

Infraspinatus

Teres minor

Teres major

Latissimus dorsi

External obliques

Gluteus medius

Gluteus maximus

Tensor fascia latae

Vastus intermedius

Gastrocnemius
Soleus

Deltoid (middle and posterior fibres)

Triceps brachii
Brachioradialis

Adductor magnus

Vastus lateralis
Semitendinosus
Biceps femoris
Semimembranosus

Figure 4.1(b) Muscles of the human body (back view)

Movements of the body

A number of terms are used to describe movements of the body. Those relevant to strength-training exercises are:

- flexion – a reduction in the angle between the bones at a joint: e.g. bending the elbow
- extension – an increase in the angle of the bones at a joint: e.g. straightening the elbow

- abduction – movement of a limb *away* from the central line of the body: e.g. moving the leg out to the side
- adduction – movement of a limb *towards* the central line of the body: e.g. moving the leg inwards.

Technique note

Every exercise listed and described in the exercise directory includes 2 photographs demonstrating the exercise at the start and at the mid-point positions. It is suggested that you use these photographs as a guide to correct technique.

◆ Before you begin . . . ◆

It is important to warm up before beginning your workout for two main reasons:

- it reduces the chances of injury
- it will improve your performance.

Here are a few quick reminders of why you should do this.

Muscles respond better to exercise if they are properly prepared for the coming workload. Warming up increases blood flow to the muscles and lubricates the joints because the fluid surrounding them becomes less viscous so the joint can move more smoothly and efficiently. At rest, muscles receive only about 15% of your total blood supply, but during exercise the requirement for fuel and oxygen sharply increases and they may need up to 80% of the total blood flow to meet the demand. Obviously, it takes time to re-route the blood, and this cannot be achieved efficiently if you omit the warm-up and start exercising vigorously.

Warming up also improves the elasticity of the muscles, enabling them to work harder, more efficiently and for longer before they fatigue, as well as allowing nerve impulses to be transmitted faster.

Finally, warming up also prepares you mentally for the work ahead; it increases your arousal level and motivation. Performing one or two warm-up sets (*see* p. 26) with light weights acts as a mental rehearsal and means that you can perform your subsequent heavier sets more effectively.

Warm-up components

The time taken on this part of your workout depends to a large extent on the temperature of your surroundings – the cooler the environment, the longer it will take to raise your body temperature. Your warm-up should include the following three components.

1. An aerobic activity that raises your body temperature and leaves you mildly sweating. This should be performed for 5–10 minutes and be continuous and rhythmic in nature – for example, stationary cycling, treadmill walking, gentle jogging, stepping or rowing.

2. Mobilisation of the major joints. This could include movements such as arm circles, knee bends and shoulder circles which take the joints through their full ROM. These are not stretching exercises as they are continuous and do not increase the ROM.

3. Warm-up sets with light weights and high repetitions. Never embark on your working sets straightaway because your muscles won't be properly warmed up and you will risk injury. Start with 1–2 sets using very light weights (around 40–50% 1RM), *see* p. 99, for 15–20 repetitions to warm up the target muscles, ligaments and joints, and to rehearse the action to be performed.

To stretch or not to stretch?

For years it was thought that stretching before strenuous activity would help prepare the muscles for exercise and reduce the risk of injury. However, more recent research suggests that stretching before you start training is unlikely to benefit your performance and may even be detrimental. Ironically, strength is lower following pre-exercise stretching compared with no stretching at all. In addition, pre-exercise stretching will not prevent post-exercise soreness or tenderness. It is now believed that stretching is best kept to a minimum prior to strength and power training. An active warm-up (such as a light jog), followed by 1–2 warm-up sets with light weights, is more effective. For example, before performing bench presses, do one or two warm-up sets with a light weight that you can comfortably manage for at least 15 repetitions.

Chapter 4

Legs, Hips and Gluteals

Strong, powerful legs give your body good symmetry, balancing the development of the upper body, and facilitating good performance in other sports.

Building a good foundation of strength in the lower body is important in all sports that require running, jumping, lifting, kicking and pushing. Hip and leg extension play a major role in:

- running – as seen in athletics, football and rugby
- jumping – as seen in volleyball and netball
- kicking – as seen in football and the martial arts.

Intense leg training not only helps build strong muscular thighs but also stimulates faster muscle growth in the upper body. In other words, the more intense the leg training, the greater the development of the chest, back, shoulders and arms. This is because intense leg training (with weights equivalent to 3–6 RM) stimulates the release of anabolic hormones – namely testosterone and growth hormone – which, in turn, improve whole-body muscle growth.

Training legs with high intensity will also elevate your heart rate and this, together with the resulting muscle mass increase, will allow you to burn fat more efficiently.

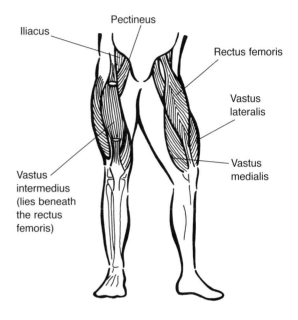

Figure 4.1 Muscles of the upper leg

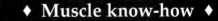

♦ Muscle know-how ♦

The leg muscles

There are four parts (heads) to the muscle at the front of the thigh, known as the quadriceps – the rectus femoris, vastus lateralis, vastus medialis and vastus intermedius – whose collective function is to extend (straighten) the knee. The rectus femoris also flexes the hip – i.e. lifts the thigh up and forwards.

The vastus medialis runs along the inside of the thigh to the rectus femoris and can be seen on the inside of the knee when the leg is locked out; the vastus lateralis runs down the outside of the thigh and can be seen on the outside of the knee; the rectus femoris can be seen when the leg is lifted up and forwards slightly; while the vastus intermedius cannot be readily seen as it lies underneath the other muscles.

The main inner-thigh muscles are comprised of three adductor muscles – adductor brevis, adductor longus and adductor magnus – whose function is to adduct or pull the legs together, while the muscles of the outer thigh – the gluteus minimus and gluteus medius – pull the legs out sideways. The muscles at the back of the leg – the hamstrings – include the biceps femoris (long and short heads), semitendinosus and semimembranosus. They have two main actions: to flex (bend) the knee and also extend the hip (pull the thigh backwards).

The calves are comprised of two muscles: the gastrocnemius and soleus. The gastrocnemius is the larger of the two and lies on top of the soleus. It is worked when the leg is fully straight, and has two distinct lobes which are visible from behind when the calf is flexed. Its role is to straighten the ankle (plantar flexion), to point the toes, and it also helps bend the knee. The soleus is a broad, flat muscle which is located beneath the gastrocnemius and which also helps straighten the ankle. It sweeps out to the sides and over across the shins, and is worked when the knee is bent at about 90°.

The gluteal muscles

There are three separate muscle groups around the backside, collectively known as the gluteals: gluteus maximus, gluteus medius and gluteus minimus.

Gluteus maximus is the largest, strongest muscle and is largely responsible for the size and shape of our backside. It attaches to the lower vertebrae and top of the rear part of the pelvis, and inserts into the top third of the back of the femur (thigh bone). Its function is to extend the hip in movements such as squatting, stair climbing and rear leg raises.

Gluteus medius is a smaller muscle, attaching at the top of the rear part of the pelvis and inserting at the top of the femur. Its function is to abduct the hip (move the legs out sideways) and also rotate the hip inwards, so it is used on the leg abductor machine or when doing leg raises to the side.

Gluteus minimus is the smallest of the three gluteals, attaching just below the gluteus medius and inserting at the top of the femur. It tends to act as a stabilising muscle, working eccentrically during impact movements such as running and jumping, and holding the hip joint in position.

The hip flexors

The main hip flexors are the iliacus, psoas (ilopsoas), rectus femoris, pectineus and tensor fascia latae. The iliacus and psoas muscles cannot be seen as they lie deep in the abdomen, running from the lower vertebrae to the top of the thigh bone. They flex the hip. The psoas muscles also help to stabilise the lower back. One of the quadriceps group of muscles, the rectus femoris, runs down the front of the thigh and crosses both the hip joint and the knee joint. It flexes the hip as well as the knee. The pectineus is a short muscle located close to the groin. It is partly covered by the rectus femoris. The tensor fascia latae can be seen on the outer front part of the hip. It helps to flex the hips as well as move the leg outwards.

♦ Barbell squat ♦

Target muscles

Gluteals, quadriceps, hamstrings, lower back, adductors, hip flexors

The squat is one of the most efficient exercises for increasing mass, strength and power in the lower body. It is a compound movement that involves many stabiliser muscles to complete the lift.

Starting position

1. Position the bar across the upper part of your back so it is resting on your trapezius muscles (not your neck).
2. Firmly grip the bar, with your hands almost double shoulder-width apart. As you lift the bar off the rack, keep your shoulder-blades together and chest up, and ensure there is a normal (stable) curve in your lower back.
3. Position your feet shoulder-width apart (or slightly wider), toes angled out at 30°.

The movement

1. Begin lowering by bending at the hips, then knees.
2. Keeping your head up and your trunk erect, slowly lower yourself down until your thighs are parallel to the ground; it is not wise to go any further than this. Keep your knees aligned over your feet, pointing in the direction of your toes. Hold for a count of one.
3. From here, press the weight up, pushing hard through your feet and keeping your body erect as you return to the starting position.

Tips

- You should maintain the natural curve in your back throughout the movement.
- If you lack ankle flexibility, it's better to work on your ankle flexibility to improve your ROM rather than to use a board under your heels. This is potentially dangerous for the knees because it moves the knees forward over the feet and can actually reduce your flexibility.
- Breathe in as you lower the weight, allowing your chest to expand and pulling your

tummy button in towards the spine. Exhale as you push upwards.

- Keep your eyes fixed on a point in front of you at about eye level.
- Make sure you do not bend forwards excessively or curve your back as this will stress your lower back and reduce the emphasis on your legs.
- Keep your hips under the bar as much as possible and your knees tracking over your toes as you rise.
- Do not rely on a weight belt unless you are using maximal weight or it could result in a weakening of the abdominal muscles. The abdominal wall should be drawn in towards the spine rather than pushing out against a belt when lifting.

Variations

Wider stance
Placing your feet just over shoulder-width apart (but not too far or you may lose stability) and taking the squat slightly deeper than parallel places more emphasis on the gluteals on the upward part of the movement. Make sure you practise perfect form and control the squat – you will have to reduce the weight on the bar, since going deeper can put greater strain on the knees. You'll find this technique will not only increase your overall strength but also better shape your gluteals!

Smith machine squats
Squats performed using a Smith machine are less effective than barbell squats and may increase injury risk when you are not using a machine as it does not develop the stabiliser muscles. Since the bar travels in a straight line, this alters your natural movement, taking much of the emphasis away from your all-important stabilising muscles. If you must use a Smith machine, position your feet so that your heels are directly under the bar.

◆ Dead lift ◆

Target muscles

Gluteals, quadriceps, hamstrings, hip flexors, lower back, adductors, latissimus dorsi, trapezius, abdominals

The dead lift is a fundamental exercise for increasing overall mass, strength and power in both the lower and upper body. Like squats, it is a maximum stimulation movement.

Starting position

1. Stand in front of the barbell with your feet parallel and shoulder-width apart.
2. Bend your legs until your hips and knees are at the same level, keeping your rib cage up and your head level. Your back should be straight, at a 45° angle to the floor.
3. Grasp the bar, with your hands just over shoulder-width apart, one overhand, the other under. This will facilitate better balance and keep the barbell in the same plane.

The movement

1. Using the power of your legs and hips, and keeping your arms straight, lift the bar from the floor until your legs are straight. The bar should be against the upper part of your thighs. Hold for a count of one.
2. Slowly return the bar to the floor, keeping your torso erect, arms straight and head up, eyes looking forwards. Your chest should be slightly forwards and over the bar.

Tips

- Keep your back straight – i.e. in its normal position – throughout the movement. Do not lean forwards.
- Keep the bar as close as possible to your legs throughout the movement.
- Make sure your knees travel in line with your toes – do not allow them to travel inwards.

Variations

On a block
Stand on a low, sturdy block or platform so that the bar is at the same level as your feet. This increases the ROM and, therefore, the benefits.

♦ Leg press ♦

Target muscles

Gluteals, quadriceps, hamstrings

Also a good strength and mass builder for the lower body, the leg press is often preferred by those with weak lower-back muscles. There is little involvement of the stabiliser muscles and, paradoxically, may lead to further weakening or imbalance of the deep muscles close to the spine and pelvis. To reduce injury risk, keep your lower back flat on the support.

Starting position

1. Sit into the base of the leg press machine (seated, lying or incline) with your back firmly against the padding.
2. Position your feet parallel and hip-width apart on the platform.
3. Release the safety bars and extend your legs.

The movement

1. Slowly bend your legs and lower the platform in a controlled fashion until your knees almost touch your chest. Hold for a count of one.

2. Return the platform to the starting position, pushing hard through your heels.

Tips

- Keep your back in full contact with the base; do not allow your lower spine to curl up as you lower the platform.
- Keep your knees in line with your toes.
- Do not 'snap out' or lock your knees as you straighten your legs back to the starting position.
- Make sure you do not bounce your knees off your chest.

Variations

Wide foot spacing
Placing your feet shoulder-width apart with your toes angled outwards puts more emphasis on the inner thigh muscles and will therefore help to develop this part of the thigh.

Feet higher on platform
Placing your feet higher on the platform so that your toes are almost off the edge puts more emphasis on the hamstrings and gluteals and will therefore help develop these muscles.

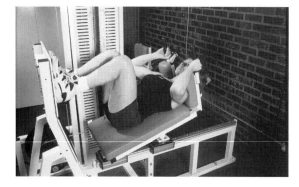

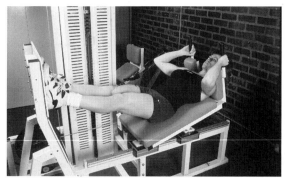

♦ Leg extension ♦

Target muscles

Quadriceps

This exercise helps to develop the front thigh muscles, particularly the teardrop muscles that hold the knee.

Starting position

1. Sit on the leg extension machine, adjusting it so that the back of your thighs are fully supported on the seat.
2. Hook your feet under the foot pads. The pads should rest on the lowest part of your shins, just above your ankles.
3. Hold on to the sides of the seat or the handles on the sides of the machine to prevent your hips lifting as you perform the exercise.

The movement

1. Straighten your legs to full extension, keeping your thighs and backside fully in contact with the bench.

2. Hold this fully contracted position for a count of two; then slowly return to the starting point.

Tips

- Do not allow your hips to raise off the seat.
- Try to 'resist' the weight as you lower your legs back to the starting point – avoid letting the weight swing your legs back.
- Make sure you fully straighten the leg until the knees are locked – do not perform partial movements.
- Avoid swinging/kicking your legs – control the movement.

Variations

One-leg extension
You can do leg extensions with one leg at a time. This allows you to concentrate fully on each repetition.

Toes outwards
Angling the feet slightly outwards places more emphasis on the vastus lateralis.

Toes inwards
Angling the feet slightly inwards places more emphasis on the vastus medialis.

◆ Front lunge ◆ (dumbbell or barbell)

Target muscles

Quadriceps, hamstrings, gluteals

Starting position

1. Place a bar across the back of your shoulders or hold a pair of dumbbells at the sides of your body with arms fully extended (palms facing your body).
2. Stand with your feet shoulder-width apart, toes pointing forwards. Lift your chest up and look straight ahead.

The movement

1. Take an exaggerated step forwards with your right leg, bending the knee and lowering your hips.
2. Lower yourself until your right thigh is parallel to the floor and your knee is at an angle of 90°. Your left leg should be about 10–15 cm above the floor. Hold for a count of one.
3. Push hard with your right leg to return to the starting position.
4. Complete the desired number of repetitions; then repeat with the left leg leading.

Tips

- Keep your front knee positioned directly over your ankle – do not allow it to extend further forwards as this can cause strain to the knee.
- Keep your body erect throughout the movement – do not lean forwards.

Variations

Step length

A shorter step forwards places more emphasis on the quadriceps and a larger step forward places more emphasis on the gluteal and hamstring muscles.

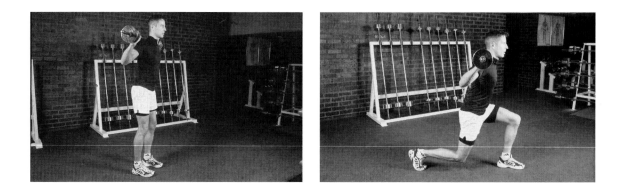

♦ Reverse lunge ♦

Target muscles

Gluteals, hamstrings, quadriceps

Starting position

1. Place a barbell across the back of your shoulders or hold a pair of dumbbells at the sides of your body with arms fully extended (palms facing your body).
2. Stand with your feet shoulder-width apart, toes pointing forwards. Lift your chest up and look straight ahead.

The movement

1. Drop your right leg behind your body, bending your left leg, lowering your hips and keeping your trunk upright.
2. Lower yourself into a one-legged squat position on your left leg until your left thigh is parallel to the floor. Your left knee should be at an angle of 90°. Hold for a count of one.

3. Push hard through your left leg, strongly contracting the gluteals, quadriceps and hamstrings to return your right leg into position. Don't push through your right (back) leg.
4. Complete the desired number of repetitions; then repeat with the left leg leading.

Tips

• Keep your front knee positioned directly over your ankle – do not allow it to extend further forwards.
• Keep your body erect throughout the movement – do not lean forwards.

Variation

Smith machine reverse lunge
Stand directly under the bar of the Smith machine so that it rests fairly low across your upper back while still allowing you to maintain an upright posture. Hold the bar and lift it from the rack, unlocking the safety catches. Perform the movement as above.

♦ Lying leg curl ♦

Target muscles

Hamstrings
Also used Gastrocnemius

Starting position

1. Lie face down on the leg curl machine and hook your heels under the roller pads. Adjust the machine if necessary so that your knees are just off the end of the bench and your thighs are fully supported.
2. Hold on to the hand grips or the edge of the bench for support.

The movement

1. Bend your knees, bringing your heels towards your backside.
2. Hold this fully contracted position for a count of two then slowly lower your heels back to the starting position.

Tips

• Keep your hips and thighs in contact with the bench throughout the movement – do not allow your hips to rise.

• Control the movement on both the upwards and downwards phase – avoid kicking your heels back fast.

Variations

Toes pointed
Performing the movement with your toes pointed intensifies the work performed by the hamstrings.

Single leg curl
You can do leg curls with one leg at a time. This allows you to focus fully on each repetition.

Using a dumbbell
If you do not have access to a leg curl machine, you can improvise with a dumbbell. Position yourself as above on a bench. Bend your knees to 90° so the soles of your feet face the ceiling. Get your training partner to place a dumbbell securely between your feet so that the plates are parallel to the ceiling. Slowly straighten your legs until almost parallel to the floor and then curl them again, until your hamstrings are fully contracted. Repeat for the desired number of repetitions.

♦ Straight-leg dead lift ♦

Target muscles

Hamstrings, gluteals, lower back

This exercise is only suitable for advanced weight trainers as it requires a high degree of technical skill. Performed correctly, it can work the hamstrings even more effectively than the leg curl.

Starting position

1. Grasp a barbell with your hands slightly wider than shoulder-width apart, using an overhand grip.
2. Stand up straight, looking directly ahead.

The movement

1. Keep your back flat and legs nearly straight.

2. Bend forwards from the hips until your back is parallel to the ground. You should feel a stretch in your hamstrings and gluteals. As you bend forwards, your hips and gluteals should move backwards and your body should be centred through your heels.
3. At the bottom of the movement, do not allow the weight to touch the floor and don't round your back.
4. Hold for a count of one then forcefully contract your gluteals and hamstrings to raise your torso back into the erect starting position.

Tips

- Keep your back flat. Rounding your back will increase the risk of injury.
- Do not lower the bar too far. The bar should be hanging at arms' length below you. Going below this point hyperflexes the spine, putting it in a vulnerable position and increasing injury risk to the lower back.

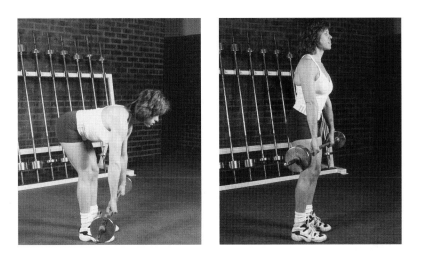

♦ Standing calf raise ♦

Target muscles

Gastrocnemius, soleus

This is perhaps the best exercise for overall development of the calves.

Starting position

1. Place your shoulders under the pads of a standing calf raise machine, or place a barbell across the back of your shoulders.
2. Step on to the platform or, if you are using a barbell, use a step or block. Allow your heels to hang off the edge.
3. Stand with your feet hip-width apart and pointing directly ahead.
4. Straighten your legs as you lift the selected weight clear of the rest of the stack.

The movement

1. Rise up on your toes as high as possible.
2. Hold the fully contracted position for a count of two; then slowly lower your heels down as far as they will go.

Tips

- Keep your legs straight throughout the movement to keep maximal emphasis on the calves and reduce the involvement of the quadriceps.
- Stretch your calves fully at the bottom of the movement – your heels should be lower than your toes.
- Do not bounce up from the bottom – keep the movement smooth and continuous.
- Keep your body straight – do not hunch.

Variations

Toes pointing out
Angling your feet outwards at 45° places more emphasis on the inner part of the calves.

Toes pointing in
Angling your feet inwards at 45° places more emphasis on the outer part of the calves.

Smith machine calf raise
Place your shoulders under the bar of a Smith machine and step on to a low platform or block with your heels hanging off the edge. Perform the calf raise as above.

♦ One-leg dumbbell ♦
calf raise

Target muscles

Gastrocnemius, soleus

This exercise is a good alternative to the calf raise if you do not have a calf raise machine.

Starting position

1. Hold a dumbbell in your right hand with your arm hanging down by your side, palm facing your body.
2. Place the ball of the right foot on the edge of a block or platform, allowing your heel to hang off the edge.
3. Hold on to a suitable support with the other hand to steady yourself.

The movement

1. Rise up as high as possible on the ball of your foot.

2. Hold the fully contracted position for a count of two; then slowly lower your heel down as far as it will go.
3. Complete the desired number of repetitions; then repeat on the left leg.

Tips

- Keep your exercising leg straight throughout the movement.
- Keep your body upright.
- Stretch your calf fully at the bottom of the movement – your heel should be lower than your toes.
- Keep the movement smooth and continuous.

Variations

Toes pointing out
Angling your feet outwards at 45° places more emphasis on the inner part of the calves.

Toes pointing in
Angling your feet inwards at 45° places more emphasis on the outer part of the calves.

◆ Leg press machine ◆ calf press

Target muscles

Gastrocnemius, soleus

Starting position

1. Position yourself in a leg press machine.
2. Place the balls of your feet on the bottom of the platform with your heels hanging off the edge. Your legs should be fully extended and feet hip-width apart. Release the safety catch.

The movement

1. Press the platform away from you as far as possible.
2. Hold the fully contracted position for a count of two; then slowly lower your heels down as far as they will go.

Tips

- Do not hurry the reps or bounce up from the bottom.
- Stretch your calves fully at the bottom of the movement – your heels should be lower than your toes.
- Keep your legs straight (not locked) throughout the movement.

Variations

Toes pointing out
Angling your feet outwards at 45° places more emphasis on the inner part of the calves.

Toes pointing in
Angling your feet inwards at 45° places more emphasis on the outer part of the calves.

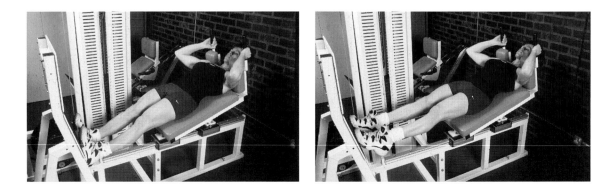

Chapter 5

Back

Training your back will change the proportions of your entire body. Well-developed latissimus dorsi muscles (lats) create that classic V-shape, making your waist appear smaller and, for women, balancing the curves of the lower body.

Strong back muscles are important in sports that involve pulling actions, such as rowing. These actions are used in rugby tackling, judo, boxing, gymnastics and swimming, especially butterfly and front crawl. A strong back will also help you develop other major muscle groups, as your back assists in key exercises such as squatting, shoulder presses and standing biceps curls; while having a strong back helps in everyday activities, such as lifting and carrying, and prevents back injuries.

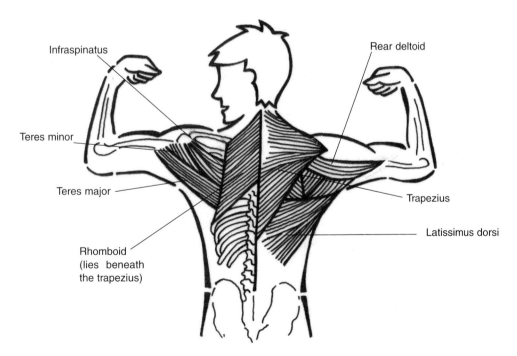

Infraspinatus

Rear deltoid

Teres minor

Teres major

Trapezius

Rhomboid
(lies beneath
the trapezius)

Latissimus dorsi

Figure 5.1 Muscles of the back and neck

◆ **Muscle know-how** ◆

The major muscles in the upper back include: the trapezius, the diamond-shaped muscle which extends from the back of the neck to the mid-back (this may be divided into upper and mid-portions) and which draws the shoulderblades backwards and upwards – as well as turning the head and bending it backwards; the latissimus dorsi ('lats'), the large wing-like muscles running from your shoulders to your waist that make up the majority of the muscle mass of the upper and mid-back and which draw the arms downwards; the rhomboids (lying beneath the mid-part of the trapezius in the central upper back) which help draw the shoulderblades backwards; and the smaller infraspinatus, supraspinatus, teres major and teres minor muscles which are located around the shoulderblades and rotate the arms outwards.

The erector spinae running along the sides of the mid- and lower spine straighten the trunk from a flexed position, as well as moving the trunk sideways. They work in concert with the abdominals and oblique muscles to stabilise the torso (*see* p. 82).

Technique note

Every exercise listed and described in the exercise directory includes 2 photographs demonstrating the exercise at the start and at the mid-point positions. It is suggested that you use these photographs as a guide to correct technique.

♦ Lat pull-down ♦

Target muscles

Latissimus dorsi, rhomboids
Also used Biceps, posterior deltoids, fore-arms

Starting position

1. Hold the bar, with your hands just over shoulder-width apart and palms facing forwards.
2. Sit on the seat, adjusting it so that your knees fit snugly under the roller pads. Your arms should be fully extended.

The movement

1. Pull the bar down towards your chest until it touches the upper part of your chest, arching your back slightly.
2. Hold for a count of two; then slowly return to the starting position.

Tips

- Keep your trunk as still as possible – avoid swinging backwards.
- Focus on keeping your elbows directly under the bar and squeezing the shoulder-blades together.
- Do not shorten the return phase of the movement – extend your arms fully.
- Do not lean back too far.
- Use wrist straps to improve your grip when using heavy weights (*see* p. xx).
- Do not pull the bar down behind your neck. This can stress the weaker muscles in the shoulders and reduce the work done by the back muscles.

Variations

Close grip
This variation works the inner portion of the latissimus dorsi rather than the outer portion, thus creating more depth to the mid-back. Use a triangle bar attachment and bring it down in front of your neck until it just touches the mid-point of your chest.

Reverse grip
This variation also thickens the latissimus dorsi rather than widening them, thus creating more depth to the mid-back. Use a short straight bar attachment and hold the bar with your palms facing towards you, about 15–20 cm apart.

♦ Chins (pull-ups) ♦

Target muscles

Latissimus dorsi, trapezius, rhomboids, infraspinatus, teres major and minor
Also used Biceps, posterior deltoids, forearms

This is a classic exercise for creating width and depth to the back. It is a difficult exercise when performed without assistance so it's best to perform it first in your back workout.

Starting position

1. Hang from a chinning bar with your hands just over shoulder-width apart, palms facing forwards.
2. Your arms should be fully extended and your ankles crossed.

The movement

1. Pull yourself up slowly until the top of your chest nearly touches the bar. Lead with your upper chest.
2. Pause for a second or two; then slowly lower back to the starting position.

Tips

- Do not swing your legs forwards or jerk as you pull yourself up – this greatly reduces the stress placed on the back muscles.
- Fix your eyes slightly upwards as you pull yourself up, slightly arching your back.
- Ensure your trunk and thighs maintain a straight line.
- Do not shorten the return phase of the movement – extend your arms fully.

Variations

Behind neck
This variation places extra emphasis on the rhomboids and posterior deltoids. Pull yourself up until the base of your neck just touches the bar.

Close grip
This variation places more stress on the lower lats and biceps. Use either an overhand or underhand grip, with your hands shoulder-width apart.

Parallel grip
This variation works the lower lats as well as the middle, adding thickness and density to these regions of the back. Hook a triangle bar over the chinning bar and pull yourself up so that your mid-chest touches the triangle bar.

♦ One-arm row ♦

Target muscles

Latissimus dorsi, trapezius, rhomboids, infraspinatus, teres major and minor
Also used Biceps, posterior deltoids

Starting position

1. Hold a dumbbell in your right hand, palm facing your body.
2. Bend forwards from the hips, placing your left hand and knee on a bench to stabilise yourself. Your back should be flat and almost horizontal and your right arm fully extended.

The movement

1. Pull the dumbbell up towards your waist, drawing your elbow back as far as it can go. Keep the dumbbell close to your body.
2. Allow the dumbbell to touch your rib cage lightly. Pause for a count of one; then slowly lower the dumbbell until your arm is fully extended.
3. After completing the required number of repetitions, perform the exercise with your left arm.

Tips

• Keep your lower back flat and still – do not twist your trunk.
• Make sure you row the dumbbell to the side of your rib cage – do not pull the dumbbell up to your shoulder.

♦ Seated cable row ♦

Target muscles

Latissimus dorsi, trapezius, rhomboids, teres major and minor
Also used Erector spinae, biceps, forearms, pectoralis major

Starting position

1. Sit facing the cable row machine and place your feet against the foot rests. Grasp the bar and bend your knees slightly.
2. Lean forwards and grasp the pulley handles, while maintaining a normal, slightly curved spinal position.
3. Pull back a little way until your torso is nearly upright and your arms are fully extended.

The movement

1. Pull the bar towards you until it touches your lower rib/upper abdomen region. You should be pulling your elbows and shoulders directly backwards as far as possible.
2. Hold for a count of two; then slowly return to the starting position, maintaining a near-upright position.

Tips

- To achieve maximum back development, keep your torso nearly upright during the entire movement – it should not move forwards or backwards more than 10°.
- Maintain a normal curve in your back – do not arch your back excessively.
- Keep your legs slightly bent and still throughout the movement.
- Inhale at the start of the movement; then hold your breath during the pulling phase – this helps stabilise your torso. Exhale only towards the end of the movement once your arms are extended.

Variations

Straight bar

Cable rows may be performed using a short straight bar instead of a triangle bar, with a palms-down grip. This emphasises the posterior deltoids, rhomboids and mid-part of the trapezius.

♦ Bent-over barbell row ♦

Target muscles

Latissimus dorsi, trapezius, rhomboids, teres major and minor
Also used Biceps, forearms

Starting position

1. Place the bar on the floor in front of you.
2. Stand with your feet parallel and shoulder-width apart.
3. Bending forwards from the hips, keeping your back flat and slightly bending your knees, grasp the bar with an overhand grip that is slightly wider than shoulder-width apart.
4. Lift the bar just a short way off the floor. Position your body so that your torso is near-parallel to the ground, arms fully extended.

The movement

1. Slowly pull the bar towards your lower chest until it just touches the lower part of your rib cage.
2. Hold this position for a count of one; then slowly lower the bar to the starting position.

Tips

- As you pull the bar up, squeeze your shoulderblades together and keep your elbows directly above your hands.
- Keep your back flat throughout the movement – do not round your back or you risk injury.
- Keep your torso still – it is tempting to move your torso upwards with the bar to generate momentum. This reduces the work on the back muscles and increases the risk of injury.

♦ Straight-arm pull-downs ♦

Target muscles

Latissimus dorsi, trapezius, rhomboids, teres major and minor

Starting position

1. Stand in front of a lat pull-down machine.
2. Hold the bar with your arms extended, palms facing downwards.
3. Pull down the bar to shoulder level.

The movement

1. Keeping your arms extended, pull the bar down until it just touches your upper thighs.
2. Hold for a count of two; then slowly return the bar to the starting position.

Tips

- Keep your wrists straight throughout the movement.
- Allow a very slight bend in the elbows – they should not be locked.
- Keep your body still and upright throughout the movement – you will need to use your abdominal muscles to stabilise your torso.

♦ Dumbbell shrug ♦

Target muscles

Trapezius (upper), rhomboids, various other neck and shoulder girdle muscles.

Starting position

1. Stand with your feet hip-width apart.
2. Hold a pair of dumbbells by your sides level with your thighs, palms facing backwards. Keep your arms straight.

The movement

1. Raise your shoulders straight up towards your ears, keeping your arms straight.
2. Hold for a count of two; then lower the dumbbells back to the starting position.

Tips

- Keep your arms straight throughout the movement.
- Lift and lower the dumbbells slowly and deliberately – don't jerk them.
- As you lower the dumbbells, allow your shoulders to drop down as far as possible – this stretches the trapezius and increases the ROM.
- Do not rotate your shoulders backwards at the top of the movement – this increases the risk of injury to the shoulder and places no further work on the trapezius.
- Use straps to improve your grip.

Variation

Barbell shrug
Shrugs may be performed with a barbell instead of dumbbells. Hold a barbell in front of or behind your thighs, keep your arms straight and move the bar up and down as described above.

◆ Back extension on the floor ◆

Target muscles

Erector spinae, gluteals

The lower back muscles rarely work through their full ROM during daily activities, nor during exercises for other muscle groups. While the lower back is often involved as a stabiliser in other exercises, such as squats, it is important to include a specific back extension movement in your back workout, which targets the muscles effectively and makes everyday activities easier to perform with less injury risk.

Starting position

1. Lie face down on the floor.
2. Place your hands by the sides of your head, elbows out to the sides. Alternatively, your arms may be placed behind on your back.

The movement

1. Slowly raise your head, shoulders and upper chest from the floor. This will be just a short distance.
2. Pause for a count of two; then lower slowly to the floor.

Tips

- Keep your head facing downwards to the floor in line with your spine.
- Keep your legs relaxed on the floor – do not raise them.
- Only raise yourself as far as you feel comfortable.

Variations

Back extension bench

Tuck your ankles underneath the pads and position your body so that your hips are resting on the middle pad, arms crossed in front of you. Raise your torso until you are parallel with the floor – do not rise higher than this. Slowly bend forwards at the waist until you are almost perpendicular to the floor. Keep your back flat.

To make the movement harder, place your hands along the sides of your head. Alternatively, if you are an advanced weight trainer, hold a small weight disc against your chest.

◆ Back extension with ◆ Swiss ball

Target muscles

Erector spinae, gluteals

Starting position

1. Lie over the Swiss ball, face down, keeping your hips halfway up the ball rather than balanced on top of it.
2. Place your arms either crossed over your chest or by the sides of your head.
3. Keep your legs wide and straight out behind you.

The movement

1. Slowly raise your upper body in a straight line towards the ceiling.
2. Hold for a count of two; then slowly lower.

Tips

- Do not arch your back.
- Keep your head in line with your spine.
- To make the movement harder, bring your legs closer together.

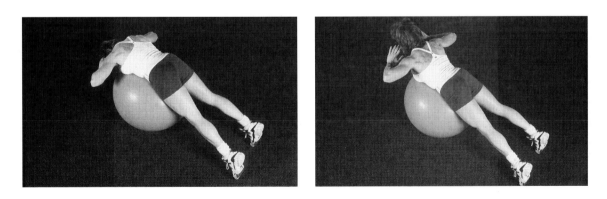

Chapter 6

Chest

The desire for a bigger, better-developed chest is perhaps the greatest motivator for men to strength train. It somehow symbolises heroism and male virility. Women, too, can benefit from chest training. Although it won't increase the size of your breasts (they are mostly fat tissue), it will create the appearance of a fuller and more shapely chest.

Strong chest muscles are advantageous in many sports. These muscles are involved in all forward- and upward-reaching actions – e.g. in rugby tackling and grabbing an opponent – and are also used in throwing and hitting movements – e.g. during forehand drives in tennis and squash; when throwing the ball overhead in netball, basketball and volleyball; and throwing the discus, shot-put and javelin. A strong chest is also advantageous in swimming (breaststroke) and several gymnastic disciplines.

♦ Muscle know-how ♦

The largest muscle of the chest is the pectoralis major, which attaches to the collarbone (clavicle) and sternum, and inserts into the upper-arm bone (humerus). It pulls the arm in front of the chest from any position, flexes the shoulder to allow pushing, and lifts the arm forwards. The smaller pectoralis minor lies beneath the pectoralis major and helps lower the shoulderblade.

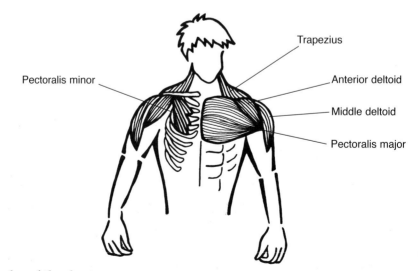

Figure 6.1 Muscles of the chest

♦ Barbell bench press ♦

Target muscles

Pectoralis major (mid-chest)
Also used Anterior deltoids, triceps

Starting position

1. Lie on your back on a flat bench, ideally with an attached barbell rack. If you have an excessive arch in your back, place your feet on the end of the bench or on a low step.
2. Hold the bar, with your hands just over shoulder-width apart, palms facing forwards.
3. Remove the bar from the barbell rack and position it directly over your chest with your arms fully extended (but not locked).

The movement

1. Slowly lower the bar down to your chest. The bar should touch your upper chest just above your nipple line. Hold for a count of two.
2. Push the bar upwards in a slightly backwards arc so that it ends up over your shoulders.

Tips

• Keep your hips firmly on the bench. If you lift your hips to generate leverage, you will risk lower-back strain.

• Do not arch your back as you push the bar upwards or you will reduce the amount of work done by the chest.
• Do not bounce the bar off your chest or use the momentum of the weight to complete the repetition. Again, this reduces the amount of chest work and risks injury to the chest muscles.
• Keep your palms facing forwards and your wrists straight.

Variations

Wide grip
Using a grip one and a half times shoulder-width apart places more emphasis on the pectorals (especially the outer part) and less on the triceps.

Narrow grip
Using a shoulder-width grip places more emphasis on the triceps and the inner pectorals.

Machine
The press may be performed on a Smith machine or a chest press machine. This has the advantage of being safer and not requiring a spotter to pass you the bar. However, you are locked into a fixed, vertical plane of movement that does not accommodate the natural arc of the movement so that there is therefore less of a contribution from the accessory muscles. As a result the muscles gain less stimulation compared with a free-weight bench press.

♦ Dumbbell bench press ♦

Target muscles

Pectoralis major (mid-chest)
Also used Anterior deltoids, triceps

This exercise develops the chest equally well as the barbell bench press but allows a slightly greater ROM, thus stimulating greater development. It requires more involvement of the stabiliser muscles to balance and control the dumbbells so you will probably need to use less weight.

Starting position

1. Lie on your back on a flat or incline bench. If you have an excessive arch in your back, place your feet on the end of the bench.
2. Hold a pair of dumbbells, with your palms facing forwards and your arms fully extended, positioned over your shoulders.

The movement

1. Slowly lower the dumbbells down to your armpit area.
2. Hold the position for a count of two; then press the dumbbells back to the starting position.

Tips

* Keep your hips firmly on the bench throughout the movement.
* Lower the dumbbells as far as you can, aiming for a maximum but comfortable stretch.
* Keep the dumbbells over your chest area – do not let them travel back towards your head.

♦ Incline barbell bench press ♦

Target muscles

Pectoralis minor (upper chest)
Also used Anterior deltoids, triceps, pectoralis major

Starting position

1. Lie on an incline bench angled at 30–60° (the steeper the incline, the greater the stress on the upper pectorals and anterior deltoids). Ideally the bench should have an attached barbell rack.
2. Hold the bar with your hands shoulder-width apart, palms facing forwards. Remove the bar from the barbell rack so it is positioned directly over your collarbone with your arms fully extended.

The movement

1. Bend your arms, allowing your elbows to travel out to the sides, and slowly lower the bar down to your chest.
2. The bar should just touch the upper part of your chest beneath your collarbone. Hold for a count of two.
3. Push the bar back to the starting position.

Tips

- Do not arch your back as you push the bar upwards. This risks lower-back strain.
- Do not bounce the bar off your chest or use the momentum of the weight to complete the repetition.
- The higher you place the bar on your chest, the greater the work placed on the anterior deltoids rather than the upper chest.

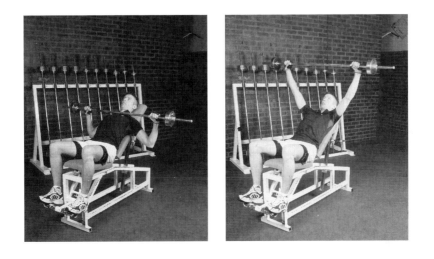

♦ Incline dumbbell bench ♦ press

Target muscles

Pectoralis minor (upper chest)
Also used Anterior deltoids, triceps, pectoralis major

Starting position

1. Sit on an incline bench, angled at 30–60° (the steeper the incline, the greater the stress on the upper pectorals and anterior deltoids).
2. Pick up a dumbbell in each hand and place them on your thighs.
3. Lie on the bench, at the same time bringing the dumbbells to shoulder level. Your palms should face forwards.

The movement

1. Press the dumbbells directly over your upper chest until your arms are fully extended. Hold for a count of two.
2. Lower the weights slowly until they are by your shoulders. You should achieve a maximal but comfortable stretch.
3. Pause for a second before pressing them up again.

Tips

- Press the dumbbells in a straight line, not back over your head.
- Do not set the angle of the bench too high otherwise the anterior deltoids will be targeted and take much of the emphasis away from the chest.

♦ Dumbbell flye ♦

Target muscles

Pectoralis major (mid-chest)
Also used Anterior deltoids, pectoralis minor

Starting position

1. Lie on your back on a flat bench with your feet flat on the floor. If you have an excessive arch in your back, place your feet on a step so that your knees are bent at 90°.
2. Hold a dumbbell in each hand and hold them above your chest with your arms extended and palms facing each other. Bend your arms very slightly.

The movement

1. Slowly lower the dumbbell out to your sides in a semi-circular arc. Keep your elbows locked in the slightly bent position throughout the ROM.

2. When your upper arms reach shoulder level and you feel a strong stretch in your shoulders, return the dumbbells to the starting position, following the same arc. Do not pause at the bottom of the movement.

Tips

- Maintain the slight bend in your elbows. Don't allow them to bend to 90° otherwise this turns the movement into a dumbbell press.
- Do not allow your upper arms to go much below shoulder level as this could place excessive stress on the shoulder joints and risk muscle or tendon tears.

Variations

Incline flye
Performing flyes on an incline bench set at 30–45° increases the stress placed on the upper chest and anterior deltoids. It is therefore particularly good for developing mass and thickness in the upper chest.

♦ Pec dec flye ♦

Target muscles

Pectoralis major (mid-chest)
Also used Anterior deltoids, pectoralis minor

Starting position

1. Sit on the seat of the pec dec machine, ensuring your lower back is pressed against the back support and adjusting the seat height so that your elbows and shoulders are level with the bottom of the pads.
2. Place your forearms against the pads. Check that your shoulders and elbows make a horizontal line.

The movement

1. Move the pads towards each other until they just touch in front of your chest.
2. Hold for a count of two; then slowly return the pads to the starting position.

Tips

- Contract your pectorals hard at the mid-point.
- Do not curl your shoulders forwards as you bring the pads together.
- Move the pads in a smooth arc – do not jerk the pads together as this reduces the work on the pectorals.

♦ Cable cross-over ♦

Target muscles

Pectoralis major (lower and mid-chest)
Also used Anterior deltoids

Starting position

1. Attach the handles to two overhead pulley machines.
2. Hold the handles, palms facing down, and stand midway between the machines with your feet hip-width apart or with one foot in front of the other for balance. Your arms should be fully extended so you achieve a good stretch in your pectorals.
3. Bend forwards slightly from the waist and maintain this position throughout the exercise.

The movement

1. Draw the handles towards each other in an arcing motion, aiming for a point approximately 30 cm in front of your hips.
2. When the handles meet, squeeze your pectorals hard and hold for a count of two.
3. Slowly return the handles to the starting position.

Tips

- Keep your back erect and elbows slightly bent (at 10–15°) throughout the movement.
- Focus on using your chest muscles to perform the movement – do not curl your shoulders forwards as you bring the handles together.
- You can vary the angle at which you pull the handles down to place emphasis on slightly different areas of the chest.

Chapter 7

Shoulders

Shoulder training can change the proportions of your physique. Well-developed shoulders draw more attention to your upper body and create an aesthetically pleasing taper, making your waist appear smaller.

Strong shoulders are advantageous in most sports involving upper body motions. The shoulder muscles are involved in:

- overhead pushing actions – e.g. tumbling and vaulting in gymnastics, and the clean and jerk in weightlifting
- overhead hitting actions – e.g. the tennis serve, the overhead smash in badminton and overhead hits and blocks in volleyball and basketball
- raising the arms forwards or sideways away from the body – e.g. tennis or squash strokes, and front crawl in swimming.

You need to use a variety of exercises to train your shoulders as there is no single exercise

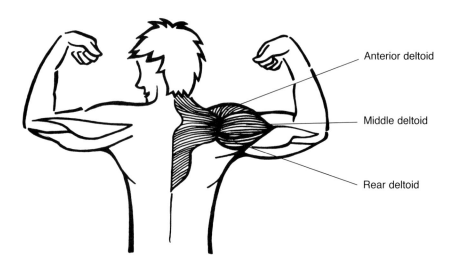

Figure 7.1 Muscles of the arms and shoulders

that works the whole area. The shoulders are comprised of three heads (*see* fig. 7.1), each of which needs to be targeted if you want full and well-balanced development.

If you are prone to shoulder injuries, however, pay attention to your training technique as poor technique can exacerbate any underlying problems.

♦ Muscle know-how ♦

The shoulder muscle comprises three distinct portions or *heads*, collectively known as the deltoids, which is a term derived from the Greek 'delta', owing to their geometrically triangular shape. The deltoids cover the front, side and back of the shoulder, from the scapula (collarbone) to the middle of the upper arm (humerus). Each head serves a particular function. The anterior (front) deltoid lifts the arm forwards and upwards; the medial (outer) deltoid lifts the arm away from the mid-line of the body to the side (abduction); and the posterior (rear) deltoid lifts the arm to the rear or draws the elbow backwards behind the shoulders. Because of their location and function, several of the following exercises that target the deltoids also use muscles in the back and chest (*see* pp. 45–6 and p. 56).

♦ Dumbbell press ♦

Target muscles

Anterior and medial deltoids, upper pectoralis major
Also used Triceps, shoulder girdle muscles (trapezius, supraspinatus)

Starting position

1. Sit on an upright bench, angled at 75–90° so that your lower back is firmly in contact with the bench.
2. Hold a pair of dumbbells, hands facing forwards, level with your shoulders.

The movement

1. Press the dumbbells upwards and inwards until they almost touch over your head.
2. Straighten your arms but do not lock out your elbows. Hold momentarily.
3. Lower the dumbbells slowly back to the starting position.

Tips

• Keep your torso upright – don't lean backwards or arch your spine as you press the bar upwards as this will strain your lower back.
• Hold your abdominal muscles taut to help stabilise your spine or, if you are using a very heavy weight, wear a weightlifting belt.
• Lower the dumbbells until they touch your shoulders – don't shorten the movement.

♦ Lateral raise ♦

Target muscles

Medial deltoids
Also used Trapezius, anterior deltoids

Starting position

1. Stand with your feet hip-width apart.
2. Hold a dumbbell in each hand, arms straight at your sides and hands facing inwards.

The movement

1. Keeping your elbows very slightly bent (at 10°), raise the dumbbells out to the sides.
2. Raise them until your elbows and hands are level with your shoulders – i.e. parallel to the floor. Your palms should face the floor. Hold momentarily.
3. Slowly return to the starting position, resisting the weight on the way back down.

Tips

• Your little finger should be higher than your thumb at the top of the movement, as if you were pouring water from a jug.
• Do not swing the dumbbells out or lean back as you raise them. Keep your body very still.
• Lead with your elbows rather than your hands.

Variations

Single arm
Lateral raises can be performed using one arm at a time. Hold on to an upright support with the other hand to help keep you steady. This allows you to concentrate fully on the movement and helps to prevent you swinging the dumbbells upwards.

Cable lateral raise
The movement can be performed using a low pulley machine. You will need to use a lighter weight but this keeps more continuous tension on the deltoids.

Seated lateral raise
You can perform the movement sitting on the end of a bench. This reduces the tendency to generate momentum by swinging your body and is, therefore, a stricter movement. You may need to use lighter dumbbells to complete the exercise in good form.

◆ Upright row ◆

Target muscles

Anterior and medial deltoids, trapezius
Also used Biceps, brachioradialis

Starting position

1. Stand with your feet shoulder-width apart.
2. Hold the barbell with your hands about 15 cm apart, palms facing towards your body. The bar should rest against the front of your thighs.

The movement

1. Pull the bar directly upwards towards your chin, bending your elbows out to the sides until the bar is level with your neck.

2. Hold for a count of two; then slowly lower the bar back to the starting position.

Tips

- Keep the bar very close to your body throughout the movement.
- Make sure you do not sway backwards as you lift the bar.
- At the top of the movement your elbows should be level with, or slightly higher than, your hands.
- Lower the bar slowly, resisting the weight.

Variations

Wide grip
Using a shoulder-width grip places more emphasis on the deltoids and less on the trapezius.

♦ Bent-over lateral raise ♦

Target muscles

Posterior deltoids
Also used Trapezius, upper back muscles

Starting position

1. Sit on the end of a bench with only half of your thighs supported.
2. Place your feet and knees together, bend forwards from the waist and hold a pair of dumbbells underneath your thighs with your palms facing each other.

The movement

1. Draw the dumbbells out to the sides, simultaneously turning your hands so that they face the floor.
2. Raise them until your elbows and hands are level with your shoulders. Hold momentarily.
3. Slowly return to the starting position, resisting the weight on the way down.

Tips

- Your little finger should be higher than your thumb at the top of the movement, as if you are pouring water from a jug.
- Keep your torso still – do not raise your body as you raise the dumbbells.
- Lead with your elbows rather than your hands.
- Keep your elbows bent at about 10° throughout to avoid straining them.

Variation

Standing bent-over lateral raise

The movement can be executed from a standing position. Stand with your feet hip-width apart, bend forwards from the waist and hold the dumbbells directly below the shoulders (arms straight). Perform the movement as described above. As your back is in an unsupported position do not use a heavy weight or attempt this if you have a weak lower back as it may place undue stress on it.

Chapter 8

Arms

Arms are the classic showpieces of strength weight trainers. Like a well-developed chest, they are visible proof of the work you put in at the gym – although for women, the result will not be a bulky masculine look (see pp. 5–6).

Developing your arm strength will help your performance in many sports. Elbow flexion (bending) and the muscles involved are important when playing forehand strokes in tennis and squash, shooting in hockey, playing a long shot in golf, pulling the body upwards in climbing, grabbing an opponent in rugby and the martial arts, and pushing movements in gymnastics.

The triceps are also involved in numerous upper-body actions, including:

• overhead hitting and throwing movements – e.g. the tennis serve, volleyball spike and basketball shot
• pushing actions – e.g. the shot-put, the chest pass in netball and basketball, throwing a punch in boxing and in the martial arts.

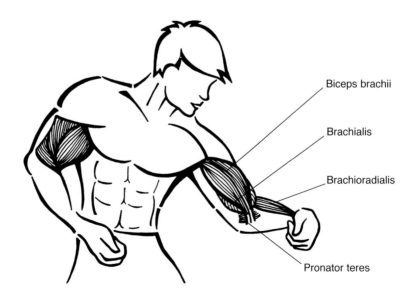

Figure 8.1 Biceps brachii

One common mistake is to train only the biceps, thinking this will produce stronger and bigger arms. However, the triceps make up the largest part of the arm muscles (see below) so it is important to devote equal time and effort to triceps training. Many men also use weights that are too heavy in their quest for bigger arms, sacrificing good technique and gaining only minimal results.

♦ Muscle know-how ♦

Approximately 60% of the upper-arm muscle mass is comprised of the triceps; 30% is comprised of the biceps brachii; and the remaining 10% comes from the brachialis muscles lying beneath the biceps.

The biceps brachii (*see* fig. 8.1 p. 70) originates above the shoulder as two muscles – the short and long heads ('bi' means 'two') – which merge at one insertion point below the elbow. These muscles are involved in flexing your arm (bending your elbow) and rotating (supinating) your forearm. The biceps brachii also assists in other arm and shoulder movements, such as raising the shoulder.

The brachialis runs under the biceps close to your elbow joint. It is also involved in arm flexion and all movements involving a palms-down position – e.g. when performing a reverse curl. The brachioradialis lies on the top side of your forearm, on the same side as your thumb but attaches just past your elbow. It is involved in all arm flexion movements, particularly when you use a neutral, or thumbs-up, grip.

The triceps brachii (*see* fig. 8.2) makes up the entire back of the arm. It has three distinct heads – the inner (long) head, the medial head and outer (lateral) head. The medial head is located on the back inner side of the arm, fairly close to the elbow. The lateral head, which works progressively

harder as the weight increases, is located on the back outer side of the arm. The long inner head, lying between the medial and lateral heads higher up on the arm gives the familiar horseshoe appearance to the outside upper arm. Whereas the medial and lateral heads only cross the elbow joint, the long head crosses both the shoulder and elbow joints.

The collective function of the triceps brachii is to partially or fully straighten the arm from a bent position. While it is difficult to isolate its individual heads, different exercises place greater emphasis on different areas. For example, the long head is best stimulated when your arm is raised overhead (e.g. in lying triceps extensions).

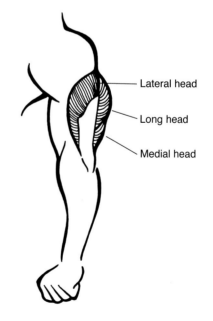

Figure 8.2 Triceps brachii

◆ Barbell curl ◆

Target muscles

Biceps brachii, brachialis
Also used Brachioradialis

Starting position

1. Stand with your feet hip-width apart.
2. Hold a barbell with your hands shoulder-width apart, palms facing forwards.
3. The bar should rest against your thighs and your arms should be fully extended.

The movement

1. Bend your elbows as you curl the bar up in a smooth arc towards your shoulders. Keep your upper arms fixed by the sides of your body.
2. Hold for a count of two; then slowly lower the bar back to the starting position.

Tips

• Do not move your upper arms or elbows at any point of the movement.

• Keep your body absolutely still – make sure you do not lean back or swing the bar up as this will strain the back and reduce the work on the biceps.
• Keep your wrists locked.
• Lower the bar under control until your arms are fully extended – shortening or rushing the downwards phase will reduce the effectiveness of the exercise.

Variations

EZ-bar curl
Arm curls can be performed using an EZ-bar instead of a straight bar. This reduces the stress on the wrists, although it puts the biceps in a biomechanically weaker position so they receive less stimulation.

Wide grip curl
Using a grip slightly wider than shoulder-width apart places more emphasis on the inner head of the biceps.

Narrow grip curl
Using a grip slightly narrower than shoulder-width apart places more emphasis on the outer head of the biceps.

♦ Preacher curl ♦

Target muscles

Biceps brachii, brachialis
Also used Brachioradialis

Starting position

1. Sit on the seat of a preacher curl machine, adjusting it so that your armpits rest over the top edge of the pad.
2. Hold a barbell with your hands shoulder-width apart, palms facing forwards.
3. Your arms should be fully extended.

The movement

1. Bend your elbows as you curl the bar up in a smooth arc towards your shoulders, stopping about 20–30 cm short of your shoulders.
2. Hold for a count of two; then slowly lower the bar back to the starting position.

Tips

- Keep your shoulders back and relaxed – avoid leaning forwards as you curl the bar up or the emphasis will shift from your biceps to your shoulders.
- Keep your body still and your wrists locked.
- Lower the bar until your arms are fully extended – shortening the downwards phase will reduce the effectiveness of the exercise.

Variations

EZ-bar preacher curl
Preacher curls can be performed using an EZ-bar instead of a straight bar. This reduces the stress on the wrists although it puts the biceps in a biomechanically weaker position so they receive less stimulation.

Dumbbell preacher curl
Preacher curls can be performed with dumbbells, allowing you to concentrate more fully on each repetition because you can perform them one arm at a time.

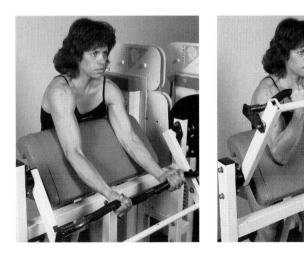

♦ Dumbbell curl ♦

Target muscles

Biceps brachii, brachialis
Also used Brachioradialis

Starting position

1. Stand with your feet hip-width apart or sit on the end of a bench.
2. Hold a pair of dumbbells, palms facing in towards your body.
3. Your arms should be fully extended.

The movement

1. Curl one dumbbell up at a time in a smooth arc towards your shoulders, rotating your forearm so that your palm faces your shoulder at the top of the movement.
2. Hold for a count of two; then slowly lower the dumbbell back to the starting position.
3. Repeat with the other arm and continue alternating arms.

Tips

- Curl the dumbbells up slowly – do not swing them up.
- Keep your upper arms fixed by the sides of your body.
- Keep your body absolutely still – make sure you do not sway backwards.
- Make sure you fully straighten your arms when you lower the dumbbells; do not shorten the downwards phase.

♦ Incline dumbbell curl ♦

Target muscles

Biceps brachii, brachialis
Also used Brachioradialis

Starting position

1. Sit on an incline bench with your back and shoulders pressed firmly against the bench.
2. Hold a pair of dumbbells by your sides, palms facing inwards.
3. Your arms should be fully extended and hang downwards.

The movement

1. Slowly curl one dumbbell towards your shoulder, rotating your forearm so that your palm faces your shoulder at the top of the movement.
2. Hold for a count of two; then slowly lower the dumbbell back to the starting position.
3. Repeat with the other arm and continue alternating arms.

Tips

- Do not allow your body to move forwards to generate momentum – keep your torso still.
- Make sure you fully straighten your arms at the bottom of the movement.

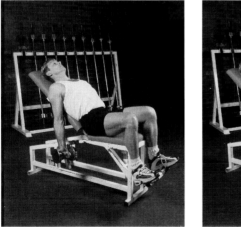

♦ Concentration curl ♦

Target muscles

Biceps brachii, brachialis
Also used Brachioradialis

Starting position

1. Sit on a bench with your legs fairly wide apart.
2. Hold a dumbbell with one hand and brace that arm against the inside of the same thigh.
3. Your arm should be full extended and your palm should be facing the opposite thigh.

The movement

1. Slowly curl the dumbbell up in a smooth arc towards your shoulder.

2. Squeeze your biceps hard at the top of the movement, hold for a count of two and then slowly lower the dumbbell back to the starting position.

Tips

- Make sure you curl the dumbbell to your shoulder and do not move your shoulder to the dumbbell. Keep your shoulder back and relaxed.
- Do not lean backwards.
- Keep your upper arm fixed.
- Make sure you fully straighten your arms when you lower the dumbbells; do not shorten the downwards phase.

♦ Triceps push-down ♦

Target muscles

Triceps (especially the outer and medial heads)
Also used Brachioradialis

Starting position

1. Attach a short, angled bar to the overhead cable of a lat machine.
2. Place your hands on the bar, palms facing downwards.
3. Bring the bar down until your elbows are at your sides and bent at about 90°.

The movement

1. Keeping your upper arms close to your body, press the bar down, moving only your forearms, until your arms are fully extended.
2. Hold for a count of two; then slowly return the bar to the starting position.

Tips

• Keep your elbows fixed firmly at your sides throughout the movement.
• Do not lean too far forwards.
• Keep your wrists locked and your palms facing you.

Variation

Short bar
You may use a short straight bar instead of the angled bar, although this places more strain on the wrists and forearms.

♦ Bench dip ♦

Target muscles

Triceps (especially the outer and medial heads)

Starting position

1. Position two benches about the length of your legs apart.
2. Place your hands shoulder-width apart, fingers facing forwards, on the edge of one bench.
3. Place your heels on the other bench so that your legs form a straight bridge between the two benches.

The movement

1. Bend your elbows and lower your body until your elbows make an angle of 90°.

2. Hold for a count of two; then straighten your arms to bring you back to the starting position.

Tips

- Keep your back close to the bench.
- Do not lock or snap out your elbows at the top of the movement.
- Keep your elbows directed backwards during both the lowering and raising phases.
- Do not shorten the downwards phase.
- Keep the movement slow – do not rush the reps.

Variations

Easier
Place your feet flat on the floor instead of on a bench.

Advanced
Place a weight disc across your lap to increase the resistance.

◆ Lying triceps extension ◆

Target muscles

Triceps (especially the long inner and medial heads)
Also used Brachioradialis

Starting position

1. Lie on your back on a flat bench. If you have an excessive arch in your back, place your feet on the end of the bench or on a low step.
2. Hold the bar with your hands slightly less than shoulder-width apart, palms facing forwards.
3. The bar should be positioned directly over your head with your arms fully extended.

The movement

1. Keeping your upper arms absolutely stationary, bend your elbows as you lower the bar until it just touches your forehead.
2. Hold for a count of two; then straighten your arms back to the starting position.

Tips

- For maximum muscle development, straighten your arms fully at the end of the movement.

- Keep your elbows perfectly still – do not allow them to move out to the sides, or backwards with the bar.
- Keep your lower back firmly down on the bench.
- Lower the bar as far back as you safely can to achieve the greatest ROM.

Variations

EZ-bar

The movement may be performed with either a straight bar or an EZ-bar. The EZ-bar places your forearms midway between supination and neutral, which you may find more comfortable.

Lying dumbbell triceps extension

Use a dumbbell instead of a barbell, placing your hands against the inner side of one of the end plates. You may also perform this exercise holding a pair of dumbbells, palms facing each other.

Lying single-arm triceps extension

Perform the movement using a dumbbell (as above), one arm at a time, palms facing inwards. You may use your free hand to steady your working elbow.

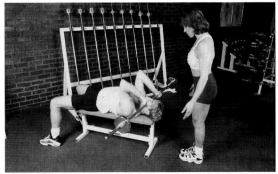

♦ Triceps kickback ♦

Target muscles

Triceps (especially the outer and medial heads)

Starting position

1. Hold a dumbbell in one hand.
2. Bend forwards from the waist until your torso is parallel to the floor.
3. Place your other hand and knee on a bench to stabilise yourself – your back should be flat and horizontal.
4. Bend the working arm to 90° at the elbow and bring it up so that your upper arm is parallel to and close to the side of your body, and the dumbbell is hanging straight down below the elbow.

The movement

1. Keeping your elbow stationary, extend your arm backwards until your arm is straight and horizontal.
2. Hold for a count of two; then slowly return to the starting position.

Tips

- Extend your arm under control – do not swing the dumbbell back.
- Keep your upper arm fixed – only your forearm moves.
- Keep your lower back flat and still.
- Use a relatively light weight as the exercise is harder to perform than many people imagine.

Chapter 9

Abdominals

A well-toned and defined mid-section reflects a lean fit body. It is the result of hard graft in the gym as well as cardio training (*see* Chapter 13) and proper nutrition (*see* Part Four). Together, they all produce strong abdominals and low body-fat levels.

Well-defined abdominals are mainly the product of low body-fat levels, which explains why even untrained people can possess washboard abs. If you are after a rippling six-pack, you need to reduce your abdominal fat layer for the muscles to show through. Increasing their size alone through exercise will not be enough. For these muscles to become visible, men need below 10–12% body fat and women need below 15–18% body fat – ranges that are below those considered healthy among the general population (*see* pp. 203–4) but which are compatible with improved sports performance.

Strong abdominals help you perform virtually every strength-training exercise and sports movement, improving core stability (*see* p. 82). Abdominal training is also important for the prevention of lower-back injuries, since these muscles help stabilise the pelvis which, in turn, helps maintain proper spine alignment. You should add a lower-back exercise such as back extensions to your abdominal routine to help balance abdominal strength.

Gadgets and machines are unnecessary – you can develop great abdominals from the basic exercises that require nothing more than

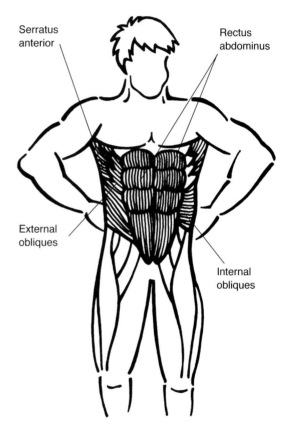

Figure 9.1 The abdominal muscles

the floor and perhaps a bench or bar. The secret to effective abdominal exercising is mental focus and technique. You should concentrate on each part of the movement, keeping it slow and controlled. Don't worry about how far you are moving – it's the *feel*

Back strain?

Weak abdominals are often associated with back problems. This is because slack abdominal muscles can become overstretched which, when combined with tight hip flexors (connecting the thigh bone to the lower vertebrae), cause the pelvis to tilt forwards (lordosis) creating an excessive arch in the lower back and potential back pain. Strong abdominals support and stabilise the pelvis and lower back. Strengthening these muscles (and stretching the hip flexors) will eliminate excessive arching in the lower back, give good posture and minimise potential back problems.

that is most important. The most common error is to perform the movements too fast, aiming for a high number of repetitions. High repetitions will only build endurance. They will not work the important FT muscle fibres that give your abdominals visible shape, nor will they increase definition or melt away fat.

The abdominals are the same as any other muscle and should be trained in the same fashion: no more than every other day and no more than 12–15 repetitions per set. So slow down, visualise your abdominals working and focus on feeling the contraction through the full ROM. When it starts to hurt (not to be confused with actual pain), take a short rest; then complete the exercise or move on to the next.

The drawback with many exercise programmes is that they isolate muscles, training them in ways that are not related to sports or everyday activities. For example, abdominal training is typically performed lying face-up on the floor with the knees bent. But no sport

or activity requires you to be in this position. Similarly, using an arm curl machine in the gym trains your biceps independently of all the other muscles you would use to stabilise and control your arm in everyday life. But the power needed, say, when sprinting for the ball in a football match is actually generated in the core of the body and transferred out to the pumping arms.

Core stability

'Core stability' describes the ability to control and link the upper- and lower-body movements and postures. It involves exercises that mimic your sport or activity and training movements. Pilates is one of the best-known stability programmes and tends not to use much equipment. Others involve exercising from an unstable base such as a wobble board or Swiss ball, which place a higher demand on the deep muscles in the core – or trunk – as well as on your motor control system because you constantly have to stabilise yourself as the ball or board rolls around. It also changes the way your neuromuscular system co-ordinates movement as you're using your legs to hold you up and your abdominals and back to keep your whole body stable. Doing abdominal exercises on a ball therefore works the muscles more effectively and more emphasis is placed on the obliques and transverse abdominis (*see* p. 83).

Repetitions

Training for muscle growth involves performing 8–12 reps.

♦ Muscle know-how ♦

The abdominals are comprised of four main muscle groups:

- the rectus abdominis (the 'six-pack' muscle), running from your pubic bone to your lower ribs, which flexes the torso so the rib cage moves toward the pelvis
- the external obliques, running diagonally from the lower ribs to the opposite hip, which bend the torso sideways and rotate it to the opposite side when flexing forwards
- the internal obliques, running in the opposite direction to the external obliques, which help the rectus abdominis bend the torso forwards, as well as rotating it to the same side to which they are located
- the transverse abdominis, a deep flat sheath of muscle running across the torso, which acts as a muscular girdle to support the contents of the abdomen.

Technique note

The first three exercises (described on the following pages) are performed with the legs lifted. At the beginning of each movement, press the lower abdominal region to the floor (imagine you are trying to press your tummy button to your spine). In this position you isolate your abdominals and remove any involvement of the hip flexors. Your lower back should not move and you should not feel any discomfort in this region. Every exercise listed and described in the exercise directory includes 2 photographs demonstrating the exercise at the start and at the mid-point positions. It is suggested that you use these photographs as a guide to correct technique.

♦ Crunch ♦

Target muscles

Rectus abdominis (mainly upper part)

Starting position

1. Lie flat on your back either on the floor or on an abdominal bench with your knees bent over your hips and your ankles touching. If you are on the floor, rest your feet on a bench with your knees bent at 90°.
2. Place your hands lightly by the sides of your head (or across your chest if you are a beginner).
3. Press your lower back to the floor or bench.

The movement

1. Use your abdominal strength to raise your head and shoulders from the floor or bench. You should only come up about 10 cm and your lower back should remain on the floor.
2. Hold in this contracted position for a count of two.
3. Let your body uncurl slowly back to the starting position.

Tips

- Focus on moving your ribs towards your hips.
- Do not pull your head with your hands – keep your elbows out and relaxed.
- Exhale as you contract your abdominals.

♦ Swiss ball crunch ♦

Target muscles

Rectus abdominis (mainly upper portion), transverse abdominis

Starting position

1. Lie across the ball, place your feet on the floor and keep your legs bent at the knees. Adjust your position so that the ball is comfortably positioned in the small of your back.
2. Cross your arms over your chest, or, to make the exercise harder, place your hands by the sides of your head.

The movement

1. Making sure that you move only your upper body and that your lower back remains in contact with the ball, slowly raise your torso.
2. Hold the position for a count of two; then lower yourself back to the starting position.

Tips

- When you lower yourself back down, keep the movement controlled.
- Do not let your upper body arch backwards or your head flop back over the ball.
- To make the movement harder, bring your whole body higher up on to the top of the ball.

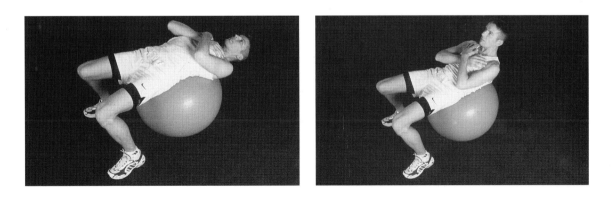

◆ **Reverse crunch** ◆

Target muscles

Rectus abdominis (mainly lower part)

Starting position

1. Lie flat on your back on the floor or on a bench with your knees bent over your hips and your ankles touching (as for crunches).
2. Place your arms on the floor alongside your body, palms flat on the floor, or hold on to the sides of the bench.
3. Press your lower back to the floor or bench.

The movement

1. Slowly curl your hips off the floor, aiming your knees towards your chest. Your hips should raise no more than 10 cm.
2. Hold for a count of two.
3. Slowly lower your hips to the starting position, maintaining constant tension in your abdominals.

Tips

- This should be a controlled, deliberate movement. Do not jerk, swing or bounce your hips off the floor; curl one vertebra up at a time.
- Do not allow your abdominals to relax at the top of the movement or while you are uncurling.
- Exhale as you contract your abdominals.

♦ Oblique crunch ♦

Target muscles

Internal and external obliques, rectus abdominis

Starting position

1. Lie on your back with your knees bent and feet either resting on a bench or flat on the floor.
2. Place your left hand by the side of your head, and your right hand on the floor for support.

The movement

1. Lift your left shoulder diagonally, aiming it towards your right knee.

2. Hold for two counts; then slowly return to your starting position.
3. After completing the required number of repetitions, repeat the exercise on the other side.

Tips

- Imagine your rib cage rotating to the side as you curl up.
- Lead with your shoulder rather than your elbow.
- Make sure you lower your upper body slowly back to the floor.
- Do not twist your head, only your torso.
- Exhale as you contract your abdominals.

♦ Side crunch ♦

Target muscles

Internal and external obliques, rectus abdominis

Starting position

1. Lie on the floor or on an abdominal bench on your side with your knees slightly bent.
2. Place your top arm behind your head.

The movement

1. Slowly exhale as you raise your head and shoulders a short distance off the floor or bench, aiming your ribs towards your top hip.
2. Hold for a count of two; then breathe in as you return to the starting position.
3. Repeat for the required number of repetitions; then perform the exercise on your other side.

Tips

• Aim to reduce the space between your ribs and hips.
• Do not worry if you don't reach up very far – concentrate on feeling the movement.
• Keep your head in line with your body – don't jerk it upwards.

♦ Hanging leg raise ♦

Target muscles

Rectus abdominis (especially lower portion), hip flexors

Starting position

1. Hang from a high bar with your hands shoulder-width apart. (You may use wrist or elbow straps for support.)
2. Your arms should be fully extended and your lower back slightly arched.

The movement

1. Take your legs slightly behind your body.
2. Keeping your legs almost straight, exhale and raise them upwards as high as possible. Ideally they should come just above the level of your hips. Focus on curling your hips towards your rib cage.
3. Hold for a count of two; then slowly return your legs to the starting position.

Tips

- Do not swing your knees up or use the momentum of your legs – use the strength of your abdominals to move your hips and legs.
- For maximal results, raise your legs to approximately 30–45° to the horizontal. The abs shorten only when your legs go past parallel – below this point, they hold a static contraction as the hip flexors raise the legs.
- To make the exercise easier, bend your knees to reduce the resistance.

Chapter 10

Stretching for strength training

Most people imagine strength trainers to be muscle-bound, lacking in mobility and graceful posture. Indeed, many strength trainers who neglect to stretch do fit that image. Stretching is highly beneficial for anyone involved in strength training. Not only does it provide numerous health benefits but it can also enhance your muscle size and shape. This chapter gives you a thorough checklist on safe and effective stretching and explains exactly what happens in your muscles when you stretch. Finally, it gives you a step-by-step guide to the essential stretches that will benefit your workouts.

♦ Why stretch? ♦

The benefits of a good stretching programme include:

- reduced risk of muscle strain, joint injuries and back problems
- reduced post-exercise muscle soreness
- speedier recovery
- increased ROM and co-ordination
- greater strength gains due to greater ROM
- improved body awareness
- better physical and mental relaxation.

♦ How can stretching help ♦ enhance muscle size and shape?

Incorporating key stretches into your strength-training programme will result in greater muscle growth and the enhancement of muscle shape. Failing to stretch will not only limit your ROM but also your growth rate.

Stretching elongates the fascia, a strong protective sheath of connective tissue covering all muscles and their cells, allowing the muscle underneath room in which to grow. Fascia tissue can become thick and tough if the muscles are not stretched and are subjected to a limited ROM. The best time to stretch the fascia is when the muscles are very warm and 'pumped' (i.e. full of blood, *see* p. 29). This occurs during and after a workout, so stretch between and after sets, and at the end of your training session.

Stretching increases flexibility, giving the muscles and joints a greater ROM. It can prevent muscle soreness and promote faster recovery between workouts, helping to release lactic acid from the muscle cells into the bloodstream so that it does not hinder further muscle contraction. Therefore, stretching during your workout may enable you to train harder and longer.

Stretching improves posture as well, and gives the body a more athletic or graceful appearance instead of that clumsy awkward gait that many bodybuilders develop.

♦ How do muscles stretch? ♦

The muscles contain receptors called muscle spindles, which register information about the muscle's length and rate of change of length.

One of their main jobs is to protect the muscles from injury. So whenever there is a rapid change in muscle length, a reflex action is set up to shorten or contract it instead.

Tendons – which attach muscles to bone – also contain receptors called *golgi tendon organs* (GTOs), registering information about the degree of tension in the tendon. When a high force is registered, the GTOs enable the muscle to relax in an attempt to reduce the tension, thus acting as a safety mechanism. If the intensity of a muscular contraction or stretch exceeds a certain critical point, an immediate reflex occurs to inhibit the contraction or stretch. As a result, the muscle instantly relaxes and the excessive tension is removed, and with it the possibility of injury. In other words, the GTOs shut down the muscle to prevent injury. If the GTOs did not exist, it would be possible to have a stretch or contraction so powerful that the muscle or tendon would be torn from its attachments!

Bouncing, uncontrolled or forced movements cause the greatest reflex response. Thus ballistic stretching can cause the muscle to contract and so increase the chance of injury. Static stretching that is carried out slowly and in a controlled manner will lead to a reflex relaxation of the muscle.

Strength through stretching is related to your GTO threshold, which limits a contraction well short of the point at which tendons would be injured. Stretching gives the muscles the ability to contract more efficiently without shutting down in response to stretched tendons. Obviously, it is desirable to have a high GTO reflex threshold, as this allows you to handle heavier weights and do more reps without the GTOs inhibiting muscle action. The higher the GTO threshold, the more intensely you can train, and the greater the gains in size and strength. Stretching your muscles regularly can help raise your GTO threshold, some experts estimate, by up to 15–20%.

♦ How to perform stretches ♦

You should only stretch when your body is warm and the muscle is receiving an increased blood flow. Stretching a cold muscle increases the risk of injury and reduces the effectiveness of the stretch. Here are some basic guidelines:

1. Ideally, stretching should be done after a workout and also in-between sets.
2. Alternatively, stretch in-between workouts as a separate session but only after a thorough warm-up – 5–10 minutes of some light aerobic activity.
3. Perform static stretches and avoid bouncing. This is a far safer method of stretching a muscle than ballistic movements.
4. Gradually ease into position, all the time focusing on relaxing the muscle.
5. Stretch only as far as is comfortable and then hold that position. As the muscle relaxes, ease further into the stretch, gradually increasing the ROM.
6. Never hold your breath. Exhale and relax as you go into the stretch and then breathe normally.
7. Never go past the point of discomfort or pain. You could pull or tear the muscle/tendon.
8. Stretches performed at the end of a workout, or during a separate session, should be held for 30 seconds or more to allow stretching in the connective tissue and muscle.
9. Release from the stretch slowly.

♦ The stretches ♦

Quadriceps

- Hold on to a sturdy support.
- Bend one leg behind you and hold the ankle.
- Keep your thighs level, knees close, and push your hips forwards until you feel a good stretch.
- Repeat on the other side.

Adductors

- Sit on the floor and place the soles of your feet together.
- Hold on to your ankles and press your thighs down using your elbows. Keep your back straight.

Hamstrings

- Sit on the floor with one leg extended and the other leg bent.
- Keeping your back straight and flat, bend forwards from the hips. Reach down towards your foot.
- Flexing your foot will increase the stretch on the calf.
- Repeat on the other side.

Hip flexors

- From a kneeling position, take a large step forwards so that your knee makes a 90° angle and is directly over your foot.
- Keep your body upright and press your rear hip forwards, keeping it square.
- Repeat on the other side.

Hips/gluteals

- Sit on the floor and cross one foot over your straight leg.
- Place your elbow on the outside of the bent knee and slowly look over your shoulder on the side of the bent leg.
- Keep your opposite arm behind your hips for stability.
- Apply pressure to the knee with your elbow.
- Repeat on the other side.

Calves

- From a standing position, take an exaggerated step forwards, keeping your rear leg straight. Hold on to a wall for support if you wish.
- Your front knee should be at 90° and positioned over your foot.
- Lean forwards slightly so that your rear leg and body make a continuous line.
- Repeat on the other side.

Neck

- In a seated position, take your hand and gently pull your head towards your shoulder – i.e. your ear towards your shoulder.
- Apply gentle pressure with your arm over your head.
- Repeat on the other side.

Upper back

- Hold on to an upright support at waist height with your arms straight.
- Bend at the hips until your torso is parallel to the floor.
- Gently pull back, ensuring your back is flat.

Lower back

- Lie on your back, knees bent and arms straight out to each side.
- Rotate both legs to each side, keeping your head, shoulders and arms in contact with the floor.

Shoulders

- Grab one elbow with your opposite hand.
- Gently pull it across your body, aiming the elbow towards the opposite shoulder.
- Repeat on the other side.

Chest/biceps

- With your arm fully extended, hold on to an upright support at shoulder level.
- Gently turn your body away from your arm, pressing your shoulder forwards.
- Repeat on the other side.

Triceps

- Place one hand between your shoulder-blades, hand pointing downwards and elbow pointing upwards.
- Use your opposite hand to gently press down on your right elbow until you feel a stretch in the triceps.
- Repeat on the other side.

♦ Summary of key points ♦

- Incorporating stretching into your strength-training programme will result in greater muscle growth and the enhancement of muscle shape.
- Stretching increases flexibility and ROM, and promotes faster recovery.
- Stretching should be performed only when the muscles are warm.
- Stretching is most beneficial when done between sets and/or after a workout.
- Ease into the stretch, hold and relax, and then gradually release.
- Avoid bouncing and any position of discomfort.
- To improve flexibility, stretches should be held for a minimum of 30 seconds.

PART THREE

The Programmes

Chapter 11

Programme Design and Training Methods

Anyone can lift weights in the gym and get a mediocre response. But you want to get great results in as little time possible, right? That requires a training programme based on scientific principles. Making serious gains requires a systematic plan as well as hard work in the gym. This chapter gets right to the heart of programme design and shows you, step by step, how to build your programme to meet your goals. It explains the essential concepts of overload, progression, training volume and intensity. These form the core of programme design. You can then use the scientifically-researched training techniques described in the SMART approach to design your programme. This approach shows you how to select and marshall your exercises, how to manipulate the weights used, sets, repetitions and rest periods, and how to increase your training intensity to achieve specific goals. The chapter also describes a variety of proven training methods – basic and advanced – designed to stimulate maximum muscle growth and help you make continual gains.

♦ Learning the training lingo ♦

Understanding the basic terms of strength training will help you make sense of your training programme.

Repetition or 'rep'

A repetition is one complete movement in the exercise, from the starting position to a position of maximum contraction and then back to the starting position. This ensures that you complete what is called full range of movement (ROM). On the bench press, for example, lowering the bar to your chest (the eccentric, or negative part of the rep) and pushing it back up from your chest (the concentric, or positive part of the rep) is one repetition.

One-rep max

One-rep max (1RM) is the heaviest weight that you can lift for one – and just one - repetition. In other words, you can do a maximum of one repetition only for a given weight. This can be calculated either directly (by performing your 1RM after a thorough warm-up) or indirectly by performing a 3RM (which is safer), then extrapolating this to what your 1RM should be from standardised tables. Alternatively, find a weight with which you can just perform six repetitions. That is equivalent to approximately 70–80% of your 1RM.

Set

A set is a group of repetitions. If you performed ten repetitions of the bench press before taking a rest, those ten repetitions constitute a set.

Training to failure

When training to failure, you perform repetitions until you can no longer lift the weight through the concentric (or positive) part of the movement using proper form. Each exercise has a 'sticking point' during the concentric phase – the part of the movement where gravity and unfavourable leverage make it hardest, and this is usually the part of the movement at which the point of muscular failure is reached. Training to the point of failure allows you to recruit the largest number of motor units, which in turn results in maximal muscle-fibre stimulation.

Overload training

Overload training is a calculated method of progressively working your muscles harder and harder to induce gains in strength, mass or endurance. When you strength train hard, you cause slight damage to the muscle fibres by overloading them. Your body then rebuilds the muscle fibres, making them stronger than they were before (*see* pp. 21–2).

Progression

As you become stronger, fewer motor units (and therefore fewer muscle fibres) are needed to perform the same exercise. In other words, your muscles become more efficient at performing particular movements. To achieve continued gains in strength, mass or endurance, your programme has to be progressive. If you were to stick to the same workout – the same exercises, weights, sets, rep schemes and rep speeds – your muscles

would stop adapting and growing and you would only maintain your strength.

♦ How to design a strength- ♦ training programme

A training programme contains five key variables, which you can manipulate to meet your goals.[1,2,3] These can be summarised by the abbreviation, SMART:

S = selection of exercises
M = marshalling of exercises
A = amount of sets
R = rest periods
T = training intensity

an easy acronym to remember because it is the same word used in goal setting (*see* pp. 12–15).

♦ Selection of exercises ♦

The exercises you select for your workout depend on your specific goals and your level of experience.

Your specific goals

For strength and mass or muscular endurance, you should select those exercises that cause greatest stimulation of the muscle fibres. Thus, your programme should include mostly compound exercises. For each muscle group, select two compound exercises and a maximum of one isolation exercise.

Alternatively, you may wish to emphasise an underdeveloped muscle group to achieve good symmetry and a balance of strength between opposing muscle groups. For

Types of exercises

- **Compound**, or **multijoint** exercises involve one or more large muscle areas (i.e. the chest, legs, shoulders, back, hips) and work across two or more major joints. For example, the bench press is a compound exercise that is used primarily to target the pectoral muscles but also involves the triceps and front deltoids. Therefore, the exercise stimulates three muscle groups. It is a multi-joint exercise because the movement involves both arm flexion (the shoulder joint) and extension of the forearm (the elbow joint).
- **Isolation**, or **single-joint** exercises involve smaller muscle groups (i.e. biceps, triceps, brachio radialis, erector spinae) and only one main joint. For example, the dumbbell flye is an isolation exercise that is used primarily to target the pectorals. The elbows are kept at a fixed angle throughout the ROM and so no other muscle groups are worked. It is a single-joint exercise as it only works around the shoulder joint.

example, many footballers and cyclists have an imbalance of strength between the quadriceps and hamstrings such that the hamstrings are comparatively weak. In this case, the solution is to add additional hamstring exercises to your programme, and perhaps reduce the workload performed by the quadriceps in order to rebalance the strength between the two muscle groups.

Your training experience

Beginners generally achieve better results from isolation exercises. This is due mainly to the fact that these exercises are easier to learn and execute using good form. Once you have mastered the basic movement patterns, plan your programme around compound exercises that stimulate a greater number of muscle fibres. The final selection of your programme should result in equal stimulation of each muscle group, and ensure that no muscle group is left out.

For advanced strength trainers, the goal is to avoid training plateaux and achieve continued gains in strength and muscle mass. Keep your muscles growing by having a greater repertoire of exercises from which to choose. You can do this by:

- frequently changing the exercises you perform for each muscle group
- using variations of standard exercises in different body positions to emphasise different parts of the muscle group.

♦ Marshalling of exercises ♦

The marshalling of your exercises means the *order* in which you perform your exercises during a particular workout. You need to get the order right because it will affect the energy and effort you are able to put into the next exercise. For example, performing two consecutive exercises that both stimulate the same muscle group reduces the effort you can put into the second one.

The order can be changed according to the aspect of strength you wish to develop, and there are four methods.

Largest to smallest

The most usual way of ordering exercises in beginners' and advanced programmes is to work from the largest muscle groups to the smallest. Therefore, compound exercises that stimulate the largest muscle groups are performed first in your workout, followed by the isolation exercises. This is because the compound exercises require the most effort and concentration, and are very difficult to perform correctly and safely if your muscles are fatigued. For example, in a leg workout you would perform compound exercises such as squats and leg presses before isolation exercises such as leg extensions and leg curls.

Advanced trainers sometimes reverse this order so as to break through a training plateau. This is called 'pre-exhaustion' and involves deliberately fatiguing a large muscle group by performing isolation exercises before the compound exercise (*see* p. 101).

Alternating upper- and lower-body circuit

Alternating upper- and lower-body exercises is particularly suitable for beginners who would otherwise find performing several exercises for one area in one go too demanding. This method allows each muscle group to recover more fully between exercises, and is also good for people with limited training time available because it minimises rest intervals – you can perform an upper-body exercise straight after a lower-body exercise without resting. Because rest periods are minimised, you also get a greater cardio-vascular effect compared with more conventional strength-training programmes. On the downside, this method generally results in less stimulation of each muscle group and can result in slower strength and mass gains. Therefore, it would be less suitable for advanced weight trainers.

Alternating 'push' and 'pull' exercises

Alternating pushing exercises (e.g. bench press) and pulling exercises (e.g. seated row) is also suitable for beginners, those resuming strength training and those with limited training time available. As with alternating upper- and lower-body exercises this method is a very good way of reducing your rest periods because, while you are performing a pulling exercise (the seated row), the opposing muscle group used in the pushing exercise (the bench press) is recovering. You will not need to rest, yet you can still use maximum effort for each set. If you were to arrange several pushing exercises together (e.g. bench press, shoulder press, triceps extensions), you might have to reduce the amount of weight or number of repetitions used because the triceps (a muscle used in all three exercises) will become fatigued.

Supersets

This training method involves two or more sets of different exercises performed consecutively with no rest period between. As it is very demanding, supersets are best suited to advanced weight trainers and are therefore covered later in this chapter (*see* p. 122).

♦ Amount of sets ♦

The number of sets you perform depends on:

1. your training experience
2. the number of muscle groups trained per session
3. the size of the muscle group being trained.

1. If you are a beginner, you should follow a muscular endurance programme, performing only one or two sets of each exercise and only one or two exercises per muscle group. For example, you could perform one set of bench presses and one set of dumbbell flyes for the chest muscles, and you would train all major muscle groups in your workout, making a total of 15–20 sets. If you are an advanced weight trainer, you can perform more sets of each exercise and more exercises per muscle group. For example, you could perform three sets of bench presses, three sets of dumbbell flyes and three sets of incline dumbbell presses for the chest. In this case, you would train only one other major muscle group, making a total of 18 sets in your workout.
2. If you are training only one or two muscle groups in a workout, you will be able to perform more sets than if you are planning to train three or four. For example, if you plan to train your chest and back, you could perform nine sets for each muscle group as shown above, making a total of 18 sets in the workout. If you plan to train your chest, back, shoulders and arms, you would reduce the total number of sets per muscle group to, say, five sets for your chest, five sets for your back, five sets for your shoulders and three sets for your arms, again making a total of 18 sets in the workout. Typically, a workout designed for muscle growth (hypertrophy) would include fewer muscle groups (1–4) than a workout designed for muscular endurance which may include every muscle group. In the latter case, you would perform only 1–3 sets per muscle group (*see* pp. 106–7).

3. The larger muscle groups (such as legs and back) generally require more sets (e.g. 8–12 for the advanced weight trainer) than the smaller muscle groups (such as arms), which require fewer sets (e.g. 3–8 for the advanced weight trainer) to achieve sufficient stimulation.

Single sets or multiple sets?

There is controversy over the benefits of single-set v. multiple-set training for achieving maximum stimulation. Some people claim that performing a single set of each exercise produces just as good gains as performing several sets.[4, 5] This opposes the majority of the research, which suggests that you do need to perform multiple sets to achieve the greatest gains, and that only beginners would benefit from single sets.[1, 6] For example, performing three near-maximal sets without going to failure has been shown to increase strength better than one maximal set going to failure. The discrepancy lies in the quality of the repetitions and the distinction between the warm-up sets and working sets (*see* p. 30). Advocates of single-set training ignore warm-up sets that could be regarded as working sets by the advocates of multiple-set training so it is not strictly single-set training. The ultimate aim, however, is to overload the muscles, so whether you achieve that on your first or tenth set depends on the quality of your set – how strict your form is and whether you reach true failure (*see* p. 100).

Rest periods between workouts

Rest between workouts is as important as the training itself. This is when replenishment, recovery, adaptation and growth take place. Let's take a look at what happens.

During and immediately after a workout your body is in a catabolic state (i.e. breaking down proteins) and levels of stress hormones such as cortisol are high. As you start to recover from your workout, levels of muscle-promoting hormones such as testosterone gradually rise, the damaged muscle proteins are replaced with new muscle proteins, and glycogen stores are also restored (*see* p. 172). Clearly, these processes take time. It is only after completion of the recovery process that the muscles can grow and strengthen. If you attempt to train your muscles before the process is complete then you will experience only minimal growth or none at all. In other words, training before you have fully recovered is counterproductive.

The rest period you need to leave between workouts depends on the intensity and duration of your workout, your training experience and your diet.

Training intensity and duration

The greater the intensity of your workout, the longer the recovery time required before your next training session. There is no easy or accurate way of predicting your recovery time between workouts. In the laboratory, scientists can measure the blood levels of muscle metabolites such as 3-methyl histidine and creatine phosphokinase, but this is clearly not a practical solution for everyday training. Instead, a certain amount of guesswork is required as you have to judge the 'feel' of your muscles. When your muscles have regained their pre-workout capacity – measured by testing your strength – you have probably recovered. Obviously, if your muscles still feel sore, stiff or weak, then they have not recovered. If you find yourself stronger and able to work out harder, then you know your muscles have fully recovered.

In practice, upper-body muscles can recover more quickly from heavy workouts than lower body muscles. Also, it takes longer to recover from compound exercises than isolation exercises.

When does detraining begin?

It is a myth that loss of strength and muscle mass begins within 72 hours of a workout. Since it may take several days for compensation to occur following a heavy workout, it would not be possible for decompensation to begin in this short time. For this reason, many experienced weight trainers train only major muscle groups once a week. Indeed, many weight trainers have experienced dramatic increases in growth using this method.

Training experience

The American College of Sports Medicine recommend that beginners train two or three times a week on non-consecutive days. As you become more experienced and better conditioned, you can increase your workout frequency to four or more times a week.

As a general guideline, beginners should leave a minimum of one day and a maximum of three days' recovery between workouts. Experienced weight trainers will need to leave 3–7 days between training the same muscle group due to the greater workout intensity. However, you can train four or more times a week by using a split routine – that is, dividing your major muscle groups into two or more separate workouts (*see* p. 101). That way, you can still allow a minimum of three days' rest between training each muscle group.

Your diet

During recovery, your muscle glycogen stores are replenished (*see* p. 172) and muscle tissue repaired. The time it takes to replenish muscle glycogen depends on the severity of depletion and the amount and timing of carbohydrate intake in your diet. On average, this takes between 24 hours and three days. You also need to ensure you consume enough protein to provide the raw material for new muscle growth. An inadequate intake will result in slower repair and growth and so your strength gains will be compromised. On the other hand, an excessive intake will not further enhance muscle growth or strength. For more detail on diet, *see* Part Four.

◆ Training intensity ◆

Training intensity serves as the major stimulus for muscle growth. By increasing your training intensity, you provide a bigger stimulus for muscle growth. You can increase the intensity by increasing the amount of weight, amount of sets or repetitions, and the number of exercises, or reducing rest intervals between sets. The exact combination you choose depends on your goals – do you want to gain strength, power, size or muscular endurance? Each requires a different way of training. Table 11.1 gives guide-

lines for the number of sets and repetitions, weight and rest intervals commonly prescribed for strength, power, hypertrophy and muscular endurance training programmes.

Maximum strength

Maximum strength is best developed using heavy weights and low-repetition sets. The consensus guideline is to perform 2–6 sets of 6 or fewer repetitions for the compound exercises.[1, 3, 7] Only 1–3 sets are necessary for isolation exercises.[5] Clearly you should select a weight that causes you to use maximum effort for that set – that is, reach the point of failure on the last repetition (between 85–100% 1RM). Your rest intervals between sets should be 3–4 minutes to allow sufficient recovery. Maximum strength workouts are centred on the compound exercises such as squats, bench presses and shoulder presses.

Power

Power is developed by performing an exercise very quickly or explosively. It can be developed with plyometrics and speed drills,

Training goal	Number of sets per exercise	Number of repetitions	Weight (% 1RM)	Rest interval	Training tempo*
Maximum strength	2–6	< 6	Heavy (> 85)	2–5 min	1:2
Power	3–5	1–5	Heavy (75–85)	2–5 min	Explosive: 1
Muscle size	3–6	6–12	67–85	30–90 s	2:3
Muscular endurance	2–3	> 12	Low (< 67)	< 30 s	2:3

Table 11.1 Sets, repetitions, weight and rest interval guidelines for different training goals

*The training tempo is the number of counts for the concentric (lifting) action, followed by the number of counts for the eccentric (lowering) action. E.g. 2:3 is 2 counts concentric, 3 counts eccentric.

as well as weightlifting exercises. For example, squat jumps and alternate leg bounding (plyometrics), 40 m dashes, shuttle runs (speed drills), power cleans, power pulls or any compound weight-training exercises (e.g. leg press, squat) performed explosively would all be suitable methods of developing neuromuscular activity and power. Power exercises would be suitable for intermediate and advanced weight trainers, Olympic lifters and athletes who use power movements in their particular sport. For example, basketball, football, sprinting and most field athletic events (such as the high jump and long jump) involve explosive activities, so power training would benefit your performance.

However, only experienced lifters and athletes should use this type of training as it could be dangerous if attempted using imperfect technique. It is important that the weight is kept under good control even when it is moved rapidly. The consensus guideline is 3–5 sets of 1–5 repetitions.[1,9] using moderate (75–85% 1RM), rather than maximal weights. Slightly lighter weights allow you to perform the exercise with maximum speed and therefore generate the greatest power output: output almost doubles when reducing the weight from 100% 1RM to 90% 1RM.[10]

Muscle size

Training for muscle size (hypertrophy) requires a higher training volume compared with pure strength and power training – in other words, more repetitions, sets and a greater cumulative amount of weight lifted per workout. The consensus guideline is a moderate number of repetitions (6–12) and 3–6 sets per exercise performed with a moderate to heavy weight (67–85% 1RM) and short to moderate rest intervals (30–90 seconds).[1, 3, 11]

You can expect parallel increases in both muscle size and strength with this type of

training programme. For overall size development, your programme should be based around compound exercises that stimulate the large muscle groups (e.g. squats, bench presses, shoulder presses, lat pull-downs). More advanced weight trainers and body-builders use 2–4 exercises per muscle group, including at least 1–2 compound exercises. They use a split training system (*see* p. 107), allowing them to train with high intensity.

Muscular endurance

Muscular endurance is the ability of a muscle or muscle group to sustain sub-maximal force over a period of time. This type of training

Fast or slow?

Perhaps the most important principle for stimulating muscle growth is the time that the muscle is under tension – i.e. the time your muscles are actually working. For example, if you blast a set of ten repetitions as fast as possible, your total time under tension will be just a few seconds. This is not sufficient to cause your muscles to grow, regardless of the amount of weight you lift.

Typically, the time under tension should be 30–70 seconds. Anything more or less would be counterproductive and result in very little gain.

The way to achieve the correct set duration is to adjust your training tempo. For example, if you are working in relatively low-rep ranges (say, 6–8), you will have to adjust your training tempo – particularly on the eccentric (lowering) part of the movement – in order for that set's time under tension to reach at least 30 seconds. If you are working in a higher rep-range (say, 10–12), the training tempo should be a little quicker so that you won't exceed the 30–70 seconds' time under tension range.

increases the aerobic capacity of the muscles rather than muscle size and strength, and is developed by using a higher number of repetitions (12 or more) per set and minimal rest intervals between sets – typically less than 30 seconds.[1, 3] The weights lifted are lighter and fewer sets are performed per muscle group, usually 2 or 3. Therefore, the intensity is very low and the overall volume is high.

This type of workout is suitable for beginners but also for advanced weight trainers wishing to improve this aspect of their fitness. Most circuit weight-training programmes, which alternate upper- and lower-body exercises or opposing muscle groups and limit rest intervals to 30 seconds or less, would promote your muscular endurance.

Pyramid training

Pyramid training is a form of multiple set training in which the weight is increased in each set and the repetitions are reduced. This allows you to warm up a muscle group gradually, and prepare it over the course of a few sets to cope with heavier weights by the end of the sets – hence allowing the muscles to achieve greater overload, and hence allowing you to develop greater size and strength. A typical pyramid is shown in Figure 11.1. Select a weight that will enable you to reach near or complete failure at the end of each set.

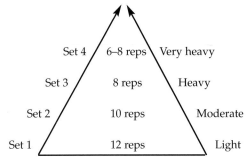

Figure 11.1 A typical pyramid pattern to increase muscle size

◆ Advanced training methods ◆

As we have seen, there are a number of different ways of arranging your sets and repetitions. All have their merits and ultimately aim to achieve the same goal: overload. Set and pyramid training form the core of any training programme for strength, power, size or endurance. However, as your body gets used to doing the same types of sets week after week, intensity tends to fall – even if you do manipulate the components of SMART training. To avoid this use one or more of the advanced training methods listed on the following pages in place of your usual workout.

The objective of all of the advanced training methods is to perform a few more repetitions after you have reached failure. In other words, they allow you to train with greater intensity, thus helping to increase hypertrophy and muscle strength. There are no hard-and-fast rules on how often you should use these advanced training methods as everyone responds differently. For best results, limit any one method to a short time period to shock your muscles when your training plateaus, and decrease your training volume to reduce the risk of overtraining and injury. To avoid overuse, use a periodised training programme, cycling weeks of low-intensity, higher-repetition training with high-intensity training that uses one or more of the advanced methods.

Eccentric training (negatives)

In eccentric training, a spotter assists you in lifting the bar (the concentric phase), and then you control the weight on the eccentric (lowering) phase. This technique allows you to use a heavier weight (110–160% 1RM) so should be performed after a thorough warm-up and particularly at the end of a set after you have reached muscular failure. Focus on lowering the weight very slowly.

The principle behind this technique is that it produces greater muscle growth than conventional (concentric) training techniques.[3, 12] During an eccentric contraction there is more mechanical load per motor unit. As a result, eccentric training can generate up to two-thirds more tension in the muscle than concentric training. Increased tension provides a greater stimulus to the muscle fibres, which, in turn, means greater strength and growth.

As this is a very intense training method, limit eccentric training to one exercise per muscle group in any one workout, performing it at the end of only one or two sets. You will need to allow longer rest intervals between sets, and following hard eccentric training you will experience greater muscle soreness because of the greater resulting muscle fibre damage. Recovery may take up to ten days, so you should allow at least 10–14 days between muscle group workouts employing this technique. For example, if you perform eccentric training on the chest on Monday, do not use it for the chest again for two weeks.

Forced, or assisted rep training

With forced rep training you enlist the help of a spotter so that you can continue past the point of failure and therefore can complete a couple of extra repetitions. The spotter should give just enough support to keep the weight moving through the sticking point.

You should only use this training technique for the last 1 or 2 reps of your heaviest sets, and should be able to complete at least 6 reps on your own in the correct form before the spotter assists you. If you cannot complete 6 reps, reduce the weight.

The advantage of forced rep training is that you can work past the point of muscular failure and thus increase the overload. For example, if you can normally complete 6 reps at 70 kg on the bench press, the forced rep training method may enable you to complete 8 reps, thus increasing the amount of stress that your pectorals receive. Whether this ultimately results in greater muscle hypertrophy, however, is a controversial issue.

Forced reps should only be used during intense training cycles and you should limit this method to once a week per muscle group.

Descending (drop) sets

This method is particularly useful for reaching overload if you are training without a partner or spotter and cannot use eccentric or forced rep training.

With descending sets you complete as many repetitions in strict form as you can, then – without resting – you reduce the weight by 20–50% and continue performing repetitions (usually 4–6) until you reach the point of failure again. Repeat this process if you wish.

Again, the objective is to stimulate as many motor units as possible. The first reps, performed with a heavy weight, stimulates the FT muscles fibres; subsequent reps performed with lighter weights stimulate mainly ST fibres. So this method allows you to train for strength, muscle size and endurance within the same set.

This method is safest for exercises with dumbbells and machines since you need to be able to return the weight safely and quickly when your muscles have reached failure. Examples of suitable exercises include: leg extensions, leg curls, dumbbell presses, flyes, lateral raises, dumbbell biceps curls, lat pull-downs, seated rows and triceps push-downs. For example, if you are performing a set of lateral raises with 10 kg dumbbells, complete as many reps as you can in strict form – say, 8. Return the dumbbells to the floor, pick up a pair of 7.5 kg dumbbells and perform as many as you can until you reach failure – say, 5. Repeat with 5 kg dumbbells.

Since this method is very fatiguing, it should only be used for selected exercises and only for the last 1–2 sets, providing maximum stimulation to the muscle when it is fatigued. You will need to leave slightly longer rest intervals between descending sets (say 2–3 minutes) and reduce the total number of sets per muscle group. Again, use this method sparingly, once every three weeks. The Phase 2 (advanced) programme incorporates descending sets (*see* pp. 120–21).

Superset training

This involves performing two or more exercises for a given body part in a row, and there are two methods:

- supersets for the same muscle group
- supersets for opposing muscle groups.

The first method involves two or more exercises for the same muscle group – for example, dumbbell shoulder press followed by lateral raises and upright rows for the shoulders. The advantage is that the stress on the muscle is increased as the muscle can be worked from slightly different angles, thus involving more muscle fibres. It also increases the blood flow to the muscle due to the increased energy demand, providing greater stimulation for hypertrophy. However, this type of superset training should not be used for every body part or at every workout as it is very intense and may lead to overtraining.

The second and less intense method involves performing two exercises for opposing muscle groups – for example, biceps curls followed by triceps extensions, or leg extensions followed by leg curls. The advantage of this method is that the blood is kept within the same area of the body, thus encouraging a greater flow and bringing more fuel, oxygen and nutrients to the muscle. Since the rest period is eliminated, it is also a good way of reducing your workout time, particularly useful if you have only a limited period in which to train.

Unlike supersetting the same muscle group, this method does not significantly increase the muscle overload. However, it does increase the demands on your cardio-vascular system since the rest periods are greatly reduced, and can therefore help to improve lactic acid tolerance, raise the anaerobic threshold and develop better stamina.

Following each superset you should take a 2–3 minute rest. An example of a superset workout is given in the Phase 2 (advanced) programme (*see* p. 122).

Pre-exhaustion training

With pre-exhaustion training the larger muscle (prime mover) is partially exhausted by performing an isolation exercise prior to performing the compound exercise. For example, performing flyes before bench presses pre-exhausts the pectorals so that when you perform the bench presses, your pectorals will fatigue before, or at the same time as, the triceps and front deltoids. (You will probably need to reduce the weight you use for the bench presses.) There is no need to change the rest intervals between sets. The objective is to change the usual recruitment pattern of the muscle fibres involved and enable you to stimulate more muscle.

Like other advanced training methods, pre-exhaustion training should only be used for selected exercises and you should limit this method to once a week per muscle group.

◆ Summary of key points ◆

- A training programme contains five key variables – selection of exercises, marshalling (ordering) of exercises, amount of sets, rest periods and the training intensity – which may be manipulated to meet your goals.
- The exercises you select for your workout depend on your specific goals and your level of experience. For strength, mass and endurance, select maximum stimulation exercises.
- The ordering of your exercises affects the energy and effort you are able to put into the next exercise. Going from the largest to the smallest muscle groups is recommended for beginners and advanced weight trainers, while performing supersets for the same muscle group is recommended only for advanced weight trainers.
- The number of sets you perform depends on the size of the muscle group being trained, the number of muscle groups trained per session and your training experience.
- The rest period you need to leave between workouts depends on the intensity and duration of your workout, your training experience and your diet.

- You can increase your training and intensity by increasing the amount of weight, amount of sets or repetitions, number of exercises, or reducing the rest intervals between sets.
- Maximum strength is developed using heavy weights and low repetition sets, typically 2–6 sets of 6 or fewer repetitions.
- Power is developed by performing a compound exercise explosively – typically, 5 sets of 1–5 repetitions using moderate weights (75–85% 1RM).
- Muscle size (hypertrophy) is best developed using moderate to heavy weights (67–85% 1RM) and moderate repetition sets, typically 6–12 repetitions for 3–6 sets.
- Muscular endurance is developed by using lighter weights, higher repetitions (12 or more) and minimal rest intervals (typically less than 30 seconds).
- Set training and pyramid training form the core of any training programme for strength, power or size.
- Advanced training methods, such as eccentric training, forced rep training, descending sets, supersets and pre-exhaustion, allow you to train with greater intensity and experience continued gains.

Chapter 12

Goal-specific Training Programmes

Just as one glove doesn't fit all, you cannot follow the same training programme as the guy training next to you. Your own programme needs to be tailored to your specific goals. This chapter gives you detailed goal-specific training programmes, based on the SMART principles described in Chapter 11. It covers four types of training goals:

- increasing muscle tone and muscular endurance
- increasing muscle size
- increasing maximum strength
- sports-specific training.

Within each programme it sets out your aims, the principles of progression that apply to that programme and your workout framework. Each workout details the exercises, sets, repetitions, workout frequency and duration and training tempo. This chapter also divides your programme into training cycles (periodisation) to enable you to make continual gains throughout each year. So, whether you want to gain muscle size or improve your performance in a particular sport, this chapter gives you all the tools to achieve your goals.

◆ Training technique ◆

Perfect technique should be the number one priority of every weight trainer whether you are a beginner or an advanced exponent. While it may mean using slightly lighter weights or fewer repetitions, in the long run it is a far more efficient way to train, producing faster and better gains and cutting the risk of muscle strain and injury. Many weight trainers get into the habit of using poor training form in order to lift more weight or squeeze out a couple of extra repetitions, but that does not produce better results. Poor technique increases the risk of injury and slows your gains. If you are unsure of an exercise, get assistance from an instructor or personal trainer who will be able to reinforce good technique. Pay close attention to the descriptions for each exercise in Part Two and the following technique tips.

Ten tips for good training technique

1. Always warm up properly before starting your workout, making sure you include the three main components outlined at the start of Part Two (*see* pp. 29–30): aerobic activity, mobilisation of the joints, and warm-up sets with light weights and high repetitions. Never train a cold muscle as that increases injury risk.
2. Select a suitable weight which will allow you to complete the desired number of repetitions safely. Do not be tempted to lift heavier weights before you have developed sufficient strength in your muscles, tendons and ligaments.
3. The general rule of thumb is to breathe out on the concentric (or positive) part of the

movement (when you lift the weight) and breathe in on the eccentric (or negative) part of the movement (lowering the weight). Never hold your breath.

4. Perform each repetition using a complete ROM, taking the muscle from its fully extended position to its fully contracted position. Partial repetitions will develop strength only in that portion of the movement, and produce only slow overall gains. Also avoid cheating movements as these will reduce the training stimulus and increase injury risk.

5. Maintain full control of the weight throughout the movement. Swinging a weight too fast means momentum takes over to bear the load rather than the target muscles, putting your joints at risk of injury.

6. Focus on both the concentric and eccentric phases of each movement. Resist the weight as you return it slowly to the starting position.

7. To find the correct training tempo, count to two as you lift the weight, and count to three as you lower the weight. Hold the fully contracted position for a count of one (but do not relax) before returning the weight to the starting position.

8. Visualising your target muscle contract and relax will not only help you perform the exercise with good technique but will also help you do more repetitions. For example, as you press the bar up for a bench press, visualise your chest muscles contracting and getting stronger. This strategy reinforces the powerful mind–body link, which gives you more control over your body and, ultimately, greater physical gains.

9. Ideally, stretch the target muscles between sets, holding each stretch for a minimum of 8 seconds.

10. Perform longer (developmental) stretches immediately after the workout. Each stretch should be held for 30–60 seconds.

◆ Personal fitness goal: increase muscular endurance and ◆ increase muscle tone (foundation)

Aims

1. Get started/resume training
2. Build a strength foundation
3. Increase muscle tone and strength
4. Increase muscular endurance

Whether you simply want to get a more toned, fitter body, enhance your performance in a particular sport, or build a good base of strength before taking your training to higher levels, start with the six-week Phase 1 programme. This foundation gradually increases in exercise volume and intensity.

◆ Phase 1 overview: circuit- ◆ training workout

The aim

Phase 1 is designed to strengthen all of the major muscle groups of your body, as well as their attachments, the ligaments and tendons. It is particularly important to build this base of strength if you plan to move on to the next phase, which will impose a greater stress on your muscles.

Phase 1 will give you good overall strength, balanced development, muscular endurance and cardio-vascular fitness. It is designed to familiarise you with the exercises and the equipment, alternating muscle groups and involving all of the major body parts to allow better recovery for each muscle group between exercises. Concentrate on feeling the movement, using a complete ROM and perfecting your training technique (*see* pp. 111–12). Don't be tempted to add more sets or push heavy weights. You need to give your body sufficient time to adjust to this type of training. Pushing yourself too hard during Phase 1 will not produce greater benefits (recovery times will be lengthened and you may end up overtraining) and may increase injury risk.

The progression

During Phase 1 you gradually step up the intensity. During the first three weeks, you perform a *single set* of each exercise. For the next three weeks, you perform *two sets* of each exercise. Thus, the training intensity is increased and a greater overload is reached – which, in turn, will produce greater increases in muscle strength and endurance.

The workout

Aim to complete the circuit twice. It should take no longer than 45 minutes (excluding warm-up and stretching) with 30 seconds' rest between exercises. Select weights that allow you to complete the prescribed number of repetitions. The last 1–2 should feel reasonably hard, so if you can complete any set easily, you need to use a heavier weight. If you cannot complete the set or you feel an intense burn in your muscles, you need to select a lighter weight. Aim to complete the workout twice a week.

Weeks 1–3: circuit-training workout

Frequency: 2/week
Number of circuits: 2
Workout time: 30–45 minutes (excluding warm-up and stretching)
Rest: allow approx. 30 s rest between sets, 30 s between exercises and 1–2 min between circuits
Training tempo: 2 counts for the concentric (lifting) action; 3 counts for the eccentric (lowering) action

Weeks 4–6: circuit-training workout

Frequency: 2/week
Number of circuits: 2
Workout time: 30–45 minutes (excluding warm-up and stretching)
Rest: allow approx. 30 s rest between sets, 30 s between exercises and 1–2 min between circuits
Training tempo: 2 counts for the concentric (lifting) action; 3 counts for the eccentric (lowering) action

Circuit-training workout 1

Muscle group	Exercise	Sets	Reps
Legs/gluteals	Leg press	1	15
Hamstrings	Seated leg curl	1	15
Chest	Bench press (machine or free weights)	1	15
Upper back	Lat pull-down	1	15
Shoulders	Shoulder press	1	15
Biceps	Barbell curl	1	15
Triceps	Triceps push-downs	1	15
Lower back	Back extension	1	15
Calves	Standing calf raise	1	15
Abdominals	Crunch	1	15

Circuit-training workout 2

Muscle group	Exercise	Sets	Reps
Legs/gluteals	Leg press	2	12–15
Hamstrings	Seated leg curl	2	12–15
Chest	Bench press (machine or free weights)	2	12–15
Upper back	Lat pull-down	2	12–15
Shoulders	Shoulder press	2	12–15
Biceps	Barbell curl	2	12–15
Triceps	Triceps push-downs	2	12–15
Lower back	Back extension	2	12–15
Calves	Standing calf raise	2	12–15
Abdominals	Crunch	2	12–15

◆ Phase 2 overview: split ◆ workout

The aim

The following six weeks are designed to challenge your body more, further increasing overall strength, symmetry, and muscular endurance. This phase should lead to noticeable increases in muscle size or tone and body shape.

The progression

You divide your body into two parts – upper body and lower body – and employ the sets training method. Slightly heavier weights and lower repetitions are used. Increase your training frequency to three workouts per week on non-consecutive days (e.g. Monday, Wednesday, Friday), so you have a minimum of one day's rest between workouts. This allows you to increase the training intensity.

The workout

Alternate the two workouts. This means that one week you will perform the first workout twice and the second workout once, and the following week you will perform the second workout twice and the first workout once. The workout should still take about 45 minutes (excluding warm-up and stretching). Select slightly heavier weights for each exercise so you are increasing the total workload for each muscle group. The last 1–2 repetitions should feel very hard (that is, grinding to a halt) but leave you just below the point of muscle failure (the point at which you can no longer lift the weight in the proper form). Maintain strict form for each repetition, using the complete ROM. Rest for approximately 60–90 seconds between sets or until your breathing rate almost returns to normal.

Weeks 7–12: split workout

Frequency: 3/week	1–2 min between exercises
Workout time: approx. 45 min (excluding warm-up and stretching)	*Training tempo:* 2 counts for the concentric (lifting) action; 3 counts for the eccentric (lowering) action
Rest: allow approx. 60–90 s between sets and	

Split workout 1: upper body

Muscle group	Exercise	Sets	Reps
	Choose 2 from list		
Chest	• Bench press (barbell or dumbbell) • Incline press (barbell or dumbbell) • Flat dumbbell flyes • Pec deck flyes	2	12–15
Upper back	• Lat pull-down • Seated row • One-arm dumbbell row	2	12–15

Split workout 1: upper body continued

Muscle group	Exercise	Sets	Reps
	Choose 2 from list		
Shoulders	• Shoulder press (barbell or dumbbell) • Lateral raise • Upright row	2	12–15
	Choose 1 from list		
Biceps	• Barbell curl • Incline dumbbell curl • Concentration curl	2	12–15
Triceps	• Push-down • Lying triceps extension • Bench dips	2	12–15

Split workout 2: lower body

Muscle group	Exercise	Sets	Reps
	Choose 1 from list		
Legs/gluteals	• Squat • Leg press	2	12–15
Quadriceps/gluteals	• Front or reverse lunge	2	12–15
Quadriceps	• Leg extension	2	12–15
Hamstrings	• Lying leg curl • Seated leg curl • Standing leg curl	2	12–15
Lower back	• Back extension	2	12–15
Calves	• Standing calf raise • Seated calf raise	2	12–15
	Choose 2 from list		
Abdominals	• Crunch • Oblique crunch • Reverse crunch • Swiss ball crunch	2	12–15

♦ Personal fitness goal: increase muscle size (bodybuilding) ♦

Aims

1. Increase muscle size
2. Increase strength

You should already have a good overall base of strength before embarking on this programme. You should have either completed the 12-week foundation programme (above) or already have several months of weight-training experience. This programme is divided into two phases: the first is a core bodybuilding programme based on sets and pyramid-training methods; the second is an adaptation of Phase 1, incorporating a variety of advanced training methods. It should therefore only be used for short periods to prevent training plateaux and promote further size and strength gains.

♦ Phase 1 overview: three-way split workout ♦

The aim

This programme is designed to increase muscle size and strength and should be followed for a minimum of six months before incorporating Phase 2 (*see* pp. 120–33). It involves a greater exercise volume than the foundation programme, as the objective is to work the muscles to exhaustion (or failure) in order to stimulate as many muscle fibres as possible and bring about muscle growth.

The progression

The number of sets per exercise and muscle group is increased and heavier weights and lower repetitions are used. It is important that

you reach failure on each set in order to reach overload. It is only when your muscles have achieved overload that the various bio-chemical changes will take place that result in muscle fibre growth. If you do not train to failure or overload, you will experience slower gains. The pyramid-training method is used in this phase of the programme, so the weight increases and the repetitions decrease progressively with each set (*see* p. 107). You divide your body into three parts, performing two upper-body workouts (one for chest and back and one for shoulders and arms) and one lower-body workout.

The workout

Perform the three workouts in rotation but not necessarily on consecutive days. Train 3–5 times a week, allowing at least two rest days per week. The important rule is to perform the three split workouts in the same order so that each muscle group is worked once every 5–7 days. For example, your workout diary might look like this:

Monday	Workout 1 (chest and back)
Tuesday	Workout 2 (shoulders and arms)
Wednesday	Rest
Thursday	Workout 3 (legs and abdominals)
Friday	Rest
Saturday	Workout 1 (chest and back)
Sunday	Rest
Monday	Workout 2 (shoulders and arms)

The last repetition of each set should feel extremely hard, and you should be unable to complete another one in proper form. Maintain strict form for each repetition, using the complete ROM. Rest for approximately 60–90 seconds between sets and 1–2 minutes between exercises.

Months 1–6: three-way split workout

Frequency: 3–5/week (rotate workouts) Leave a minum of two rest days per week
Workout time: approx. 45 min (excluding warm-up and stretching)
Rest: allow approx. 60–90 s between all sets, except squats, dead lifts and leg presses, which require 2–3 min rest, and 1–2 min between exercises
Training tempo: 2 counts for the concentric (lifting) action; 3 counts for the eccentric (lowering) action

Three-way split workout 1: upper body (chest and back)

Muscle group	Exercise	Sets	Reps
	Choose 1–2 from list*		
Chest	• Flat bench press (barbell or dumbbell) • Incline bench press (barbell or dumbbell)	4	12, 10, 8, 6
	Choose 1 from list		
Chest	• Flat dumbbell flye • Incline dumbbell flye • Pec deck flye • Cable cross-over	4	12, 10, 8, 6
	Choose 1–2 from list*		
Back	• Chins • Lat pull-down	4	12, 10, 8, 6
	Choose 1 from list		
Back	• One-arm row • Seated row • Bent-over row	4	12, 10, 8, 6
	Choose 1 from list		
Lower back	• Back extension • Back extensions on Swiss ball	4	12, 10, 10, 10

*Only more advanced weight trainers, with at least one year's training experience, may choose two exercises.

Three-way split workout 2: upper body (shoulders, biceps and triceps)

Muscle group	Exercise	Sets	Reps
Choose 1–2 from list*			
Shoulders	• Lateral raise • Upright row • Bent-over (rear) lateral raise	4	12, 10, 8, 6
Choose 1 from list			
Chest	• Barbell shoulder press • Dumbbell shoulder press	4	12, 10, 8, 6
Choose 2 from list			
Biceps	• Barbell curl • Incline dumbbell curl • EZ barbell curl • Concentration curl	3	12, 10, 8
Triceps	• Lying triceps extension • Triceps push-down • Bench dips • Triceps kickback	3	12, 10, 8

Three-way split workout 3: lower body

Muscle group	Exercise	Sets	Reps
Choose 1–2 from list*			
Legs/gluteals	• Squat • Dead lift • Leg press	4	12, 10, 8, 6
Quadriceps/gluteals	• Front or reverse lunge	4	12, 10, 8, 6
Quadriceps	• Leg extension	4	12, 10, 8, 6
Hamstrings	• Lying leg curl • Seated leg curl • Standing leg curl • Straight-leg dead lift	4	12, 10, 8, 6
Choose 2 from list			
Calves	• Standing calf raise • Dumbbell calf raise • Seated calf raise	3	15, 12, 10
Choose 3 from list			
Abdominals	• Crunch • Oblique crunch • Reverse crunch • Hanging leg raise • Swiss ball crunch	2	10–15

*Only more advanced weight trainers, with at least one year's training experience, may choose two exercises.

◆ Phase 2 overview: three- ◆ way split workout (advanced)

The aim

You may incorporate Phase 2 into your training programme only when you have followed Phase 1 for a minimum of six months. This is necessary, as you need significant muscle mass, strength and central nervous system adaptation to benefit from the higher-intensity training required.

The aim of Phase 2 is to achieve greater overload and therefore increased muscle growth, and to avoid training plateaux. It should be used only during the high-intensity phases.

Progression

Each programme incorporates one of three advanced training methods – descending sets, supersets and pre-exhaustion – alongside the established basic methods of sets and pyramid training. These methods allow you to perform a few extra repetitions after reaching failure, thus increasing your training intensity. Your training volume is reduced (e.g. fewer sets or exercises) and you may need to leave a longer recovery period between workouts to avoid overtraining. Detailed explanations of each training method are given in Chapter 11 (*see* pp. 99–100).

The workout

For best results follow one of the three workouts that follow only during the high-intensity training periods within a periodised training programme (*see* pp. 126–30). The objective is to shock your muscles when your training plateaus. Using high-intensity training for longer periods or too frequently would deplete your glycogen stores (*see* pp. 104–5), increase the rate of muscle breakdown and decrease the rate of muscle building. The result would be reduced or no training gains!

Month 6 onwards: three-way split workout (advanced), with descending (drop) sets

Frequency: in place of your regular Phase 1 bodybuilding workout (*see* pp. 117–19) *Workout time:* approx. 45 min (excluding warm-up and stretching) *Rest:* allow approx. 60–90 s between all sets except squats, dead lifts and leg presses, which require 2–3 min rest, and 2–3 min between exercises	*Training tempo:* 2 counts for the concentric (lifting) action; 3 counts for the eccentric (lowering) action *Drop sets:* where drop sets are indicated, on your last set complete the prescribed number of repetitions, reduce the weight by 20–30%, then immediately complete an additional four repetitions (or more) until you reach failure

Three-way split workout (advanced) 1: upper body (chest and arms)

Muscle group	Exercise	Sets	Reps
Chest	• Flat bench press (barbell or dumbbell) • Incline bench press (barbell or dumbbell) • Dumbbell flye (flat or incline)	3 3 3	10, 8, 6 drop set + 4 10, 8, 6 drop set + 4 10, 8, 6
Biceps	• Barbell curl (straight or EZ bar) • Preacher curl	3 3	10, 8, 6 drop set + 4 10, 8, 6
Triceps	• Lying triceps extension • Triceps push-down	3 3	10, 8, 6 drop set + 4 10, 8, 6

Three-way split workout (advanced) 2: upper body (shoulders and back)

Muscle group	Exercise	Sets	Reps
Shoulders	• Shoulder press (barbell or dumbbell) • Lateral raise • Upright row	3 3 3	10, 8, 6 drop set + 4 10, 8, 6 drop set + 4 10, 8, 6
Back	• Chins/pull-up • Bent-over barbell row • Straight-arm pull-down	3 3 3	10, 8, 6 10, 8, 6 drop set + 4 10, 8, 6 drop set + 4

Three-way split workout (advanced) 3: lower body

Muscle group	Exercise	Sets	Reps
Quadriceps/gluteals	• Squat	4	12, 10, 8, 6
Quadriceps	• Leg extension	4	12, 10, 8, 6 drop set + 4
Hamstrings	• Straight-leg dead lift	4	12, 10, 8, 6 drop set + 4
Calves	• Seated calf raise	3	10, 8, 6 drop set + 4
Abdominals	• Crunch • Oblique crunch • Reverse crunch	2	15–20

Month 6 onwards: two-way split workout (advanced), with supersets

Frequency: two in place of your regular Phase 1 bodybuilding workout (*see* pp. 117–19)

Workout time: approx. 45 min (excluding warm-up and stretching)

Rest: do the first exercise of the superset first (e.g. barbell bent-over row), followed immediately by the second exercise (e.g. bench press). That is one superset. Rest for 2–3 min and repeat the process. Once you complete the prescribed number of supersets, rest for 2 min; then move on to the next superset (e.g. lat pull-downs and incline dumbbell presses)

Training tempo: 2 counts for the concentric (lifting) action; 3 counts for the eccentric (lowering) action

Superset workout 1: chest/back, shoulders/trapezius and abdominals/lower back

Superset No.	Muscle group	Exercise	Sets	Reps
1	Back	Barbell bent-over row	3	8–12
	Chest	Bench press	3	8–12
2	Back	Lat pull-down	2	8–12
	Chest	Incline dumbbell press	2	8–12
3	Shoulders	Dumbbell press	3	8–12
	Trapezius	Upright row	3	8–12
4	Shoulders	Lateral raise	2	8–12
	Trapezius	Dumbbell shrug	2	8–12
5	Abdominals	Swiss ball crunch	2	8–12
	Lower back	Back extension (Swiss ball)	2	8–12
6	Abdominals	Hanging leg raise	2	8–12
	Lower back	Back extension	2	8–12

Superset workout 2: legs and arms

Superset No.	Muscle group	Exercise	Sets	Reps
1	Quadriceps	Squat	3	8–12
	Hamstrings	Straight-leg dead lift	3	8–12
2	Quadriceps	Lunge (front or reverse)	2	8–12
	Hamstrings	Lying leg curl	2	8–12
3	Biceps	Barbell curl	3	8–12
	Triceps	Triceps push-down	3	8–12
4	Biceps	Dumbbell curl	2	8–12
	Triceps	Triceps kickback	2	8–12

Month 6 onwards: two-way split workout (advanced), with pre-exhaustion training

Frequency: in place of your regular Phase 1 bodybuilding workout (*see* pp. 117–19) *Workout time:* approx. 45 min (excluding warm-up and stretching) *Rest:* 60–90 s between sets, 2–3 min between exercises	*Training tempo:* 2 counts for the concentric (lifting) action; 3 counts for the eccentric (lowering) action *Pre-exhaustion:* the pre-exhaustion training method is used for chest, shoulders and legs. An isolation exercise is performed, followed by a compound exercise

Pre-exhaustion workout 1: upper body (chest, back and shoulders)

Muscle group	Exercise	Sets	Reps
Chest	• Dumbbell flye • Bench press (barbell or dumbbell)	4 4–6	8–12 8–12
Back	• Lat pull-down • Seated row	4–5	8–12
Shoulders	• Lateral raise • Shoulder press (barbell or dumbbell)	4 4–6	8–12 8–12

Pre-exhaustion workout 2: lower body (legs, arms and abdominals)

Muscle group	Exercise	Sets	Reps
Quadriceps	• Leg extension	4	8–12
Hamstrings	• Lying leg curl	4	8–12
Quadriceps/hamstrings/gluteals	• Leg press	4–6	8–12
Calves	• Standing calf raise • Seated calf raise	3	8–12
Biceps	• Barbell curl • Concentration curl	3	8–12
Triceps	• Lying triceps extension • Triceps pushdown	3	8–12
Abdominals	• Crunch • Oblique crunch • Reverse crunch	2	15–20

♦ Personal fitness goal: maximum strength ♦

Aims

1. Increase pure strength
2. Increase muscle density
3. Increase muscle size

This programme should only be followed after a minimum of two years bodybuilding or weight training experience because of the very heavy weights used and the stress imposed on the central nervous system.

Maximum strength workout overview

The aim

The aim of this maximum strength programme is to increase pure strength as well as muscle density. There will be little increase in muscle size but the density of the myofilaments in the muscle will increase. In addition to power lifters, anyone training for muscle size would benefit from including a maximum strength phase in their training cycle (*see* pp. 128–9). It can help you get through a sticking point by allowing you to lift more weight and further increase your muscle size when you resume your regular routine. This type of training will produce harder, stronger muscles, improved joint stability, better symmetry and greater aesthetic appeal.

The progression

You can incorporate this programme into your bodybuilding programme for a period of 4–6 weeks. It involves heavier weights than the bodybuilding programme since maximum strength is only developed by using near-maximal weights – at least 85% 1RM. This type of training causes maximum stimulation of the powerful FT muscle fibres and hence greater muscle strength. If you do not know your 1RM, find a weight that you can just lift for six strict repetitions. This will approximate to 70–80% 1RM. As with the bodybuilding programme, you need to increase the weight you lift gradually over time.

The workout

The workout comprises mostly compound exercises and should be performed twice a week. It is important to warm up thoroughly – perform two or three sets of that exercise using very light weights – before embarking on the heavy sets. You should also allow longer rest periods between sets (3–4 minutes) than in the bodybuilding programme to allow full recovery of your fuel system. Ensure you use the full ROM for each exercise and train using perfect technique.

Maximum strength workout

Frequency: 2/week
Workout time: approx. 45 min (excluding warm-up and stretching)
Rest: 3–4 min between sets and 3–4 min between exercises

Training tempo: 1 count for the concentric (lifting) action; 2 counts for the eccentric (lowering) action

Muscle group	Exercise	Sets	Reps
Quadriceps/hamstrings/ gluteals	• Squat	(2–3 warm-up sets) 4 working sets	3–8*
Chest	• Bench press (flat or incline)	(2–3 warm-up sets) 4 working sets	3–8*
Hamstrings	• Leg curl (lying, seated or standing)	(2–3 warm-up sets) 4 working sets	3–8*
Shoulders	• Shoulder press	(2–3 warm-up sets) 4 working sets	3–8*
Back	• Seated row	(2–3 warm-up sets) 4 working sets	3–8*
Calves	• Standing calf raise	(2–3 warm-up sets) 4 working sets	3–8*
Biceps	• Dumbbell curl	(2–3 warm-up sets) 4 working sets	3–8*
Triceps	• Lying triceps extension	(2–3 warm-up sets) 4 working sets	3–8*
Abdominals	• Crunch	(2–3 warm-up sets) 4 working sets	3–8*

*Begin with weights equal to 70–80% 1RM and perform 6–8 repetitions. Progress to 80–90% 1RM, performing 3–4 repetitions.

◆ Periodisation (training cycles) ◆

Periodisation refers to the planned manipulation of training volume and intensity throughout a series of specific training phases or cycles. It is an application of the principles of progressive training – you vary your repetitions, sets, weight and intensity during each cycle – and is a method used to make continual improvements in performance throughout the year, thus avoiding reaching plateaux. If you follow the same workout for any length of time, the body soon adapts to the constant load and your gains diminish. However, by structuring your long-term training goals in a number of training cycles, you will be able to make gains in strength, mass and definition all year round, and will also avoid overtraining and injuries.

Proof that periodisation works better than sticking to the same routine week after week comes from a study at Apalachian State University in Boone, North Carolina, and the USA Weightlifting Development Center in Shreveport, Louisiana.[4] The experienced weight trainers who followed a periodised programme made significant improvements in strength (as measured by their 1RM for the squat), whereas those who followed a standard programme did not show any improvement.

A periodisation programme is divided into a number of distinct cycles. The longest cycle is called a *macrocycle* and usually spans a period of one year, although shorter macrocycles can be used – for example, two macrocycles per year are used in a double-periodisation programme. This would suit those who cannot commit themselves to a year-round programme or those who want greater variety in their training.

The year is then broken down into 2–6 shorter training cycles (*mesocycles*), each spanning several weeks. Each mesocycle emphasises a particular training goal (e.g. muscle size or muscular endurance) and involves a gradual increase in training intensity. The aim is to peak at the end of your mesocycle. For strength trainers, this may be gauged by the amount of weight that can be lifted.

Each mesocycle is then followed by a short period (1–2 weeks) of relative rest, which is important to allow your body to recover and recuperate before beginning the next mesocycle. Provided this rest phase lasts no longer than four weeks, you will not experience a detraining effect (*see* also p. 104). During this time, you should do only very light training, or a completely different activity such as golf or recreational swimming that does not tax your energy systems or central nervous system in the same way.

Each mesocycle is then divided into week-long *microcycles*, around which you plan your day-to-day workouts.

There are many variations on periodisation programmes, dependent on your goals, training experience and lifestyle. The examples given on the following pages may be used as a basis for designing your own programme. You may commence training at any time during the year – simply change the month headings. Also you may change the timing of the rest periods to fit around holidays and other lifestyle commitments. The important point is to follow the mesocycles in the given order, and to gradually increase your training intensity within each mesocycle.

Periodisation programme 1: muscular endurance

Aims

1. Improve muscular endurance
2. Improve muscle tone

This periodisation programme emphasises muscular endurance and comprises four mesocycles of circuit training, each progressively increasing in intensity. This is achieved by shortening the rest intervals from 30 seconds to 20 seconds, adding more circuits to your allocated workout time and changing the reps and weight. If you are training for a particular sport, include exercises that work the main muscle groups involved in that sport and which also mimic the movements used – e.g. lat pull-down if you are a swimmer. You can also concentrate on particular goals:

- Muscular strength and endurance – use slightly heavier weights for 12–15 reps, with slightly longer rest intervals between exercises
- cardio-vascular fitness/fat loss – use lighter weights for up to 20 reps, with a cardio-vascular exercise such as the stationary bike or jogging between stations.

Periodisation programme 1 – to improve muscular endurance (beginners)

						Macrocycle						
Jan.	Feb.	Mar.	Apr.	May	June	July	Aug.	Sept.	Oct.	Nov.	Dec.	
Mesocycle 1			Mesocycle 2			Mesocycle 3			Mesocycle 4			
12 weeks ME		1 week R	12 weeks ME		1 week R	12 weeks ME		1 week R	12 weeks ME			1 week R

Progression

- Reduce rest interval between sets from 30 to 15 seconds
- Increase reptitions from 15 to a maximum of 20
- Increase number of circuits performed in 45 minutes
- Use slightly heavier weights if you can exceed 20 reps

Key:
ME = muscle endurance training (*see* pp. 106–7)
R = rest/low-intensity activity

Periodisation programme 2: muscle size (beginners)

Aims

1. Increase muscle size
2. Increase strength

This cycle includes a 12-week muscular endurance mesocycle to build a good base of conditioning and prepare the muscles for the next mesocycles. The exact length of the muscle size mesocycles will depend on your level of conditioning and any holiday commitments. For example, you may need to shorten mesocycle 1 to avoid overtraining. As you become progressively adapted to training, however, you should be able to sustain the full training cycles. Increase the intensity gradually by using progressively heavier weights.

Periodisation programme 2 – to improve muscle size (beginners)

Jan.	Feb.	Mar.	Apr.	May	June	July	Aug.	Sept.	Oct.	Nov.	Dec.
Macrocycle											
Mesocycle 1			Mesocycle 2			Mesocycle 3			Mesocycle 4		
12 weeks ME		1 week R	10 weeks MS		3 week R	10 weeks MS		3 week R	4 weeks MS	2 weeks AMS / 4 weeks MS	2 weeks AMS / 1 week R

Progression

- Gradually increase weight used in each mesocycle

Key:
ME = muscle endurance training (*see* pp. 106–7)
MS = muscle size training (*see* pp. 117–19 Phase 1 only)
AMS = advanced muscle size training (*see* pp. 120–223 – descending (drop) set workout)
R = rest/low-intensity activity

Periodisation programme 3: muscle size (advanced)

Aims

1. Increase muscle size
2. Increase strength

This plan is suitable for weight trainers with at least 1–2 years' training experience. Following a six-week mesocycle building muscle endurance and strength, this periodisation programme emphasises muscle hypertrophy. Muscle size cycles dominate, interspersed with short periods that incorporate advanced training methods (descending (drop) sets, supersets and pre-exhaustion) and maximum strength-training methods. The objective of this approach is to avoid training plateaux and produce long-term muscle size gains.

Periodisation programme 3 – to improve muscle size (advanced)

	Jan.	Feb.	Mar.	Apr.	May	June	July	Aug.	Sept.	Oct.	Nov.	Dec.
Macrocycle												
	Mesocycle 1			Mesocycle 2			Mesocycle 3			Mesocycle 4		
	6 weeks ME	1 week R	6 weeks MS	1 week R	6 weeks MS	2 wks AMS	4 weeks MS	1 week R	2 wks AMS	4 weeks MS	1 week R	4 weeks MS	4 weeks MS	4 weeks MXS	1 week R

Progression

- Gradually increase amount of weight used

Key:
ME = muscle endurance training (*see* pp. 115–16 – phase 2 only)
MS = muscle size training (*see* p. 117–19 – phase 1 only)
AMS = advanced muscle size training (*see* pp. 120–23 – any of the three workouts)
MXS = maximum strength training (see pp. 124–5)
R = rest/low-intensity activity

Periodisation programme 4: maximum strength (advanced)

Aims

1. Increase maximum strength
2. Promote long-term hypertrophy

This periodisation programme is suitable for advanced weight trainers who want to develop stronger muscles and long-term hypertrophy. Following a 6-week conditioning mesocycle to prepare the body for the forthcoming intense training, it incorporates both maximum strength-training methods as well as advanced muscle size training methods. Muscle strength-training cycles dominate and they are interspersed with advanced training method cycles and maximum strength training.

Periodisation programme 4 – to increase maximum strength (advanced)

	Jan.	Feb.	Mar.	Apr.	May	June	July	Aug.	Sept.	Oct.	Nov.	Dec.
Macrocycle												
	Mesocycle 1		Mesocycle 2			Mesocycle 3		Mesocycle 4			Mesocycle 5	
	6 weeks ME	1 week R	6 weeks MS	6 weeks MXS	1 week R	6 weeks MXS	3 weeks AMS	3 weeks MS	3 weeks MXS	3 weeks AMS	1 week R	4 weeks MXS	2 wks AMS	3 weeks MXS	3 weeks AMS	2 weeks R

(Timeline blocks: 6 weeks ME — 1 week R — 6 weeks MS — 6 weeks MXS — 1 week R — 6 weeks MXS — 3 weeks AMS — 2 weeks R — 3 weeks MS — 3 weeks MXS — 3 weeks AMS — 1 week R — 4 weeks MXS — 2 wks AMS — 3 weeks MXS — 3 weeks AMS — 2 weeks R)

Progression

● Gradually increase amount of weight used

Key:
ME = muscle endurance training (*see* pp. 115–16 – phase 2 only)
MS = muscle size training (*see* p. 117–19 – phase 1 only)
AMS = advanced muscle size training (*see* pp. 120–23 – any of the three workouts)
MXS = maximum strength training (*see* pp. 124–5)
R = rest/low-intensity activity

◆ Personal fitness goal: training for sports ◆

Aims

1. Improve sports performance
2. Improve strength, power, muscle size or muscular endurance
3. Reduce injury risk

While fitness athletes and bodybuilders train primarily to change the appearance of their physiques, other athletes can tailor a strength-training programme to improve various aspects of their sports performance. When designing a sports strength-training programme, however, it has to be specific to the requirements of your sport. You need to consider the following:

- the movement patterns of your sport, and which muscles are used
- the relative importance of strength, power, hypertrophy and muscular endurance in your sport
- which muscles or joints are most prone to injury and therefore need strengthening

- the priorities of your sport's season – i.e. off-season, pre-season, in-season and post-season
- Your fitness level and training experience.

General guidelines for strength training for sport

1. Use different programmes for each season, focusing on developing only one of these goals (e.g. strength). Attempting to improve in two or more areas (e.g. strength and muscular endurance) simultaneously will produce only mediocre improvements.
2. During the off-season focus on developing your strength and hypertrophy.
3. Pre-season training should focus on one particular fitness aspect (e.g. power, muscular endurance or strength) that is relevant to the sport. Use one of the programmes detailed in the first part of this chapter.
4. During the season, concentrate on maintaining your fitness and staying

Season	Sports-specific training	Strength training	Strength-training goal
Off-season	Low	High	Hypertrophy and strength
Pre-season	Medium	Medium	Strength/power/ muscular endurance – depending on the sport
In-season	High	Low	Maintain strength/power/ muscular endurance

Table 12.1 Priorities for a sports-specific strength-training programme

injury-free. The frequency and duration of your strength-training workouts should be reduced and the exercises should be more sport-specific.

5. Include mostly compound exercises in your programme. They will increase your balance and co-ordination while increasing strength. Keep isolation exercises to a minimum and schedule at the end of your workout.

6. Keep rest periods fairly short (between 60 and 90 seconds) to mimic the demands of your sport.

7. Choose a weight with which the set becomes difficult by the last 1–2 repetitions.

8. Maintain strict form for each repetition, using the complete ROM.

9. Emphasise quality rather than quantity.

Athlete's off-season strength-training workout

The workout includes exercises for each muscle group, with a particular emphasis on compound exercises, to cause maximum muscle stimulation. There is equal emphasis on lower- and upper-body exercises to build balanced muscle development. Moderate to heavy weights should be used and the prescribed sets and reps are designed to develop muscle strength and hypertrophy.

You may change the exercises according to your particular athletic event. This programme is more suitable for sprinting events but the amount of upper-body work should be increased and lower-body work reduced for events such as javelin or discus. Longer-distance running events require more muscular endurance and less muscle mass, so the reps should be inceased and the weights reduced.

Frequency: 3/week on non-consecutive days, alternating workout 1 (lower body) and workout 2 (upper body)
Workout time: approx. 45 min (excluding warm-up and stretching

Rest: 60–90 s between sets and 1–2 min between exercises
Training tempo: 2 counts for the concentric (lifting) action; 3 counts for the eccentric (lowering) action

---

Athlete's off-season workout 1 (lower body)

Muscle group	Exercise	Sets	Reps
Quadriceps/gluteals	• Squat • Dead lift	2–3	8–12
Quadriceps/gluteals/hamstrings	• Lunge (front or reverse)	2	8–12
Hamstrings	• Straight-leg dead lift	2	8–12
Calves	• Standing calf raise	3	8–12
Abdominals	• Swiss ball crunch • Hanging leg raise	2	10–15

Athlete's off-season workout 2 (upper body)

Muscle group	Exercise	Sets	Reps
Chest	• Bench press (flat or incline)	2–3	8–12
Back	• Bent-over row	2–3	8–12
Shoulders	• Shoulder press (barbell or dumbbell) • Dumbbell shrug	2–3 2	8–12 8–12
Biceps	• Barbell curl	2	8–12
Triceps	• Lying triceps extension	2	8–12

Athlete's in-season strength-training workout

The in-season workout places more emphasis on isolation exercises and less on compound movements. As the goal shifts to strength and mass maintenance, and developing muscle endurance, the number of repetitions are increased and the total number of sets are reduced slightly. Like the off-season workout, the exercises are designed to promote balanced development of all muscle groups.

Frequency: 2/week on non-consecutive days, alternating workout 1 (lower body) with workout 2 (upper body)
Workout time: approx. 30 min (excluding warm-up and stretching

Rest: 60–90 s between sets and 1–2 min between exercises
Training tempo: 2 counts for the concentric (lifting) action; 3 counts for the eccentric (lowering) action

---

Athlete's in-season workout 1 (lower body)

Muscle group	Exercise	Sets	Reps
Quadriceps/gluteals	• Squat or leg press	2	10–12
Hamstrings	• Lying leg curl	2	10–15
Quadriceps/gluteals/hamstrings	• Lunge (front or reverse)	2	12–15
Abdominals	• Swiss ball crunch • Hanging leg raise	2	10–15
Lower back	• Back extension on Swiss ball	2	15–20

Athlete's in-season workout 2 (upper body)

Muscle group	Exercise	Sets	Reps
Chest	• Bench press	2	12–15
Back	• Incline dumbbell press • Chins/pull-ups	2 2	12–15 10–12
Shoulders	• Shoulder press (barbell or dumbbell)	2	12–15
Biceps	• Dumbbell curl	2	12–15
Triceps	• Triceps push-down	2	12–15

Footballer's off-season strength-training workout

Like the athlete's workout, this workout includes exercises for each muscle group to promote balanced development, as all muscles are important in football. Rather more emphasis – i.e. more sets – is placed on compound exercises for the lower body, as these muscle groups are used more than upper-body muscles in football. Moderate to heavy weights should be used as the goal is strength and hypertrophy. It is important to include a hamstring exercise as these muscles receive less work compared with the quadriceps in this sport, which can lead to imbalanced strength and increased injury risk.

Frequency: 3–4/week on non-consecutive days, alternating workout 1 (lower body) and workout 2 (upper body)
Workout time: approx. 45 min (excluding warm-up and stretching

Rest: approx. 60–90 s between sets and 1–2 min between exercises
Training tempo: 2 counts for the concentric (lifting) action; 3 counts for the eccentric (lowering) action

---

Footballer's off-season workout 1 (lower body)

Muscle group	Exercise	Sets	Reps
Quadriceps/gluteals	• Leg press • Dead lift	4	8–12
Quadriceps	• Leg extension	3	8–12
Hamstrings	• Lying leg curl	3	8–12
Calves	• Standing calf raise	3	8–12
Abdominals	• Crunch • Hanging leg raise	2	15–20

Footballer's off-season workout 2 (upper body)

Muscle group	Exercise	Sets	Reps
Chest	• Bench press (flat or incline)	4	8–12
Back	• Lat pull-down	3	8–12
Shoulders	• Shoulder press (barbell or dumbbell)	4	8–12
Triceps	• Lying triceps extension	3	8–12
Biceps	• Barbell curl	3	8–12

Footballer's in-season strength-training workout

The in-season workout continues to include exercises for each muscle group. The workout is designed to maintain muscle strength and increase muscular endurance, hence the reduction in sets and increase in reps.

Frequency: 2/week on non-consecutive days, alternating workout 1 (lower body) with workout 2 (upper body)	Rest: 60–90 s between sets and 1–2 min between exercises
Workout time: approx. 30 min (excluding warm-up and stretching	Training tempo: 2 counts for the concentric (lifting) action; 3 counts for the eccentric (lowering) action

Footballer's in-season workout 1 (lower body)

Muscle group	Exercise	Sets	Reps
Quadriceps/gluteals	• Squat or leg press	2	12–15
Hamstrings	• Lying leg curl	2	12–15
Quadriceps/gluteals/hamstrings	• Lunge (front or reverse)	2	12–15
Biceps	• Dumbbell curl	2	12–15
Abdominals	• Swiss ball crunch • Hanging leg raise	2	15–20
Lower back	• Back extension on Swiss ball	2	15–20

Footballer's in-season workout 2 (upper body)

Muscle group	Exercise	Sets	Reps
Chest	• Bench press	2	12–15
Back	• Chins/pull-ups	2	12–15
Shoulders	• Shoulder press (barbell or dumbbell)	2	12–15
Biceps	• Barbell curl	2	12–15
Triceps	• Triceps push-down	2	12–15

Swimmer's off-season strength-training workout

The workout comprises supersets for opposing muscles, allowing more work to be completed – and greater strength and mass to be developed – in less time. The movement patterns in many of the exercises (e.g. lat pull-down) replicate those in swimming, although you may change the exercise selection within each muscle group to mimic the actions in a particular stroke more closely.

Frequency: 2–3/week on non-consecutive days *Workout time:* approx. 45 min (excluding warm-up and stretching	*Rest:* approx. 60–90 s between exercises *Training tempo:* 2 counts for the concentric (lifting) action; 3 counts for the eccentric (lowering) action

Swimmer's off-season workout

Superset No.	Muscle group	Exercise	Sets	Reps
1	Back	Lat pull-down	1	8–12
	Chest	Bench press	1	8–12
2	Back	Seated cable row	1	8–12
	Chest	Dumbbell flye	1	8–12
3	Shoulders	Shoulder press (barbell or dumbbell)	1	8–12
	Trapezius	Dumbbell shrug	1	8–12
4	Shoulders	Lateral raise	1	8–12
	Trapezius	Upright row	1	8–12
5	Quadriceps/gluteals	Squat or leg press	1	10–12
	Quadriceps/gluteals/hamstrings	Lunge (front or reverse)	1	10–12

Swimmer's in-season strength-training workout

This in-season workout is designed to increase muscular endurance and simply maintain strength and hypertrophy. Greater emphasis is placed on back and shoulder movements as these muscles are used to the greatest extent in most swimming disciplines. No specific exercises for the arms are included as they receive sufficient stimulation for the sport's requirements with the other exercises. A circuit format is used, and the total workout time reduced slightly to allow more time to be devoted to swimming training.

Frequency: 2/week on non-consecutive days
Workout time: approx. 30 min (excluding warm-up and stretching
Number of circuits: 3

Rest: approx. 20–30 s between exercises and 2 min between circuits
Training tempo: 2 counts for the concentric (lifting) action; 3 counts for the eccentric (lowering) action

---

Swimmer's in-season strength training workout

Muscle group	Exercise	Sets*	Reps
Quadriceps/gluteals/hamstrings	• Lunge (front or reverse)	1	12–15
Back	• Chins/pull-ups • One-arm row	1	12–15
Chest	• Bench press	1	12–15
Shoulders	• Lateral raise	1	12–15
Shoulders/trapezius	• Upright row	1	12–15
Lower back	• Back extension	1	15–20
Abdominals	• Hanging leg raise	1	15–20

*Complete one set of each exercise, then repeat the circuit two more times.

◆ Summary of key points ◆

- It is essential to warm up before training to reduce injury risk and enhance your subsequent performance. Include 5–10 minutes of a light aerobic activity, mobility movements, and 1–2 warm-up sets with a light weight.
- Good training technique is crucial for injury prevention and maximum strength gain. Use full ROM, maintain full control of the weight at all times and avoid cheating movements.
- A circuit-training workout is most appropriate for beginners wishing to build a good base of strength. It is also suitable for those who desire increased muscle tone and increased muscular endurance.
- A split workout is most appropriate for increasing muscle size and strength. It should only be followed by those with previous training experience.
- Advanced training techniques such as descending (drop) sets, supersets and pre-

exhaustion can be incorporated into a split programme to provide greater overload and allow you to make continued gains in muscle size and strength.
- Maximum strength training, involving heavier weights and lower repetitions, increases pure strength and muscle density. It helps bodybuilders and Olympic lifters get through sticking points and further increase muscle size.
- Periodisation is a planned manipulation of training volume and intensity throughout a series of training cycles that allows you to make continual improvements in strength and size.
- Strength training may be tailored to improve various aspects of sports performance. Different programmes should be used to develop key areas of fitness (i.e. strength and hypertrophy, muscular endurance) during the off-, pre- and in-season.

Chapter 13

Fat-burning Training Programmes

Building good-looking muscles is only part of your quest. If you want to improve your muscle definition and reduce your body fat, you need to incorporate cardio-vascular ('cardio') training into your programme. Contrary to popular belief, cardio training is not counterproductive to a weight-training programme. It will not burn hard-earned muscle nor prevent gains in muscle size. In fact, cardio training is essential for any fitness or sports training programme, not just for fat-burning but for its performance-boosting and immunity-boosting effects.

This chapter explains which activities are best for fat-burning, and how often and how long you need to train. It gives you the straight facts on high-intensity versus low-intensity cardio, shatters the popular myth of the 'fat-burning zone' and reveals the true fat-burning formula. Exactly how cardio-vascular training reduces your body fat store is explained, as well as the effect of cardio-vascular exercise on your metabolic rate. More is not always better so this chapter also summarises the risks of excessive cardio for strength trainers. And to get you well on your way to a leaner physique, it gives you three scientifically based cardio workouts for optimal fat-burning and cardio-vascular health.

♦ Cardio terms ♦

Before going any further, here are the key terms associated with cardio-vascular exercise.

Maximum heart rate (MHR)

This is the highest heart rate value you can achieve in an all-out effort to the point of exhaustion. It remains constant from day to day and decreases only slightly from year to year – by about 1 beat per year beginning at 10–15 years of age.

To estimate your MHR, subtract your age from 220. For example, if you are aged 30, your MHR would be estimated at 190 beats per minute (bpm).

$$MHR = 220 - 30$$

Maximal oxygen uptake, or maximal aerobic capacity (VO$_2$max)

This is the maximum amount of oxygen that can be consumed per minute during exercise. It is regarded as the best single measurement of cardio-vascular fitness.

Training heart rate (THR)

When prescribing exercise intensity, it is appropriate to establish a THR range. This is the intensity at which you would need to exercise to gain a training effect. The general guideline for improving cardio-vascular fitness is 65–75% of your MHR.[1] For example, if you are aged 30, your THR zone would be calculated as follows:

THR zone = (65% x 190)–(75% x 190)
= 123–142 bpm

This is equivalent to about 55–65% of your VO_2max, since oxygen uptake values are approximately 5–10% lower at any given intensity than those predicted using MHR values. A heart rate monitor is a valuable tool for performing the cardio workouts below.

Rating of perceived exertion (RPE)

This is a subjective rating of how hard you feel you are exercising. The most popular rating scale is the Borg scale. The 10-point scale ranges from 0 (nothing at all) to 10 (very, very hard) (*see* Figure 13.1), although there are 15-point scales that may be used. Used correctly, this is a very accurate system for monitoring exercise intensity.

% HR max	Rating	Intensity
	0	Nothing at all
	1	Very light
< 35%	2	Light
	3	Moderate
35–59%	4	Somewhat hard
	5	Hard
60–79%	6	
	7	Very hard
80–89%	8	
	9	
> 90%	10	Very, very hard

Figure 13.1 The Borg scale of perceived exertion (10-point scale)[2]

High-intensity cardio-vascular exercise

This is generally accepted as an intensity corresponding to more than 70% of VO^2max, or approximately 80% MHR.

Low-intensity cardio-vascular exercise

This is generally accepted as an intensity corresponding to less than 70% of VO^2max, or approximately 80% MHR.

◆ Cardio facts ◆

Which activity?

Cardio workouts can be any exercise that raises and maintains your heart rate – running, cycling, swimming, stepping or elliptical machine. Cardio training provides numerous benefits for strength trainers. It:

- reduces body fat and maintains a low body fat percentage
- increases the body's fat-burning capacity during exercise and rest
- improves body composition
- increases the metabolic rate
- reduces stress and anxiety
- improves confidence, self-esteem and mood
- reduces blood pressure, blood cholesterol and the risk of heart disease
- boosts the immune system.

Any of the following activities may be included in your cardio programme:

- running/treadmill
- fitness/power walking
- stepping machine/stair climber
- cycling/stationary bicycle
- swimming

- aerobic classes/aqua aerobics/step aerobics
- climbing machine
- elliptical training machine
- rowing/rowing machine.

The choice depends on your personal preference, and the equipment and time available to you. It's important to plan your workouts around activities that you enjoy, and also to vary the exercise mode as far as possible. If you dislike running, choose activities that you like better. The more enthusiastic you are about an activity, the more likely you are to work hard and keep it up. In fact, frequently changing the mode of cardio may produce better results than simply increasing the duration of time you spend doing it as your body becomes more efficient in performing a movement over time, using less energy. For example, perform your cardio training on a stationary bike on one day, a stepping machine on another and a rowing machine on another.

How much and how often?

For cardio-vascular fitness, the Health Education Authority recommends 20 minutes of high-intensity aerobic activity repeated three times a week. As this level of training can only be managed by very well-conditioned athletes, an alternative recommendation of 30 minutes of moderate-intensity activity repeated five times a week would be suitable for beginners and intermediate fitness participants. Both workout 1 and workout 2 (*see* pp. 146–7) involve a high level of intensity for 20 minutes, while workout 3 is a low-intensity workout suitable for beginners, in which cardio is maintained for a minimum of 30 minutes.

High- or low-intensity cardio?

Whether you choose a high- or low-intensity cardio programme depends on your goals, fitness level and time available. Both types will develop cardio-vascular fitness and burn fat but high-intensity cardio (over 70% of your VO_2max) is more effective. If time is a premium, shorter periods of high-intensity cardio will give you the same results in terms of fat loss as longer periods of low-intensity cardio.

Is low-intensity cardio best for burning fat?

It's been a long-held belief that low-intensity cardio is the best way to burn fat. While this may be appropriate for beginners and is certainly more attractive for many casual exercisers, serious fitness trainers and athletes will reap greater benefits from training at a higher intensity. In fact, it is a myth that training in the so-called 'fat-burning zone' (around 60–70% MHR) is optimal for fat burning.

The theory about the fat-burning zone came from a study that showed that low-intensity exercise burns a greater percentage of calories from fat than from carbohydrate.[3] When high-intensity exercise is practised, the percentage of fuel from carbohydrate is increased. However, the amount of fat burned is greater than or equal to that burned during low-intensity exercise.[4] When it comes to fat loss it is not the proportion of each fuel metabolised but the *total calorie expenditure* that is most important. For the same workout time, you will burn more calories and more fat with high-intensity cardio. For example, walking (low-intensity cardio) for 60 minutes will burn about 270 kcal, of which approximately 60% (160 kcal) come from fat, while jogging (high-intensity cardio) for 60 minutes will burn about 680 kcal, of which approximately 40% (270 kcal) come from fat. Thus, the higher intensity exercise results in a greater fat loss over the same workout time.

Exactly how does cardio reduce your fat stores?

Regular cardio training enhances the body's ability to burn fat for energy both at rest and during activity. Not only do you burn extra fat calories during aerobic exercise but regular training has a long-term effect on your body's metabolism.

For example, regular cardio training increases the body's production of the enzyme lipoprotein lipase, which breaks down fat into its component fatty acids. These fatty acids are released into the bloodstream and transported to other tissues such as muscle where they are taken up by the cells, transferred into the mitochondria and broken down to release energy. Thus, cardio training increases the body's ability to break down fat. The more aerobically fit you are, the greater the percentage of fat you burn at any given exercise intensity. Just as you can train your muscles to become stronger and bigger, so you can train your aerobic system to burn fat more efficiently. Including aerobic training in your strength-training programme will therefore help you to achieve and maintain a lower body fat percentage and better muscle definition.

However, the benefits of high-intensity training don't end with your workout. Following exercise, your metabolic rate remains elevated above resting levels for some time as your body replenishes its energy systems. This 'excess post-exercise oxygen consumption' (EPOC) is fuelled almost entirely by fat. Following low-intensity training, the EPOC is very small. On the other hand, the EPOC following high-intensity

training may be quite large. Also, high-intensity cardio can lead to a significant increase in the resting metabolic rate (RMR), when performed at least three times a week. That means you continue burning more calories throughout the day, even when you are at rest.

What is the best fat-burning exercise?

While all forms of aerobic activity burn fat, the best method for burning fat – and simultaneously increasing cardio-vascular fitness – is high-intensity interval training.[5] Performing a series of intervals at 80–90% MHR, or an RPE of 8–9 (very hard), as opposed to maintaining a steady intensity, burns up to 50% more fat than low-intensity exercise. But before you rush into it, you must be aware that this type of training is only suitable for very well-conditioned athletes and should not be attempted by beginners.

Once you have built up to it, high-intensity interval training is a very effective way of improving your body composition. Not only does it burn more calories during your workout compared with low-intensity training, it produces the greatest EPOC and speeds up your metabolic rate for some time after your workout.

Interval training can easily be applied to any mode of exercise – e.g. running, cycling, stationary bike, stepping machine or any other cardio machine. During the interval phases, you increase either your speed or the resistance of the machine (e.g. the incline of a treadmill or the 'level' setting on a stationary bike) in order to reach the required RPE level of 8–9 or 80–90% MHR. This is maintained for 15 seconds–3 minutes, depending on the intensity, followed by a recovery period at an RPE of 4 (somewhat hard) or 60% MHR for 30 seconds to 3 minutes. An interval training workout is detailed on p. 147.

Is it possible to do too much cardio?

More isn't always better, as excessive cardio can result in muscle breakdown and a loss of muscle size and strength. During cardio training, small amounts of protein can be used for energy, although the misconception that it significantly depletes muscle mass relates more directly to poor dietary habits.

The biggest problem is the combination of dieting – or an inadequate calorie intake – and excessive cardio. Dieters who go overboard with cardio training don't realise that a large proportion of their weight loss may be due to muscle loss. When the body doesn't get enough calories it draws upon its reserves, mainly in the form of fat but also from protein, which is found in muscle. Too much cardio takes calories away from muscle growth and you can end up literally canabalising your own muscle tissue to help your body meet its energy needs. That's the last thing a strength trainer wants.

For this reason cardio should be done in moderation, as per the guidelines detailed on p. 142. As we have seen, moderate amounts of cardio will help you lose fat, and give you numerous cardio-vascular health benefits.

The downside of running

Long-distance running can result in a loss of muscle tissue. This is induced by the release of the catabolic hormone cortisol (released during all types of high-intensity activity), which outstrips the production of anabolic hormones such as testosterone. Under these conditions there is a net catabolism or breakdown of muscle tissue. One study measured a decrease in the size of FTI fibres following a three-month period of aerobic training on a treadmill.[6] This may help explain the low muscle mass of many endurance runners.

When is the best time for cardio?

This depends on your individual lifestyle. Choose a time of day that fits in well with your daily schedule; that way you will be less likely to miss a workout.

If fat loss is your main goal, the best time to do your cardio workout is first thing in the morning. There is evidence that, when performed on an empty stomach, cardio enhances fat burning during and after your workout.[7] According to research from the Human Performance Laboratory at the University of Texas at Austin, fat burning is suppressed when carbohydrates are eaten during the six hours before exercise. This is due to the rise in insulin levels in the blood (caused by carbohydrates), which suppresses the breakdown of fat stores in adipose tissue and reduces the release of fatty acids into the bloodstream. Thus, fatty acids are less readily available as a fuel for the exercising muscles, an effect that can last for several hours after eating carbohydrates. Doing your cardio workout after a period of fasting (e.g. first thing in the morning), when blood insulin levels are relatively low, will optimise the rate of fat breakdown and fat burning, and would be a more effective fat-burning strategy than doing your cardio workout later in the day after you have eaten a few meals. However, it is more important that you fit your cardio workout comfortably into your daily schedule than risk omitting it if you are unable to fit it in in the morning.

Research suggests that it may be better to perform your cardio and strength training as separate sessions to minimise catabolism (the breakdown of lean mass).[8] But if you prefer to do both in one session, complete your weight-training workout first when glycogen stores are high. Performing cardio prior to your strength-training workout may be counterproductive, resulting in reduced strength and early fatigue due to muscle glycogen depletion.

Weight training burns fat too

It's not only cardio that burns body fat – weight training will also help you get lean.[9] Researchers at Colorado State University measured the RMR of volunteers following an hour's strenuous weight training and discovered that their RMRs remained significantly elevated for three hours after the workout. Even after 16 hours the RMR remained a little higher than normal, as did the rate of fat oxidation. Since RMR makes up the major proportion (60–70%) of total daily energy expenditure, any increase in RMR would have a big impact on your daily calorie output. Therefore, regular strenuous weight-training workouts are a very effective strategy for upping calorie burning and losing fat.

◆ The fat-burning workouts ◆

Three workouts follow which have been designed around the latest cardio research and which have been proven to get great results.

For maximum fat burning and time efficiency, use either 1 or 2, which are both high-intensity sessions. Workout 3 is a low-intensity programme that may be more appropriate for beginners or at certain times when you are easing back for various reasons – e.g. following illness or injury.

For each programme, select the pace or machine resistance according to your individual level of cardio-vascular fitness. If you have a heart rate monitor, you can work out the appropriate intensity needed to bring your heart rate to the prescribed level. Alternatively, use the Borg RPE in Figure 13.1 to ensure you are exercising at the right intensity.

As you adapt to cardio training and your cardio-vascular fitness improves, you will need to increase the machine's resistance or your pace to continue gaining benefits. When the exercise feels a little easier, it's time to make it harder again! For example, if you started at level 2 on the stationary bike with an RPE of 5 (hard) , you may need to increase to level 3 after a few weeks to elicit the same RPE. Alternatively, keep changing the type of cardio you do to keep your body guessing (*see* p. 142).

1. High-intensity cardio workout (steady state)

Frequency: 3/week
Workout time: 30 min (including warm-up and cool-down)
THR zone: 75–85% MHR
RPE: 6–7 (hard–very hard)

This workout is suitable for *very well-conditioned weight trainers only*. Start with a 5-minute warm-up, then gradually build up your pace or machine resistance until you reach your training zone (75–85% MHR) or an RPE of 6–7. Maintain your intensity in this zone for 20 minutes, although you may vary the intensity between the lower and upper ends of the zone if you wish. Gradually reduce your pace or resistance for a 5-minute cool-down before stretching out.

Intermediate
Aim to maintain a slightly lower THR of 70–80% MHR or an RPE of 6. Maintain this for 10–15 minutes to start with, and increase your workout time by 1 minute each time you train, until you reach 20 minutes.

Beginners
Do not attempt this workout until you have achieved a good level of cardio fitness using workout 3 (low-intensity) on p. 148.

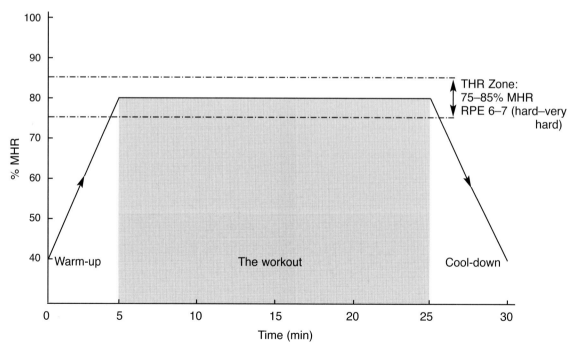

Figure 13.2 High-intensity cardio workout (steady state)

146

2. High-intensity cardio workout (interval)

Frequency: 3/week
Workout time: 30 min (including warm-up and cool-down)
THR zone: 80–90% MHR – high-intensity intervals; 60% MHR – low-intensity intervals
RPE: 8–9 (very hard) – high-intensity intervals; 4 (somewhat hard) – low-intensity intervals

This workout is suitable for *very well-conditioned weight trainers only* and is the most efficient way to burn fat. Start with a 5-minute warm-up, then perform 9 sets of 2-minute intervals. Adjust your pace or machine resistance to reach your training zone (80–90% MHR) or an RPE of 8–9 for 1 minute, followed by 2 or 1 minute at 60% MHR or an RPE of 4. Gradually reduce your pace or resistance for a 5-minute cool-down before stretching out.

Intermediate
Monitor your intensity using RPE instead of % MHR, and perform moderately intense intervals at an RPE of 6–8. Begin with 3 or 4 sets of 3-minute intervals to start with, and each week add one more 3-minute interval until you can perform 7 sets.

Beginners
Do not perform this workout until you have achieved a good level of cardio fitness using workout 3 (low-intensity) on p. 148.

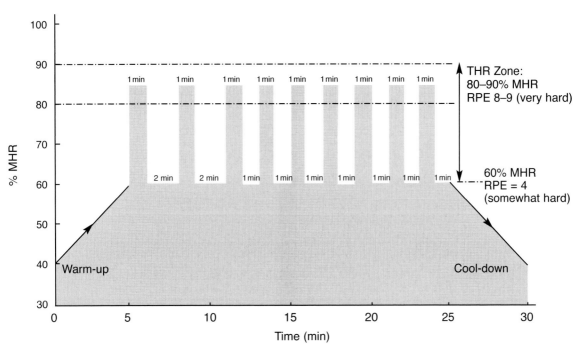

Figure 13.3 High-intensity cardio workout (interval)

3. Low-intensity cardio workout

Frequency: 3/week
Workout time: 40–60 min (including warm-up and cool-down)
THR zone: 50–60% MHR
RPE: 3 (moderate)

This workout is suitable for beginners, intermediate and well-conditioned weight trainers. Start with a 5-minute warm-up, then gradually build up your pace or machine resistance until you reach your training zone (50–60% MHR) or an RPE of 3 (moderate). Maintain your intensity in this zone for 30–50 minutes, although you may vary the intensity between the lower and upper ends of the zone if you wish. Gradually reduce your pace or resistance for a 5-minute cool-down.

Beginners
Monitor your intensity using RPE instead of % MHR. Perform the 5-minute warm-up and cool-down, but only do 10 minutes within your training zone at an RPE of 3. Each time you work out, increase your training time by 1–2 minutes until you reach 30–50 minutes.

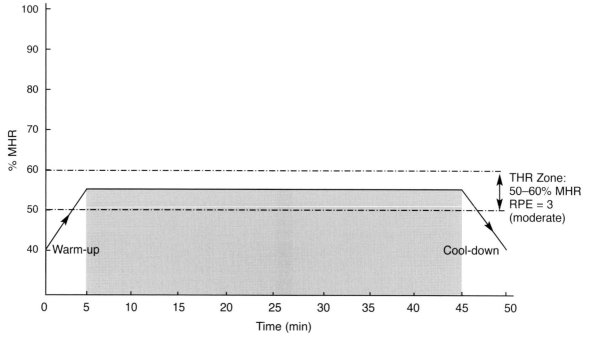

Figure 13.4 Low-intensity cardio workout

♦ Summary of key points ♦

- It is important to include cardio training in a strength-training programme to improve body composition, increase the RMR, and improve cardio-vascular fitness.
- Muscle definition depends on body fat percentage, in particular subcutaneous fat, and is therefore increased by reducing total body fat.
- Performing three 20-minute high-intensity cardio workouts per week will reduce body fat.
- It is a myth that low-intensity exercise – the so-called fat-burning zone – is optimal for fat burning.
- High-intensity cardio (over 70% of VO_2 max) burns more body fat than low-intensity cardio, and your body continues to burn more fat after training. It produces a greater EPOC and raises your RMR.
- High-intensity interval training produces the greatest fat-burning and cardio-vascular benefits
- Excessive cardio, together with an inadequate calorie intake, can result in muscle breakdown and loss of size.
- Performing cardio training after a short period of fasting (e.g. first thing in the morning) when insulin levels are low enhances fat burning.

Chapter 14

Re-sculpting Your Body

Wouldn't it be great if you could create the perfect physique? Well, strength training can go a long way to helping you improve your body symmetry and the ratio of muscle to fat. You may not be able to change your basic shape – that is determined by your genes – but by adding a little extra muscle here, removing a little fat there, you can refine your dimensions and develop your physique to its best potential.

This chapter shows you how to re-sculpt your body through specific training programmes. Whether you were born skinny (and have trouble gaining muscle) or you're a natural chubby (who can put on muscle but can't shift the fat), you can improve your shape by following the training guidelines for your body type. Most people have certain body parts that require more work than others – for example, you may have narrow shoulders or particularly thin legs. This chapter helps you diagnose your symmetry problems and gives you specific routines to improve each area.

♦ Which body type am I? ♦

The Sheldon system classifies body types into three basic categories:

- ectomorph
- mesomorph
- endomorph.

Most people are a mixture of these three types but tend to resemble one type more strongly.

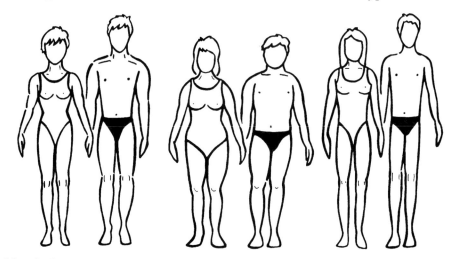

Figure 14.1 Sheldon body types. Mesomorph (left); endomorph (centre); ectomorph (right)

For example, you may share most of the characteristics of a mesomorph (wide shoulders and narrow hips) but have slight endomorphic tendencies as well (gain fat readily).

The true ectomorph is lean and thin with little muscle bulk and low body-fat levels. This person has narrow shoulders and hips and a fast metabolism, which makes it difficult to gain muscle or fat. At the other side of the spectrum, the true endomorph has a naturally stocky, rounded build with wide shoulders and wide hips. This person has an even distribution of fat and gains both muscle and fat easily, making muscle gains less visible. The genetically gifted mesomorph has a naturally athletic build with wide shoulders and narrow hips. This person gains muscle readily and finds it easy to shed fat, so tends to make the best bodybuilder.

How should an ectomorph train?

If you are an ectomorph, your muscle gains will be slower than those of the other body types. Realistically, you cannot expect to gain much more than 0.5 kg/month, although your initial gains may be higher during the first 3–6 months. However, don't get discouraged if your gains come slowly – once you have developed a good foundation of strength, follow the hypertrophy training programme detailed in Chapter 12 (*see* pp. 117–23), concentrating on basic compound movements such as squats, bench presses and dead lifts. These exercises will stimulate larger amounts of muscle mass and a greater number of muscle fibres. Keep isolation exercises to a minimum, and limit your cardio training to just two sessions/week, opting for low-intensity rather than high-intensity training (*see* pp. 142–3). Also follow the weight-gain eating plan in Chapter 17 (pp. 195–202).

How should an endomorph train?

Endomorphs are naturally strong and generally have little trouble gaining muscle and strength. However, your gains are hidden under a thick layer of fat, so the main focus of your training programme should be fat-burning aerobic activity. Aim to perform a cardio workout 3–6 days/week, including at least two high-intensity interval workouts (*see* pp. 146–7) in addition to your strength training. High-intensity cardio training burns more fat than low-intensity training both during your workout and afterwards. If you do your cardio workout first thing in the morning, your muscles will also burn more calories from fat (*see* p. 144). Another way to encourage fat being used for fuel is to avoid eating within 3–4 hours of either your cardio or strength-training workouts (*see* p. 205), and wait one hour before having a post-workout meal. For your strength-training workouts follow the foundation programme (*see* pp. 124–5), which emphasises muscular endurance and muscle tone until you achieve a good base of strength and an acceptable body-fat percentage. You can also afford to do more sets and higher repetitions (10–15) than the ectomorph – the emphasis being on calorie burning.

How should a mesomorph train?

As a mesomorph, you tend to get good gains from just about anything you do in the gym. However, that's not to say that you can train mindlessly. A well-designed programme will keep you focused and optimise your gains. The key is to use a periodised programme, breaking your training into shorter cycles to achieve year-round gains in strength and size (*see* pp. 128–30). This will help you avoid over-training. You should vary your routines frequently, using advanced training techniques such as supersets and descending sets once you have sufficient experience. Change the order of your exercises, the number of sets and repetitions, and the rest intervals used to provide plenty of variety and increase your motivation. Your workout can include a mixture of compound and isolation exercises, and should include cardio training three times per week to keep your body-fat levels low and improve your cardio-vascular fitness. Follow the bodybuilding programme (*see* pp. 117–19) progressing to the advanced workouts (*see* pp. 120–23) once you have at least one year's training experience.

Table 14.1 Training principles for different body types

Body type	Exercise selection	Sets and reps	Intensity	Cardio
Ectomorph	• Mainly compound exercises such as squats, rows and presses • Avoid isolation exercises such as leg extensions and flyes	• 8–10 sets for larger muscle groups; 4–6 sets for smaller muscle groups • Train within the 6–10 rep range	• Use heavy weights and train to failure on your working sets • Increase rest intervals to 2 min, but up to 4–5 min for squats • Train each muscle group once a week • Allow sufficient rest and recovery	• Too much cardio will reduce your gains • Limit cardio to 20–30 min, 2 times per week • Low-intensity cardio will burn fewer calories than high-intensity
Endomorph	• Include mostly compound exercises – they burn more calories • Include some isolation exercises	• 8–12 sets for large muscle groups; 6–8 for smaller muscle groups. This burns more calories • Train mostly within the 10–15 rep range • Include a few lower rep (6–10) sets to maintain size	• Include a mixture of heavy and light weights • Use shorter rest intervals (30–90 s) • Include advanced methods such as descending sets and supersets to increase the intensity and calorie-burning effect	• Increase your cardio training to 3–6 sessions per week, lasting 20–40 min • Include a minimum of 2 high-intensity interval workouts per week

Table 14.1 continued

Mesomorph	• Include both compound and isolation exercises	• Use a wide variety of sets and reps • 6–12 sets for larger muscle groups; 4–8 for smaller muscle groups • Train mostly in the 8–12 rep range	• Include different training methods in your routine, both basic (e.g. pyramid) and advanced (e.g. supersets, eccentric) • Use periodisation to optimise strength and size gains, and avoid training plateaux • Avoid over-training	• Maintain low body-fat levels and cardio-vascular fitness with 3 20-min sessions per week

♦ Leg clinic ♦

Symmetry problem: thin legs and difficulty gaining size

Skinny legs produce an overall weak appearance. The symmetry problem is exacerbated if you have a well-developed upper body – a particularly common fault in men who put more emphasis on training their chest, shoulders and arms but neglect to train their legs!

The solution

You can increase muscle mass in the leg area by concentrating on compound exercises which cause maximum stimulation of the FT muscle fibres: squats, dead lifts and leg presses. These are, admittedly, harder to perform than isolation exercises such as leg extensions and curls (which should be avoided) as they require a great deal of physical and mental effort. However, they will produce faster and better results. Perform 3–4 sets per exercise for 6–10 repetitions, using heavy weights that allow you to reach failure.

Symmetry programme for thin legs

Exercise	Sets	Reps
Squat	3–4	6–10
Dead lift	3–4	6–10
Leg press	3–4	6–10

Symmetry problem: lack of hamstring development relative to quadriceps

The back of your thigh appears straight and flat when viewed from the side, as it is underdeveloped compared with the quadriceps. This imbalance is a common problem in long/middle-distance cyclists and runners as these activities stress the quadriceps more than the hamstrings. It is also seen in weight trainers who have concentrated on exercising the quadriceps and neglected to balance their leg programme with hamstring exercises.

The solution

The imbalance can be corrected by cutting back on quadriceps isolation exercises such as leg extensions, and by including more exercises for the hamstrings, such as leg curls and straight-leg dead lifts. Use relatively heavy weights and keep the reps in the 6–10 range. All-round mass builders such as squats and leg presses should still be included as they stimulate all the leg muscles equally.

Symmetry programme for hamstrings

Exercise	Sets	Reps
Squat or leg press	3–4	6–10
Straight-leg dead lift	3–4	6–10
Lying or seated leg curl	3–4	6–10

Symmetry problem: fat thighs

Fat thighs are more common in women than men, partly due to hormonal influences (oestrogen and progesterone favour fat deposition in the upper thighs and hips) and partly due to lifestyle. Eating more calories than you need, and under exercising over a period of time, causes an increase in body-fat stores. The only way to reduce fat is to combine increased aerobic exercise with a lower calorie/fat diet. Fat or cellulite cannot be removed by creams, massage, body brushes or 'detox' supplements.

The solution

The solution for fat thighs is to include both strength and aerobic (cardio) exercise in your programme, and reduce the fat content of your diet. Aim for a minimum of 20 minutes cardio training 3–5 times a week, gradually increasing this to 45 minutes as you get fitter (*see* pp. 146–8)

Symmetry programme for fat thighs

Exercise	Sets	Reps
Squat or leg press	2–3	12–15
Front or rear lunge	2–3	12–15
Lying or seated leg curl	2–3	12–15

Symmetry problem: shapeless legs

Although you may have good strength in your legs, they may lack shape. Viewed from the front, your legs make a straight line from the hips to the knees, with no obvious outer sweep to the thigh. From the side, your legs also look straight and neither the quadriceps nor hamstrings make an aesthetic arc. This is due mainly to a lack of muscle development, a symmetry problem common among long-distance runners and people who exercise regularly but relatively infrequently (e.g. once a week).

The solution

Your programme should include a combination of compound exercises such as squats, and isolation exercises such as lunges and leg extensions to stimulate overall development. Use moderate to heavy weights and a mixture of low and high repetitions (8–15).

Symmetry programme for shapeless legs

Exercise	Sets	Reps
Squat or leg press	2	8–15
Front or rear lunge	2	8–15
Lying or seated leg curl	2	8–15
Leg extension	2	8–15

Symmetry problem: small calves

Small calves are partly due to genetics and partly due to lack of direct calf work. Some people have naturally thin calves due to a high percentage of ST fibres. This means they have a low capacity for growth and are better suited to endurance work. It is a common mistake to neglect calf training, however. Many weight trainers leave them to the end of their workout when they are tired and perform little work on them.

The solution

If you have naturally thin calves you need to perform exercises that stress the small percentage of FT that you have there. Unfortunately, everyday activities such as walking and running work only the ST endurance fibres and provide minimal stimulation for growth. Therefore, your programme should include more emphasis on calf exercises. Perform 6–10 sets of 8–12 repetitions using heavy weights.

Symmetry programme for small calves

Exercise	Sets	Reps
Standing calf raise	2–4	8–12
Leg press machine calf press	2–4	8–12
Dumbbell calf raise	2–4	8–12

Symmetry problem: bulky calves

Bulky calves are usually due to the genetic endowment of a high percentage of FT fibres coupled with previous participation in sports such as sprinting, rugby, football and step aerobics. If you have a high percentage of FT fibres, your calves respond readily to any type of high-intensity exercise.

The solution

The only way to reduce the size of a muscle is to stop training it and allow it to atrophy (waste away). Realistically, you should minimise the amount of direct calf work you perform. They will receive sufficient stimulation from everyday activities, such as walking and running, your leg training and any sports that you play.

◆ Back clinic ◆

Symmetry problem: narrow back

Viewed from behind, your torso is straight, narrow and lacks a pleasing 'V' taper. This is mainly due to the under development of the back muscles and is a very common problem, especially in people who do little exercise. It is also seen in long-distance runners, joggers, cyclists, aerobics participants, and many other sportsmen since relatively few sports and activities work this muscle group.

The solution

You can build and develop the muscles of the upper and mid-back using heavy compound exercises, such as chins and rowing movements. Perform 3–4 sets of each exercise for 6–10 repetitions. The exercises in this programme build both width and thickness.

Symmetry programme for a narrow back

Exercise	Sets	Reps
Chins	3–4	6–10
Bent-over barbell row or one-arm row	3–4	6–10
Seated cable row	3–4	6–10

Symmetry problem: weak lower back

The muscles of your lower back, the spinal erectors, are easily over stretched and weakened through poor posture, bearing uneven and heavy loads, sudden twisting, poor exercise technique and lack of direct exercise. This leaves you prone to injury and back pain.

The solution

The lower-back muscles can be strengthened by specific exercises, but also by practising safe training technique during exercises such as the squat and dead lift which place considerable stress on this area. By holding the abdominals taut during these exercises – indeed during all exercises – you will help avoid injury and strain to the lower-back muscles. Include 3–4 sets of back extensions performed for 10–15 repetitions twice a week with your abdominal routine.

You should also strengthen your abdominal muscles, in particular the deep (core) muscles in the abdomen and near the lower spine. Perform back extensions and abdominal exercises with the Swiss ball (*see* p. 55).

Symmetry programme for a weak back

Exercise	Sets	Reps
Back extension with Swiss ball	2–3	8–12
Crunch with Swiss ball	2–3	8–12

◆ Chest clinic ◆

Symmetry problem: narrow chest

A narrow chest has a straight appearance and makes the shoulders appear rounded and dominating. Viewed from the side it appears flat or even hollow. The width and circumference of your chest depends partly on your bone structure, in particular the size and shape of your rib cage and your clavicles (collarbones), and the size of your pectoral muscles.

The solution

A narrow chest can be improved by building up the pectorals and stretching the muscles between the ribs (serratus and intercostals). Poor posture can also exacerbate the symmetry problem, making the chest appear concave. This programme is designed to develop the pectorals. You should use maximum ROM, particularly for the isolation exercises, and perform chest stretches between exercises to improve the flexibility of the pectorals and muscles of the rib cage. Perform 2–3 sets per exercise for 6–10 repetitions.

Symmetry programme for a narrow chest

Exercise	Sets	Reps
Barbell or dumbbell bench press (wide grip)	2–3	6–10
Incline barbell or dumbbell press	2–3	6–10
Dumbbell flye or cable cross-over	2–3	6–10

Symmetry problem: flat upper chest

Viewed from the side, the upper part of your chest appears flat or concave and lacks a pleasing aesthetic curve from your clavicles (collarbones). This symmetry problem is very common, particularly in women who have dieted, since the upper pectorals easily atrophy when calorie and protein intake is reduced over a period of time. A concave upper chest is due to under development of the upper portion of the pectorals.

The solution

Building the upper-chest muscles corrects this problem and creates a fuller, more symmetrical chest. It also adds cleavage! Perform all pressing and flye movements on an incline bench set at 30–45°. Use moderate–heavy weights, and perform 2–3 sets of 6–10 repetitions.

Symmetry programme for a flat upper chest

Exercise	Sets	Reps
Incline bench press	2–3	6–10
Incline dumbbell press	2–3	6–10
Incline dumbbell flye	2–3	6–10

♦ Shoulder clinic ♦

Symmetry problem: narrow shoulders

Narrow shoulders greatly affect your total body symmetry. In women, narrow, under-developed deltoids accentuate a pear shape, making the hips appear wider than they actually are. In men, they make the whole body look weak and undeveloped, or detract from an otherwise athletic physique. Sometimes, the medial (outer) head is poorly developed relative to the anterior (front) head. This is common in weight trainers who focus on chest exercises such as the bench press, at the expense of shoulder exercises.

The width of your shoulders is determined partly by the length of your clavicles (collarbones) and partly by the amount of muscle mass development. Obviously, you cannot change the former but you can significantly increase the width of your shoulders and greatly improve your overall body symmetry by developing your deltoids. The medial head is mostly responsible for creating width but all three heads need to be developed equally to create good symmetry and avoid injury.

The solution

To widen the shoulders you need to build up the muscle mass by focusing on compound exercises such as shoulder presses and up-right rows. These place the greatest stimulus on the shoulders and therefore lead to fastest gains in size and strength. You should also include lateral raises, as these directly work the medial head and create width. Perform 3–4 sets of 6–10 repetitions of each exercise, using heavy weights for the pressing movements.

Symmetry programme for narrow shoulders

Exercise	Sets	Reps
Dumbbell press	3–4	6–10
Upright row	3–4	6–10
Lateral raise	3–4	6–10

Symmetry programme for rounded shoulders

Exercise	Sets	Reps
Upright row	2–3	8–12
Bent-over lateral raise	2–3	8–12
Shrug	2–3	8–12
Shoulder press	2–3	8–12

Symmetry problem: rounded shoulders

Rounded shoulders are the result of poor posture, bad sitting position, poor muscle strength in the upper back and lack of flexibility in the chest muscles. Viewed from the side, your head juts forwards, your upper back is rounded, your rib cage is reduced or even hollowed and your shoulders droop. It is one of the most common postural faults in men and women. Rounded shoulders are also common in weight trainers who have overly developed the anterior head of the deltoids relative to the posterior head. Thus, the anterior head receives a disproportionate amount of stress compared with the medial and posterior heads, creating muscular imbalance.

The solution

Strengthening the trapezius and muscles of the upper back will pull the shoulders back into correct alignment. Increasing the flexibility of your chest muscles will expand the rib cage and allow the shoulders to move back easily into alignment. You should also strengthen the deltoids, especially the posterior head, which will help correct any muscular imbalance. Perform 2–3 sets of 8–12 repetitions of each exercise using a moderate weight.

♦ Arm clinic ♦

Symmetry problem: skinny arms

Poorly muscled arms are the result of a lack of direct biceps and triceps exercise. Your muscles are small and under developed, lack density and appear straight and flat with no discernible shape.

The solution

The problem can be easily corrected by including mass-building exercises for your arm muscles, such as barbell curls, triceps extensions and triceps push-downs. These movements recruit the largest number of muscle fibres and therefore place maximum stress on the muscles, producing the fastest gains in size and strength.

Your programme should include more triceps work than biceps work because the triceps provide a much greater proportion of the upper-arm muscle mass than the biceps (*see* p. 71). (Many weight trainers make the mistake of over training their biceps and neglecting their triceps in an attempt to get bigger arms.) Select a total of 4–6 sets for your biceps, and 6–9 sets for your triceps, performing 6–10 repetitions per set with a heavy weight.

Symmetry programme for skinny arms

Exercise	Sets	Reps
Barbell curl	2–3	6–10
Preacher curl	2–3	6–10
Lying triceps extension	2–3	6–10
Triceps push-down	2–3	6–10
Bench dip	2–3	6–10

Symmetry problem: bulky, shapeless arms

Viewed from the side, your arms appear chunky, straight and lacking in definition. You have developed good muscle mass in them but there is no real peak to the biceps, nor a discernible horseshoe outline to the triceps. This problem is partly due to excessive subcutaneous fat covering the muscles' outline, and partly due to poor exercise technique, shortening the ROM which leads to sub-optimal development of the muscle along its whole length.

The solution

By reducing your body fat you will reduce the fat layer covering your triceps and biceps and improve your muscle definition. So include more cardio training (aim for 3–5 sessions of 20–30 minutes per week) and follow the fat-burning eating plan (*see* pp. 203–9). The programme includes only one mass-building exercise for biceps and triceps, and two isolation exercises, which place greater demand on different parts of the muscles' length. Ensure that you use the full ROM and do not shorten the motion. Use slightly higher repetitions (up to 15), moderate weights and concentrate on the feel of the movement.

Symmetry programme for bulky arms

Exercise	Sets	Reps
Concentration curl	2	10–15
Incline dumbbell curl	2	10–15
Dumbbell preacher curl	2	10–15
One-arm triceps extension	2	10–15
Bench dip	2	10–15
Triceps kickback	2	10–15

♦ Abdominal clinic ♦

Symmetry problem: lower tummy bulge

Viewed from the side, the lower part of your tummy appears rounded and protruding. This may be due to one or more of the following:

- poor posture
- poor muscle tone in the lower and deep abdominals
- overstretched abdominals
- an accumulation of fat.

The posture problem – lordosis – is caused by an excessive forward pelvic tilt. The hip flexors (which connect the thigh bone with the lower vertebrae) become tighter, and pull and compress the lower vertebrae, leading to excessive arching in your lower back.

The solution

Lordosis can be corrected by retraining the tilt of your pelvis (aim to maintain a neutral tilt), stretching the hip flexors and strengthening the abdominals (especially the lower part of the abdominis rectus and the transverse abdominis). Body fat should be reduced if necessary by increasing aerobic activity (aim for 3–5 cardio sessions per week of 20–45 minutes), and following the fat-burning eating plan in Chapter 18 (*see* pp. 203–9). This programme emphasises the lower part of the rectus abdominis and the transversus abdominis, one of the deeper 'core' muscles (*see* p. 82) but also includes exercises for the other abdominal muscles to maintain good overall development. Performing the abdominal exercises using a Swiss ball will strengthen the core muscles and improve stability (*see* pp. 84–5). Read the technique notes on pp. 111–12 also.

Symmetry programme for a lower tummy bulge

Exercise	Sets	Reps
Reverse crunch with Swiss ball	2	10–15
Hanging leg raise	2	10–15
Hip flexor stretch	2*	30–60 s
Crunch with Swiss ball	1	10–15
Oblique crunch	1	10–15

*Perform twice on each leg.

Symmetry problem: wide waist

Viewed from the front, your waist appears wide relative to your hips and chest and your tummy may protrude slightly. This may simply be due to a 'short' waist structure, or to an excess of fat stored at the sides of the waist and poor muscle tone of the obliques.

The solution

Fat stored at the sides of the waist cannot be spot-reduced by diet or exercise. However, it can be reduced when overall body-fat levels are reduced through increasing aerobic activity (3–5 cardio sessions per week of 20–45 minutes) and following the fat-burning eating plan in Chapter 18 (*see* pp. 203–9).

Unfortunately, your basic skeletal structure cannot be changed. A naturally short mid-section is determined by the distance between your ribs and pelvis and can make the waist appear wider than it actually is. However, you can still improve your appearance by working the abdominal muscles and particularly the obliques. This will create a narrower waistline and better posture. This programme emphasises the internal and external obliques but also includes exercises for the rectus abdominis to maintain good overall development. Performing the abdominal exercises with a Swiss ball will strengthen the core muscles, i.e. the deeper abdominal muscles and the muscles close to the lower spine and pelvis, that improve your stability, co-ordination and posture (*see* pp. 84–5). Read the technique notes on pp. 111–12.

Symmetry programme for a wide waist

Exercise	Sets	Reps
Oblique crunch (with Swiss ball	1–2	10–15
Side crunch	1–2	10–15
Reverse crunch	1–2	10–15
Crunch (with Swiss ball)	1–2	10–15

♦ Summary of key points ♦

- Your personal training programme should be tailored to suit your natural body type, with a different emphasis placed on exercise selection, sets, repetitions, intensity and cardio training.
- Ectomorphs should focus on mass-building, using compound exercises, heavy weights, a high training intensity and limited cardio training.
- Endomorphs require more cardio training to burn fat, and can afford to do more sets and repetitions to increase calorie burning.

- Mesomorphs experience good gains from most programmes but should employ periodisation and plenty of variety to optimise developments and avoid over-training.
- Most symmetry problems can be remedied by using the SMART principles of programme design (*see* pp. 100–1) – selecting specific exercises, performed in a particular order for the right amount of sets and repetitions and at the correct intensity.

Chapter 15

Troubleshooting

Many people fail to make significant progress despite many months or years of training. Initial gains in muscular endurance or improved muscle tone are relatively rapid in beginners but gains in muscle size and strength are often painstakingly slow. This chapter reveals the most common reasons why weight trainers fail to achieve their goals of increased muscle mass and strength.

♦ Choosing the wrong ♦ exercises

The selection of exercises in your programme depends on your specific goals and your training experience. For example, if your goal is to increase muscle size, you have to prioritise maximal-stimulation or compound exercises (e.g. squats, bench presses, barbell rows, shoulder presses) in your programme. These stimulate the largest muscles and the greatest proportion of fibres in those muscles. Isolation exercises (e.g. triceps kickbacks, biceps curls), which work smaller muscle groups or a smaller proportion of the muscle fibres in that muscle group, should be kept to a minimum and performed last in your workout.

♦ Doing too many repetitions ♦

If you can do more than about 12 repetitions, it means that you are using too light a weight to stimulate growth in the FT muscle fibres. Doing more than 12 repetitions will improve muscular endurance but produce only small improvements in strength and size. Therefore, if it is muscle growth you want, select a weight that will allow you to perform 6–12 repetitions. Using a heavier weight that allows you to perform no more than six repetitions will improve your maximum strength. This method will not produce maximum size but can be useful for overcoming training plateaux within a hypertrophy programme.

♦ Doing too many sets ♦

Research has established that less is best when it comes to building size and mass. The exact number of sets required to achieve maximal stimulation of the muscle fibres is debatable. The general recommendation for muscle size is 8–12 sets for larger muscle groups and 3–8 for smaller muscle groups, but the most important goal is to achieve overload. Whether you achieve this after one set or 12 is less important.

Advocates of single-set training claim overload can be achieved by performing a strict set of 6–10 repetitions with a heavy weight to failure, following a few warm-up sets (*see* pp. 29–30). Once overload has been achieved, there is no benefit in performing further sets. Doing too many sets also leads to glycogen depletion and increased protein (muscle) breakdown, creating a net catabolic (breakdown) state – just the opposite of your goal! If you can perform more sets than the recommended range, this means you have failed to train hard enough to reach overload and stimulate growth.

♦ Not enough rest ♦

If you don't give your body enough rest between workouts, you will not experience gains in mass or strength. One of the biggest mistakes made by beginners in their desire to make rapid gains is training too frequently. It is tempting to think that the more often you train, the faster you will gain mass, but in fact the converse is true. Growth can only take place after compensation and full recovery. In other words, training before you have fully recovered can lead to a net protein (muscle) breakdown and, over time, can lead to over-training. As a general guideline, beginners should leave 1–3 days' recovery between workouts, while experienced weight trainers should leave 3–7 days between training the same muscle group due to the greater workout intensity (*see* p. 104).

♦ Lack of progression ♦

Many weight trainers become disheartened when strength gains slow down or plateau, despite maintaining a consistent workout programme. Indeed, it is easy to get stuck in a rut if you use the same weights, same exercises and same number of sets and reps. The muscles can soon adapt to a routine programme if the stimulus remains the same. In order to continue making strength and mass gains your training programme must be progressive. That is, you must continue to increase the amount of stimulus applied. This may be achieved in one of the following ways:

- change the *number of reps* – either increase them up to a maximum of 12 (for developing muscle size), or decrease them to 3–6, using a heavier weight (for developing maximum strength)
- increase the *number of sets* – up to a maximum of 12 for major muscle groups and 8 for smaller muscle groups
- change the *type of exercises* you perform and vary your workout – e.g. if you always perform lat pull-downs, seated rows and close-grip chins for your back, change to wide-grip chins, one-arm dumbbell rows and pullovers
- use *different variations of exercises* – e.g. different grip distances or feet positions. *See* the wide range of variations outlined in Chapters 4–9
- change the *order of your exercises* – e.g. instead of always working from the largest to the smallest muscle groups, use the pre-exhaustion method for one workout (*see* p. 123), or try new sequences such as alternating pushing and pulling exercises or using supersets either for the same muscle group or for opposing muscle groups (*see* p. 122)
- change the *training tempo* – e.g. taking shorter rest periods between sets
- use *advanced training methods* – e.g. eccentric training, forced or assisted reps, descending sets or supersets
- change the *training split* – e.g. train your shoulders and back together instead of your shoulders and arms.

♦ Partial range of movement ♦

If you use an incomplete ROM, the muscle fibres receive only partial stimulation. You may be able to use a heavier weight doing partial repetitions but the overall stimulus applied will be greatly reduced. This is a very common fault made by weight trainers keen to increase the weight lifted – but it is at the expense of correct form. Research has proved that taking a movement to the end of its natural range produces a more powerful anabolic stimulus than exercising over an incomplete ROM. It also produces better muscle shape and prevents muscle shortening and reduced flexibility. You will therefore achieve considerably greater gains by performing each repetition through its complete ROM, even if it means using a lighter weight.

♦ Poor technique ♦

Many weight trainers sacrifice technique in an attempt to lift heavier weights. Not only does this increase the risk of injury but it limits gains in strength and mass. 'Cheating' movements – such as arching the back and bouncing the bar off the chest when performing a bench press, bending excessively forwards when squatting or swinging backwards when doing barbell curls – reduce the work done by the prime mover muscles and put the back at risk of injury. Correct technique is therefore vital in order to make continued gains in strength and mass.

♦ Lack of goal setting ♦

Setting SMART goals is essential if you want to achieve results (*see* pp. 12–14). First, be clear about exactly what you want to achieve, setting *specific* goals (e.g. ' I want to gain 5 kg of muscle') that are *measurable* and *realistic*. Secondly, write down the reasons *why* you want to change. Thirdly, set a *timescale* for achieving your goals and finally, *monitor* your progress by filling in a training diary. Reward your progress once you reach each mini-goal.

♦ Summary of key points ♦

- Failure to make progress is often due to a combination of reasons centred around programme design, training technique and goal setting.
- Slow gains may be the result of poor programme design – for example, choosing inappropriate exercises, performing too many repetitions or sets, or taking inadequate rest.
- A lack of programme progression leads to training plateaux as muscles require continual changes in stimulus in order to grow.
- Progression can be achieved by changing any one of the following variables: the number of repetitions and sets, the type and order of exercises, the training tempo and training split.
- Poor technique and incomplete ROM are common faults that reduce your gains.
- Failure to set SMART goals and make a plan of action sets you up for failure.

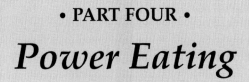

• PART FOUR •

Power Eating

Chapter 16

The Menu for Muscle

Strength training and good nutrition go hand in hand. There is little point sweating it out, giving it your all in the gym, unless you support your training programme with sufficient fuel and nutrients. Strength training simply provides the stimulus for muscle growth – your diet provides the raw materials for new muscle.

This chapter explains what you should eat to maximise muscle and minimise fat. It covers seven key topics – carbohydrate, protein, fat, fluid, vitamins and minerals, antioxidants and supplements – each of which addresses the issues most relevant to strength trainers to give you the straight facts about eating before, during and after training, what and how much you should drink, and which supplements are most helpful for reaching your goals.

♦ Carbohydrate ♦

Carbohydrate, in the form of muscle glycogen and blood glucose, is the major source of fuel for strength training. You need to eat enough to fuel your workouts. Eating too little results in low muscle glycogen levels, early fatigue in the gym, reduced training intensity, slower gains and an increased breakdown of muscle proteins. Eating too much results in unwanted body fat. As a general guideline, you should aim to consume 5–7 g/carbohydrate/kg body weight/day.[1]

How much carbohydrate exactly?

Carbohydrate recommendations for the general population and endurance athletes are usually expressed as a percentage of total daily energy. For example, the International Conference on Foods, Nutrition and Performance in 1991 recommended that carbohydrates provide 60–70% of daily calories for most athletes.[1] This method focuses only on the ratio between carbohydrate and fat and works best for endurance athletes with high energy needs. For strength athletes, however, this method works less well as they require less carbohydrate than endurance athletes to fuel their workouts. In other words, they don't deplete their muscles of glycogen to the same extent that endurance athletes do. Bear in mind too that strength trainers tend to train different muscle groups every day so their muscles have plenty of time to recover. That's why it is more accurate to calculate your carbohydrate requirement according to the *muscles'* needs rather than your total calorie intake. Carbohydrate needs for strength trainers should therefore be given in terms of grams per unit of body weight and hours of training.[2]

For moderate-intensity training lasting up to one hour, you should aim to consume 5–7 g carbohydrate/kg body weight/day. This range is suitable for everyone following any of the programmes described in Chapter 12. However, if you do additional training for a specific sport or you average 2–4 hours of moderately intense training daily, you should aim to consume 7–10 g/kg body weight/day.

Example:
For a 75 kg male weight trainer:
    Carbohydrate needs = (75 x 5)–(75 x 7)
                       = 375–525 g/day

What type of carbohydrates should strength trainers eat?

Carbohydrates can be grouped in different ways. The traditional method divides them according to their chemical structure – simple (sugars) and complex (starch and fibre) – but it is more meaningful for strength trainers to group carbohydrates according to their glycaemic index (GI). This is a measure of how quickly your blood glucose will rise after eating a specific amount of a given carbo-hydrate.

All foods containing carbohydrate are ranked on an index from 0 to 100 relative to pure glucose, which has the highest GI value of 100. Thus, high GI foods produce a relatively rapid rise in blood glucose and low GI foods produce a slower, more sustained rise in blood glucose. Figures 16.1–3 show the GIs of various foods, divided into high, medium and low GI foods. According to this index, many complex carbohydrates – such as potatoes, bread and rice – give a quick rise in blood glucose, while many simple carbo-hydrates – such as fruit – give a slower rise. It is important to realise, however, that the GI values relate to single foods being consumed. When two or more foods are eaten together, the GI changes. High GI foods eaten with protein or fat moderate the glucose response, so the GI values matter more when eaten alone. For example, if you eat potatoes on their own, your blood glucose level will rise quickly. If you eat the potatoes with a high-protein food (e.g. tuna) or a high-fat food (e.g.

butter), the resulting GI will be lower and so your blood glucose will rise more slowly.

Low GI diets are beneficial for both strength trainers and the general population. They can help control diabetes, lower blood fats, reduce the risk of heart disease and control body weight.[3] For strength trainers a low GI daily diet is particularly important for encouraging glycogen recovery between workouts. It produces more steady blood glucose and insulin levels, which facilitates a steady uptake of glucose by the muscle cells for glycogen storage, and minimises the conversion of blood glucose into body fat.

The best way to plan a low GI diet is to balance each meal by including:

- a lean source of protein (e.g. chicken breast or cottage cheese)
- a nutrient-rich carbohydrate (e.g. potatoes or pasta)
- vegetables (e.g. broccoli or green salad)
- a little unsaturated fat (e.g. olive oil dressing or nuts) (*see* Table 16.2 p. 169).

Eating a mixed meal like this evens out the effects of the high GI carbohydrates.

There are times, however, when high GI carbohydrates may be beneficial for strength trainers: when they are eaten immediately after a workout they replenish glycogen more quickly.[4]

Should I eat carbohydrate before training?

Most of the research on pre-exercise meals has been with endurance athletes. In these studies, those athletes who consumed approximately 1 g carbohydrate/kg body weight about one hour before exercise were able to keep going longer than those who consumed nothing. However, the benefits of eating before strength training are less clear.

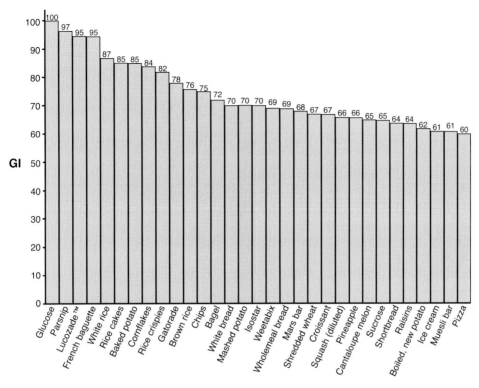

Figure 16.1 The Glycaemic Index of selected high GI foods (60–100)

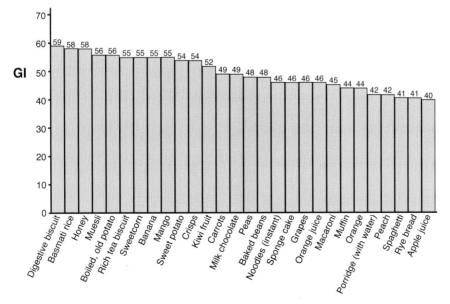

Figure 16.2 The Glycaemic Index of selected medium GI foods (40–60)

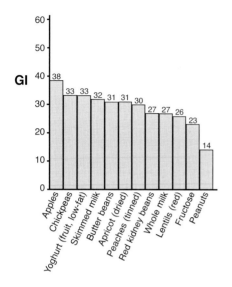

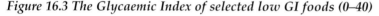

Figure 16.3 The Glycaemic Index of selected low GI foods (0–40)

Sources
1. Leeds, A. et al. (2000) *The Glucose Revolution* (London: Hodder & Stoughton)
2. MAFF/RSC (1991) *McCance and Widdowson's The Composition of Foods*, 5th ed. (Cambridge: MAFF/RSC).
3. *CompEat 5 software* (Grantham: Nutrition Systems)

It really depends on your goals – whether you are mass-building or trying to lose body fat – and on your personal preference.

If you are mass-building and not trying to lose fat, a pre-workout carbohydrate drink or snack may give you a little more energy to train. The more sets you do, the more stimulation your muscles receive, so this may help you perform a few more sets at the end of your workout when fatigue would normally set in. However, if you are trying to lose fat, skip that pre-workout drink or snack. Your body will then burn a little more fat during the recovery periods to replenish the fuel systems (*see* p. 104).

By working out without pre-workout carbohydrate you theoretically force your body to dip into its fat stores. One study at Appalachian State University, North Carolina, found that pre-workout carbohydrate (1 g/kg body weight) had no effect on the ability to perform strength training exercises.[5] Those weight trainers who consumed a high-carbohydrate diet prior to working out were not able to lift more weight than those who did not eat extra carbohydrate. It seems, then, that it is your overall daily diet that is more important for fuelling your workout.

But there is a downside. Exercising on an empty stomach may result in earlier fatigue and, if your muscle glycogen stores become depleted, you will break down more protein (muscle). Certainly, low-carbohydrate dieting will reduce your performance and produce progressively smaller gains in the gym.[6]

If you feel more comfortable training after a snack and it does not impede your workout, there is no reason not to continue. It may improve your performance. If your goal is to lose fat, then training on an empty stomach (as well as cardio training) will help you to achieve this goal a little faster.

Should I consume carbohydrate during training?

There is certainly lots of evidence that consuming carbohydrate during exercise lasting more than one hour improves endurance and performance.[7] Blood glucose levels are maintained for longer and fatigue is delayed. But does this apply to a strength-training workout lasting less than one hour?

Researchers at California State University gave ten male weight trainers either a liquid meal (a meal replacement product (MRP) shake containing carbohydrate, protein and a little fat) or a placebo immediately before and during an intense weight-training workout lasting two hours).[8] Those who had consumed the liquid meal maintained higher blood glucose and insulin levels throughout the workout, which – conclude the researchers – could promote even greater muscle growth. This is because insulin increases the uptake of amino acids into muscle cells and reduces protein breakdown – the ideal state for muscle hypertrophy. Although the workout in this study lasted longer than one hour, it is possible that carbohydrate or carbohydrate/protein liquid meals during a shorter workout may be beneficial too.

A study with cyclists also found that drinking a carbohydrate drink before and during a time trial lasting approximately one hour improved performance time.[9] It is possible, therefore, that consuming a carbohydrate-containing drink during a strenuous strength-training workout lasting 45–60 minutes may encourage faster muscle growth and offset or delay fatigue, giving

you a little more energy to perform those last few sets. It may also reduce the risk of excessive protein (muscle) breakdown during the latter stages of your workout, which is a clear advantage.

If you wish to lose body fat or prevent fat gain, make sure you don't consume *excessive* carbohydrate during your workout. Many 'energy' drinks are high in calories so, if you drink a lot of them, you can end up taking in more carbohydrate than you burn off!

When should I eat carbohydrate after my workout?

Eating carbohydrate immediately after training is definitely beneficial for endurance athletes. Many studies have proved that eating within two hours of exercise speeds glycogen recovery[10] and can improve your performance if you work out the next day.[11] But the exact timing of your post-workout snack has always hung in the balance. Recent research presented at the Experimental Biology 99 conference, Washington, D.C., suggests that waiting one hour after training may result in greater muscle size and allow your body to burn more fat after training.[12] In this groundbreaking study, researchers gave strength trainers a carbohydrate-protein drink immediately, one hour or three hours after a strength-training workout on three separate occasions. They found that protein manufacture was highest when the drink was taken either one or three hours after working out – there was no difference between these two times. Therefore, waiting about one hour after training before having a carbohydrate–protein shake seems like the best strategy for promoting muscle growth and burning fat.

Which is best: high fibre or low fibre?

Aim to get the majority of your carbohydrates from 'whole' foods, that is, foods which have undergone minimal processing and are as close to their natural state as possible. These foods, generally, have a higher content of vitamins, minerals and dietary fibre. For example, whole grains such as wholemeal bread, porridge oats, wholegrain pasta and wholemeal flour have a higher content of B vitamins, iron and dietary fibre compared with processed or 'white' versions.

There is one downside to these higher-fibre foods if you have very high-calorie and carbohydrate needs: bulk. These foods can be very filling and you may find it difficult to eat enough food to satisfy your calorie and nutritional needs. For example, it is more filling and takes longer to eat four apples (48 g carbohydrate) than to drink a large glass (480 ml) of apple juice (48 g carbohydrate). Similarly, a large bunch of grapes (150 g) is more filling than a tablespoon (30 g) of raisins, yet both supply 21 g carbohydrate. So, to reduce the bulk of your diet, choose foods with either a lower fibre content (e.g. fruit juice instead of fruit; white pasta instead of wholemeal) or a lower water content (e.g. dried fruit instead of fresh fruit).

What should I eat after my workout?

For glycogen replenishment the obvious choice would be to consume carbohydrate. However, several studies have found that combining carbohydrate with protein is a more effective strategy than consuming carbohydrate alone.[13, 14, 15, 16] A study at the University of Texas at Austin found that a carbohydrate–protein shake (112 g carbohydrate plus 40 g protein) accelerated glycogen restocking in the muscle by 38% compared with carbohydrate-only drinks.[13]

Protein combined with carbohydrate stimulates insulin release more than carbohydrate alone, which promotes faster uptake of glucose by the muscles cells and faster glycogen storage. Protein-only drinks fail to increase muscle glycogen,[13] so save them until later or, better still, add some carbohydrate to them to make them more useful.

However, the benefits of a post-exercise carbohydrate–protein supplement don't stop there. A further study at the University of Texas at Austin found that such supplements taken after strength training also promote greater growth hormone (GH) release.[16] Thus, the combination of higher insulin and GH levels create the ideal anabolic (muscle-building) environment. Carbohydrate-plus-protein also improves your mood state after training. Researchers at Ithaca College, New York, carried out a psychological survey on weight trainers after consuming either a carbohydrate–protein drink or meal, a carbohydrate-only drink or a placebo drink.[17] Those who consumed the carbohydrate–protein combination, either in liquid or solid form, experienced less mental distress, less irritability and less fatigue than the others.

Aim for a balance of 2–3 times as much carbohydrate as protein in your post-workout snack or drink. A good rule of thumb for strength trainers (based on the mixtures used in the studies) is 20–40 g protein plus roughly double that amount of carbohydrate. Small amounts of fat can also reduce the rate of glycogen storage so make sure your recovery snack is low in fat. Some ideas for suitable post-workout snacks are given in the box opposite.

Is carbohydrate loading beneficial for bodybuilders?

Competitive bodybuilders sometimes use carbohydrate loading to increase muscle size

Suitable post-workout snacks

Carbohydrate and protein in a ratio of about 2:1

- Meal-replacement shake (carbohydrate–protein formula)
- Protein shake and bananas
- Roll filled with a slice of chicken breast
- Baked potato topped with cottage cheese
- Porridge (oatmeal) made with skimmed milk or protein powder and water
- Sandwich filled with tuna
- Bran or wheat flakes with skimmed milk and yoghurt
- Fruit yoghurt
- Protein/energy bar

and fullness before a competition. Whether this really is beneficial is debatable. In one study, researchers measured the muscle girth of nine male bodybuilders before and after a control and a high-carbohydrate diet.[18] This carbohydrate-loading diet involved three days of heavy weight training on a low-carbohydrate diet (10% calories from carbohydrate), followed by three days of light weight training on a high-carbohydrate diet (80% calories from carbohydrate). The control diet involved the same weight-training programme but the men ate a standard diet providing the same number of calories. So what happened? Carbohydrate loading did not increase the muscle circumference in any of the bodybuilders, which suggests that it probably has no benefit after all.

Obviously, this is just a single study so its findings are not conclusive. There is plenty of anecdotal evidence from experienced bodybuilders that carbohydrate loading before a competition improves muscle fullness. If you decide to try this regime, however, you may achieve equally good results by omitting the three-day depletion phase and simply eating a high-carbohydrate diet for the three days prior to competition.

What should I eat between workouts?

To promote efficient recovery between workouts, you should divide your food intake into several small meals – ideally all with a low GI value. Frequent feedings tend to produce more stable blood sugar and insulin levels, promote efficient glycogen storage and increase the metabolic rate. So, for optimal muscle-building and fat-burning effects, you should consume approximately six balanced meals or snacks throughout the day. Each meal should include 1–2 portions of carbohydrate-rich foods and at least 1 portion of a protein-rich food. Include plenty of vegetables with at least two of your daily meals, and eat a minimum of three portions of fruit each day. Table 16.1 lists nutrient-rich carbohydrate- and protein-rich foods and practical advice to help you plan your daily meals.

♦ Protein ♦

Protein is important for muscle growth. Protein from your food is broken down into individual amino acids during digestion and absorption. The amino acids are then taken up by the body for various functions such as manufacturing tissue and the enzymes needed for metabolism. Everyone needs protein, but the needs of strength trainers are higher than those of endurance athletes.

Why should strength trainers eat more protein?

Heavy strength training stimulates an increased uptake of amino acids from the

Protein-rich food: choose 1 portion/meal	Carb-rich food: choose 1–2 portions/meal	Vegetables: choose 3+ portions/day	Fruit choose 3+ portions/day	Omega-3-rich fats:* choose 1–2 portions/day	Omega-6-rich fats:* choose 1/day	Sample meal combinations
Chicken breast	Potato	Broccoli	Apples	Omega-3 enriched margarine	Sunflower oil	Baked potato with omega-3 enriched margarine, grilled chicken and broccoli; stewed apples
Turkey breast	Pasta	Carrots	Cherries	Cod liver oil	Corn oil	Pasta tossed with flaxseed oil; turkey and vegetable stir fry; cherries
White fish, e.g. tuna tinned in water/brine cod, haddock, plaice	Wholegrain bread	Salad leaves	Oranges/clementines/satsumas	Rapeseed oil	Olive oil	Tuna sandwich (with olive oil margarine); side salad with walnut oil dressing; oranges
Oily fish, e.g. salmon, sardines, mackerel	Rice	Cauliflower	Nectarines	Salmon	Soya oil	Baked salmon; boiled rice; cauliflower
Tofu	Noodles	Peppers	Plums	Flaxseeds	Margarine made with sunflower/soya/corn/olive oil	Noodles with stir-fried peppers and tofu; plum crumble sprinkled with flaxseeds
Low-fat cheese	Rice cakes/crackers	Tomatoes	Apricots	Mackerel	Mayonnaise made with sunflower/olive oil	Rice cakes with low-fat cheese and tomatoes; apricots
Yoghurt*	Wholegrain breakfast cereal	Brussel sprouts	Kiwi fruit	Walnuts	Nuts	Muesli with yoghurt, walnuts and almonds; kiwi fruit
Quorn	Beans and lentils*	Mangetout	Melon	Walnut oil	Sunflower seeds	Quorn and bean stew; mangetout; melon
Lean cuts of meat	Sweet potato	Spinach	Mango	Sardines	Salad dressing made with sunflower/olive oil	Grilled lean sirloin steak; sweet potato; spinach salad with dressing; mango
Milk*	Porridge oats	Cabbage	Strawberries	Pilchards		Porridge with milk; strawberries
Cottage cheese	Sweetcorn	Green beans	Papaya	Omega-3 enriched egg		Cottage cheese mixed with papaya (snack)
Egg	Milk*		Bananas	Flaxseed oil		Banana milkshake with flaxseed oil (snack)
Beans and lentils*	Yoghurt*	Onions	Grapes	Trout		Lentil dahl (with onions) topped with yoghurt

Table 16.1 Meal planning for strength training

*These foods contain roughly equal amounts of protein and carbohydrate. Only count them once for each meal.

bloodstream. These amino acids are then built up into new contractile muscle proteins, actin and myosin (*see* p. 176). To build muscle, you must take in more protein than you excrete – i.e. be in a 'positive nitrogen balance'. A deficiency will result in slower gains in strength, size and mass, or even muscle loss – despite hard training. However, there is not a linear relationship between protein intake and muscle growth. Muscle growth depends not only on your protein intake but also on the intensity of your training (i.e. the training stimulus) and your genetic potential for muscle growth.

In practice the body can adapt to variations in protein intake. For example, as you gain experience the body becomes more efficient in conserving it so you break down less muscle proteins during intense training. This is often sufficient to maintain an anabolic environment and induce muscle growth.[19] Therefore, advanced strength trainers may need less dietary protein/kg body weight compared with novice strength trainers. One study found that the protein requirement/kg body weight of advanced strength trainers was 40% less than those of novice sstrength trainers.[20]

It is generally recommended that strength trainers need 1.4–1.8 g/kg body weight/day[19, 20] compared with the Recommended Daily Allowance (RDA) of 0.75g/kg body weight/day.

Example
For a 75 kg strength trainer:
$$\text{Protein needs} = (75 \times 1.4)–(75 \times 1.8)$$
$$= 105–135 \text{ g/day}$$

Could I eat too much protein?

Consuming more than 1.8 g protein/kg body weight/day will not make you stronger or more muscular. As mentioned, there is not a linear relationship between protein intake and strength or muscle size.[21] In a study of strength athletes carried out at McMaster University, Ontario, athletes consuming either 1.4 g/kg body weight/day or 2.3 g/kg body weight/day experienced similar increases in muscle mass.[19] Those with the higher protein intake gained no further benefits. Once your optimal intake has been reached, additional protein is not converted into muscle.

How can I meet my protein needs?

You should get the majority of your protein from food sources rather than supplements. Animal sources (chicken, turkey, fish, lean cuts of meat, low-fat dairy products and eggs) generally have a higher biological value (BV) (*see* p. 176) than plant sources (tofu, quorn, beans, lentils, nuts and cereals) but the key with protein is to include as great a variety as possible. If you eat a mixture of animal and plant sources, you get a good variety of amino acids as well as a better range of other nutrients (fibre, vitamins, minerals and carbohydrate). The protein content of various foods is given in Table 16.2.

Food	Portion size	Protein (g)
Meat and fish		
Beef – fillet steak, grilled	105 g	31
Chicken breast – grilled, meat only	130 g	39
Turkey – light meat, roasted	140 g	47
Cod – poached	120 g	25
Mackerel – grilled	150 g	31
1 small tin tuna – canned in brine	100 g	24
Dairy products		
Cheese, cheddar (1 thick slice)	40 g	10
1 small carton cottage cheese	112 g	15
1 glass skimmed milk	200 ml	7
1 carton low-fat yoghurt – fruit	150 g	6
Eggs (size 2)	1	8
Nuts and seeds		
Peanuts – roasted and salted (handful)	50 g	10
Peanut butter on 1 slice bread	20 g	5
Cashew nuts – roasted and salted (handful)	50 g	10
2 tbsp sesame seeds	24 g	4
Pulses		
1 small tin baked beans	205 g	10
3 tbsp red lentils – boiled	120 g	9
3 tbsp red kidney beans – boiled	120 g	10
Soya and quorn products		
2 tbsp dry soya mince	30 g	13
Tofu burger	60 g	5
4 tbsp quorn mince	100 g	12
Grains and cereals		
2 slices wholemeal bread	76 g	6
1 bowl pasta – boiled	230 g	7

Table 16.2 The protein content of various foods

Protein and amino acids – the lowdown

There are dozens of amino acids but the body uses only 20 of them as the building blocks of proteins. Eight of these are 'indispensable' (IAA) – that is, they are essential and must be supplied in the diet as the body cannot make them itself. The remaining 12 can be made from other amino acids and are termed 'dispensable' – in other words, they are non-essential.

Three IAAs – valine, leucine and isoleucine – are termed BCAAs, due to their branched structure. These are used as fuel for energy by the muscles during intense exercise when glycogen stores are low.

Food proteins with a high IAA content in proportions closely matched to the body's requirements are said to have a high biological value (BV). This is a measure of the usefulness of a protein – that is, the proportion of the protein that can be absorbed and used for growth and repair. Eggs have the highest BV (100) of all foods, although, according to supplement manufacturers, whey protein supplements have even higher values.

To maximise the benefits of protein in your diet, eat a mixture of protein foods so that the shortfall of amino acids in one is complemented by higher amounts in the other. For example, combining beans and rice means that the shortfall of lysine in rice is complemented by higher amounts in the beans. Other combinations suitable for vegetarians include: tortillas filled with refried beans; cous cous with spicy chickpeas; cashew nut roast with rice; quorn burger in a bun; and stir-fried tofu with noodles.

Should I take protein and meal replacement supplements?

There are two main reasons for taking protein and meal replacement supplements: convenience and to increase protein intake. Protein foods require a certain amount of preparation; supplements just need mixing with water or milk. However, supplements offer nothing intrinsically different from food, and possess no miracle ingredient that will enhance your muscle size.

From a nutritional viewpoint, supplements can be justified if:

- you have particularly high protein requirements (e.g. high body weight and/or you are undergoing heavy training) and find it difficult to consume sufficient quantities from food
- you are on a calorie-restricted diet – additional protein can offset muscle breakdown and a supplement can provide protein without extra calories from carbohydrate or fat
- you eat a vegetarian or vegan diet – most plant sources contain considerably less protein per gram compared with animal sources, making it more difficult to meet your needs from food alone.

If in doubt, keep a record of your usual food intake over a few days, then compare your actual protein intake (*see* Table 16.2, p. 176) with your requirement. If there is a consistent shortfall, consider adding a supplement. For example, if you weigh 80 kg, you may need as much as 144 g protein/day (based on 1.8 g/kg body weight/day), which is difficult to get from food alone – and more so if you are vegetarian.

Which type of supplement should I choose?

First you need to decide whether you need a protein powder or an MRP. Protein powders basically supplement your protein intake; MRPs are designed to provide a well-balanced 'meal'. In addition to protein, they also provide carbohydrate, vitamins, minerals and various ergogenic substances and as such they are particularly convenient as a post-workout meal (*see* p. 173). You should also consider the source of the protein (whey, casein, soya, milk etc.), the taste, cost, ease of mixing and whether you are intolerant to any of the ingredients (e.g. lactose, casein). The various pros and cons of protein sources are summarised in Table 16.3.

◆ Fat ◆

Athletes should aim to limit fat to 15–30% of total calories[1] although, in practice, most strength trainers achieve an intake of around 20% in an effort to maintain low body-fat levels. Be careful not to drop your fat intake too low or you will almost certainly miss out on certain vitamins – such as vitamin E – and a vital sub-group of fats called the 'essential fatty acids'. Eating them in the right quantities could even boost your performance in the gym.

What are essential fats?

The two essential fatty acids – linoleic acid and alpha-linolenic acid – are vital to your health and cannot be made in the body. When you eat linoleic acid, your body converts it into a number of other fatty acids, including gamma-linolenic acid (GLA) and docosa-pentanoic acid (DPA). Linoleic acid and its derivative fatty acids are called omega-6 fatty

Protein source	Derived from	Pros	Cons
Whey	A by-product of cheese manufacture	• Excellent ratio of IAAs including the BCAAs • Higher BV than other proteins • Raises glutathione levels, which stimulates immune system	• Relatively expensive • Needs a blender to mix well
Casein	Milk	• Slower to digest, longer transit through gut, so protein may be asborbed more completely • High glutamine content makes it immune-boosting • 'Anti-catabolic' – i.e. reduces muscle breakdown • Good ratio of IAAs	• Lower BCAA content than whey • Relatively expensive
Soy	Soybeans	• 'Supro' soy isolate has high BCAAs content of glutamine and arginine • Numerous health benefits, including cholesterol lowering and prevention of certain cancers	• Variable quality depending on manufacturing process • Relatively expensive
Milk protein	Skimmed milk	• Good amino acid profile • Low cost	• Unsuitable for those with lactose intolerance • Lower BV than whey or casein

Table 16.3 Protein pros and cons

acids (there is a rigid link, or 'double bond', on the sixth carbon atom in the fatty acid chain). When you eat alpha-linolenic acid, your body converts it into eicosapentanoic acid (EPA) and docosahexaoic acid (DHA), and these are called omega-3 fatty acids (the rigid link occurs on the third carbon atom).

Both omega-6 (from most vegetable oils and margarines) and omega-3 (from oily fish and certain nuts and seeds) fatty acids are essential for good health. They are involved in cell membrane structure, especially in the retina of the eye, the brain and the heart, and the body also uses them to produce a group of hormone-like substances called 'eicosanoids'. These regulate many processes in the body, such as the inflammatory and immune responses. Many experts believe that it is the wrong ratio of omega-3s to omega-6s that contributes to many health problems, such as heart disease, inflammation, rheumatoid arthritis and pain, even slow post-workout recovery. In other words, a high omega-6 intake and low omega-3 intake causes your body to make too many eicosanoids, promoting inflammation and pain.

For optimal health and performance you therefore need to consume them in the right proportions – roughly five times more omega-6s than omega-3s.[22] That means you should consume 1 g of omega-3s for every 1–5 g of omega-6s each day. Most people consume far more omega-6s than omega-3s.

How can omega-3s help strength trainers?

There is mounting evidence to suggest that a high intake of omega-3s reduces inflammation, pain and joint stiffness.[23] Eating more omega-3s and less omega-6s could help you recover faster after a heavy workout in the gym and reduce any pain and swelling in your joints.

Omega-3s can also benefit your cardio workouts. Eating more omega-3s enhances aerobic metabolism, which means increased endurance and fat burning. Oxygen delivery to your cells is improved because omega-3s reduce blood viscosity and make red cell membranes more flexible. So, your cardio workouts will be more effective.

How can I get the right amount of omega-3s?

Oily fish – such as mackerel, pilchards, trout, salmon, herring and sardines – are the richest sources of EPA and DHA, the very long chain omega-3s (*see* above). However, alpha-linolenic acid (the precursor to EPA and DHA) is also found in other foods – like sweet potatoes, walnuts, almonds, rapeseed oil, walnut oil, soya oil, flaxseed oil, flaxseeds, chicken and beef. Alternatively, supplements and foods fortified with omega-3s (e.g. omega-3 enriched eggs, margarine and bread) can also help increase your intake. The best sources of both omega-3 and omega-6 fatty acids are given in Table 16.4.

There is no RDA for omega-3s, although the government advises eating at least 1 portion of oily fish per week, which will provide around 2–3 g EPA and DHA. A separate recommendation of 0.65 g EPA and DHA/day has also been made.[21]

Food	Portion	Omega-3s	Omega-6s	Omega-6: Omega-3 ratio
Good sources of omega-3s				
Rapeseed oil	1 tbsp	1.5	3.1	1:0.49
Cod liver oil	1 tbsp	2.7	0.9	1:3
Flaxseed oil	1 tbsp	7.5	1.8	1:4.2
Walnut oil	1 tbsp	1.4	7.5	5.3:1
Salmon	100 g	1.5	0.6	1:2.5
Herring	100 g	1.8	0.6	1:3
Trout	100 g	2	1.4	1:1.4
Omega-3 fortified egg	1	0.7	0.7	1:1
Typical fatty-acid supplement*		0.5	0.1	1:5
Good sources of omega-6s				
Corn oil	1 tbsp	0.1	7.9	79:1
Soya margarine	1 tbsp	0.1	3.5	25:1
Mayonnaise	1 tbsp	0.4	7.2	18:1
Safflower oil	1 tbsp	0.05	10.1	202:1
Soya oil	1 tbsp	1	7.2	7.2:1
Goal				**5:1**

Table 16.4 The omega-3 and omega-6 fatty acid content of various foods

*8 capsules (the recommended daily dose) of 'Efalex'
Source: Simopoulos, A.P. and Robinson, J. (1998), *The Omega Plan* (New York: HarperCollins).

♦ Fluids ♦

Of all the nutrients, water is the most important. Without any water or fluid, you'll last less than a week. It makes up more than 60% of your body weight and is vital to all cells.

Water is the medium in which all metabolic reactions take place, including energy production. One key fluid – blood – carries nutrients and oxygen to the cells and helps rid the body of toxins. Fluid acts as a cushion for your nervous system and acts as a lubricant for your joints and eyes. On top of that, proper hydration helps to keep your body temperature stable – you sweat when you get too hot.

You need to top up your fluid levels frequently because you lose water through sweat, breathing and urine. Most experts recommend consuming at least 1 litre of water for every 1000 kcal expended. Since about one-third will come from the food you eat, the British Dietetic Association recommends drinking at least 1.5–2 litres/day. That's equivalent to roughly eight 250 ml glasses, although you'll need to drink more during hot weather and when you exercise. Table 16.5 gives some tips on how to drink more water and keep properly hydrated.

Why should I drink before, during and after a workout?

Drinking water before and during exercise will help you to perform at your best and keep going longer. One of the most important roles of water is to get rid of the excess heat produced by your exercising muscles. Water from your blood and extracellular (outside the body cells) spaces is transported to the skin's surface, and evaporated by heat (sweating). If you're low on water, your muscle control and strength will diminish. A

Thirst

Thirst is the most important mechanism for ensuring you take in enough fluid. When you experience thirst – a dry mouth and throat, a craving for drinking – your body is signalling dehydration. This is detected by 'osmoreceptors' in the hypothalamus region of your brain. They are able to detect changes in the osmotic pressure and volume of body fluids. When your body's fluid level becomes low, the sodium concentration and, therefore, osmolality of your blood rises, signalling the thirst sensation in the hypothalamus. So, you get the urge to drink.

It is important to realise that feeling thirsty is like a red flag – it means you are already dehydrated by at least 2% of your body weight. You should not wait until you get into this state before topping up. To keep properly hydrated, drink before, during and after a workout.

loss of just 2% of your body weight can reduce your muscle strength and your aerobic capacity by at least 10%. Your thirst mechanism only kicks in when you have lost 2% of your body weight – by which time your performance will have suffered.

If water is not replaced during exercise, your blood volume drops, your cardio-vascular system becomes stressed, your heart rate increases, your blood pressure rises and exercise feels much harder. You also begin to lose concentration and feel more tired. A 4% drop in body weight due to dehydration causes a 20–30% drop in strength. You may also get headaches, cramping, dizziness and nausea. Severe dehydration (8–10% loss of body weight) can lead to heat stroke and death.

How much should I drink?

Make sure you are properly hydrated before your workout. As a guideline, drink 500 ml of fluid two hours before you train, then

- Keep a bottle of water on your desk
- Carry a waterbottle with you throughout the day
- If you don't like the taste of tap water, try bottled water or flavour it with a slice of lemon or lime
- Other options include flavoured water and 'low calorie' soft drinks (but try to avoid those laden with artificial sweeteners and flavours), herb and fruit tea, weak tea, and coffee substitutes
- Have a 'water break' at least once an hour – set the timer on your watch to remind yourself
- Get into the habit of having a water break instead of a coffee break
- Drink water before, during and after your workout – take a 1-litre bottle of water to the gym.

Table 16.5 How to keep hydrated

another 125–250 ml immediately before your workout.[24] During your workout, drink 125–250 ml every 10–20 minutes. In hot or humid conditions you will lose more fluid so you will need to drink more. Make regular drink breaks a part of your workouts and start drinking early in your workout. If you wait until you are thirsty, you will become dehydrated and your performance will have already suffered by the time you drink. If you feel nauseous when you drink, this indicates that you are dehydrated, so ensure you drink plenty of water. After your workout is the time to replace any fluid you have lost. Drink 1.5 litres for every kg you have lost. Have 500 ml immediately after your workout, then continue drinking at regular intervals.

What should I drink?

Water is the best drink for replacing lost body fluids if you are training for less than one hour. Sports drinks containing carbohydrate and sodium also replace fluid rapidly, but are more beneficial for athletes exercising hard for longer than one hour. Most contain 4–8 g carbohydrate/100 ml, and are designed to help maintain blood glucose levels and combat fatigue when muscle glycogen levels run low. It is possible that they may help you do a few more repetitions or sets at the end of your workout if you are training for longer than one hour but, so far, there have not been any studies on the benefits of sports drinks on strength-training exercise lasting less than one hour (*see* p. 171).

If you are aiming to reduce body-fat levels, definitely choose water as sports drinks can add unnecessary calories.

Sports drinks are more helpful to strength trainers after exercise as opposed to during training. Getting carbohydrate into your body within two hours of training is definitely beneficial as it speeds glycogen recovery. However, a carbohydrate–protein drink (i.e. MRP) would be even better than a carbohydrate-only drink (*see* p. 171).

Dehydration check

Check the colour of your urine – the more transparent it is (i.e. the less yellow), the better hydrated you are. If it is a golden colour or a deep colour with a strong odour, you are dehydrated. Passing a small volume of urine having experienced a strong sensation to visit the toilet is also an indicator.

◆ Vitamins and minerals ◆

Getting the right balance of vitamins and minerals is important not only for good health but also for your performance in the gym. Regular heavy strength training places additional demands on your body that increase your requirement for many vitamins and minerals, higher than the RDAs set for the general population. Coupled with busy lifestyles, erratic eating habits, or calorie-restricted diets, many athletes end up with vitamin and mineral intakes below the RDAs.[25] This could leave you lacking in energy, failing to make gains in size and strength, susceptible to minor infections and illnesses or at risk of more serious conditions such as stress fractures and anaemia. Table 16.6 (*see* pp. 183–4) summarises the exercise-related functions, best food sources, and requirements of 12 key vitamins and minerals.

Should I take a multivitamin supplement?

A multivitamin can act as an insurance policy if you aren't getting enough nutrients from your food. Regard supplements as top-ups rather than main providers of your intake. They should not be substitutes for a badly planned diet but they may be beneficial if:

- you eat erratically and fail to consume five portions of fruit and vegetables a day
- you are on a calorie-restricted diet providing less than 1500 kcal/day
- you exclude one or more major food groups (e.g. a dairy-free diet).

One study of competitive bodybuilders found that those who consumed roughly 1500 kcal/day had worryingly low intakes of several minerals, which put them at risk for

calcium, zinc, copper and chromium deficiencies.[26] Researchers at the University of Alabama at Birmingham, Alabama, also found that competitive bodybuilders consumed less than 70% of the RDA for folic acid, vitamin E, calcium, potassium and zinc.[27] These low intakes were due partly to their low-calorie (food) intakes during the pre-competition diet, and partly due to their avoidance of dairy products. One of the biggest problems is that many bodybuilders eat very monotonous diets, centred on only a few foods. This is bad news because the more restricted your diet is, the less likely you are to obtain all the vitamins and minerals you need. By increasing the variety of foods in your diet, you will automatically be getting more vitamins and minerals.

Will supplements enhance my performance?

The idea of supplements giving you a performance advantage or enhancing your strength is certainly an attractive one. Unfortunately, there is no evidence in the scientific literature to support this. In studies, those athletes who were given vitamin and mineral supplements for a period of eight months did not experience greater gains in strength, power or endurance compared with athletes who had a placebo (dummy pill).[27, 28] On the other hand, the studies did not measure the health-enhancing effects of supplements, or their effect on post-workout recovery. Given that vitamins and minerals are essential for energy production, muscle manufacture, red blood cell formation, cell division and virtually every other metabolic process, it seems logical that an adequate intake will optimise all of these processes. And a supplement may just help you achieve this. A sub-optimal intake would clearly reduce the efficiency of these processes, slow down your recovery, and have a negative effect on your

Vitamin/ mineral	RNI and USL*	Major functions	Why strength trainers may need more	Best food sources	Dangers of high doses
Carotenoids	• No official RNI: 15 mg beta-carotene suggested • USL = 100 mg	• Vision in dim light • Healthy skin • Converts into vitamin A	Exercise increases need for antioxidants Antioxidants may protect against certain cancers and reduce muscle soreness	• Intensely coloured fruit and vegetables e.g. apricots, peppers tomatoes, mangoes, broccoli	Excessive doses of beta-carotene can cause harmless (and reversible) orange tinge to skin
Thiamin	• RNI = 0.4 mg/1000 kcal • USL = 20 mg	• Converts carbo- hydrates to energy	To process the extra carbohydrates eaten	• Wholemeal bread and cereals • Pulses • Meat	Excess is excreted, so toxicity is rare
Riboflavin	• RNI = 1.3 mg (men); 1.1 mg (women) • USL = 200 mg	• Converts carbo- hydrates to energy	To process the extra carbohydrates eaten	• Milk and dairy products • Meat • Eggs	Excess is excreted (producing yellow urine!), so toxicity is rare
Niacin	• RNI = 6.6 mg/1000 kcal • USL = 150 mg (2 g)	• Converts carbo- hydrates to energy	To process the extra carbohydrates eaten	• Meat and offal • Nuts • Milk and dairy products • Eggs • Wholegrain bread and cereals	Excess is excreted, but high doses may cause hot flushes
Vitamin C	• RNI = 40 mg • USL = 2000 mg (2 g)	• Healthy connective tissue, bones, teeth, blood vesels, gums and teeth • Promotes immune function • Helps iron absorp- tion	Exercise increases need for antioxidants, may help reduce free radical damage, protect cell membranes and reduce post-exercise muscle soreness	• Fruit and vegetables (e.g. raspberries, blackcurrants, kiwi, oranges, peppers, broccoli, cabbage, tomatoes)	Excess is excreted, but doses over 2 g may lead to diarr- hoea and excess urine formation. High doses (> 2 g) may cause vitamin C to behave as a pro-oxidant (enhance free radical damage)
Vitamin E	• No RNI in UK; 10 mg in EU USL = 800 mg	• Antioxidant which helps protect against heart disease • Promotes normal cell growth and development	Exercise increases need for antioxidants; may help reduce free radical damage, protect cell membranes and reduce post-exercise muscle soreness	• Vegetable oils • Margarine • Oily fish • Nuts and seeds • Egg yolk • Avocados	Toxicity is rare

Table 16.6 The essential guide to vitamins and minerals ... continues overleaf

Vitamin/ mineral	RNI and USL*	Major functions	Why strength trainers may need more	Best food sources	Dangers of high doses
Calcium	• RNI = 1000 mg (men); 700 mg (women) • USL = 1500 mg	• Builds bone and teeth • Blood clotting • Nerve and muscle function	Low oestrogen in female athletes with amenorrhoea increases bone loss and need for calcium	• Milk and dairy products • Sardines • Dark green leafy vegetables • Pulses • Nuts and seeds	High intakes may interfere with absorption of other minerals; take with magnesium and vitamin D
Iron	• RNI = 8.7 mg (men); 14.8 mg (women) • USL = 15 mg	• Formation of red blood cells • Oxygen transport • Prevents anaemia	Female athletes may need more to compensate for menstrual losses	• Meat and offal • Wholegrain bread and cereals • Fortified breakfast cereals • Pulses • Green leafy vegetables	Constipation, discomfort. Avoid unnecessary supplementation – may increase free radical damage
Zinc	• RNI = 9.5 mg (men); 7.0 mg (women) • USL = 15 mg	• Healthy immune system • Wound healing • Skin formation • Cell growth	Exercise increases need for antioxidants; may help immune function	• Eggs • Wholegrain cereals • Meat • Milk and dairy products	Interferes with absorption of iron and copper
Magnesium	• RNI = 300 mg (men); 270 mg (women) • USL = 300 mg	• Healthy bones • Muscle and nerve function • Cell formation	May improve recovery after strength training; increase aerobic capacity	• Cereals • Fruit and vegetables • Milk	Take with calcium and vitamin D. May cause diarrhoea
Potassium	• RNI = 3.5 mg • USL = no value	• Fluid balance • Muscle and nerve function	May help prevent cramp	• Fruit and vegetables • Cereals	Excess is excreted
Selenium	• RNI = 75 µg (men); 60 µg (women) USL = 200 µg	• Antioxidant which helps protect against heart disease and cancer	Exercise increases free radical production	• Cereals • Vegetables • Dairy products • Meat • Eggs	Nausea, vomiting and hair loss

Table 16.6 The essential guide to vitamins and minerals

*RNI = Reference Nutrient Intake (Dept. of Health, 1991). This is the amount of a nutrient that should cover the needs of 97% of the population. Athletes in hard training may need more.
*USL = Upper Safe Levels for daily supplementation. It defines the intake of nutrients from supplements that could be consumed on a long-term basis. This term was used in a report issued by the European Federation of Health Product Manufacturers (EHPM) and the UK Council for Responsible Nutrition (CRN) in 1997. It is not a definition of levels that could be advocated to promote general health and should not be exceeded.

performance. The whole point of taking a supplement is to ensure 'normal' levels of vitamins and minerals that will support health and performance.

Is it possible to overdose on supplements?

Supplements taken in excess of your requirements will not give you any further benefit and some may even be harmful in high doses. For example, regular daily doses of vitamin A greater than 1500 micrograms during pregnancy can cause birth defects in unborn babies. A single dose of 150,000 micrograms may cause weakness and vomiting.

To avoid excess doses, it is best taken in the form of beta-carotene or carotenoid supplements (these can be converted into vitamin A in the body as required). Regular daily doses of vitamin D greater than 50 micrograms can cause constipation or diarrhoea, nausea and heartbeat irregularities, and can ultimately cause calcium to accumulate in the muscles. Most supplements contain up to 10 micrograms of vitamin D. High doses of vitamin B6 (more than 2000 mg/day) can cause nerve damage if taken over a period of time. So, always check the amounts of these vitamins on the label and follow the recommended dose given by the manufacturer. Upper safe levels for supplementation have been determined by the Council for Responsible Nutrition and the European Federation of Health Product Manufacturers. These are also given in Table 16.6.

A balance of nutrients is also important, so avoid single-nutrient supplements, unless you have taken the advice of a nutritionist or health professional. A common mistake is to take only some vitamins, when a full range is needed. This can result in imbalances as many nutrients interact and work as a team. For example, most of the B vitamins work together to help

convert food into energy. Each B vitamin must be present for the team to do its job, but if one is in short supply, this reduces the functioning of the rest of the team. It is always safer to take a multivitamin formulation rather than individual supplements.

◆ Antioxidants ◆

Antioxidants are substances that quench free radicals (*see* below) and include enzymes, vitamins, minerals and plant substances called phytochemicals. The most popular antioxidant supplements include beta-carotene and other carotenoids (such as lycopene found in tomatoes), vitamin C, vitamin E, selenium, Coenzyme Q10, lipoic acid, conjugated linoleic acid, N-acetyl-cysteine (NAC), proanthocyanidins (found in pine bark and grape seed extract), curcumin (found in turmeric), the amino acids cysteine and methionine, and catechins (found in green tea).

What are free radicals?

A free radical is an atom or molecule containing an unpaired electron. It is highly unstable and reactive, and capable of damaging fat- and protein-containing tissues.

Free radicals are continually produced during normal cell processes and at low levels even have a useful role: they help manufacture prostaglandins, kill bacteria and heal wounds. It's only when free radicals are present in excessive numbers that they cause problems. They can destroy cell membranes, membrane proteins, DNA (the genetic material found in every cell), enzymes, blood cholesterol and mitochondria membranes and, over a period of time, free radicals damage is thought to be responsible for the development of atherosclerosis, several cancers and the ageing process.

Should athletes take antioxidant supplements?

The more you exercise, the more free radicals you generate. This is due partly to the 10–20-fold increase in oxygen consumption, the increase in lactic acid production and the increase in heat generation. Heavy weight training is one of the worst. It results in micro-tears in the muscle that generate more free radicals, and this is partly responsible for post-exercise soreness and tenderness.

The body tends to adapt – thankfully – by producing higher levels of antioxidant enzymes to deal with the additional amount of free radicals. So could supplements provide any further benefit?

Well, antioxidant supplements will not stop you producing free radicals nor will they enhance your strength and performance.[29] However, they will bolster your body's defences against increased free radical attack, and studies have found that supplementation helps reduce the damage to muscles and other tissues caused by exercise.[30] You also get less post-exercise discomfort, swelling and soreness.

What are the optimal doses of antioxidants?

Professor Anthony Diplock from the University of London at Guys Hospital has proposed optimal intakes, which would give greater protection from disease. For beta-carotene, the optimal level would be 15–25 mg, for vitamin E, 50–80 mg and for vitamin C, 100–150 mg, all of which are considerably greater than current average intakes. Mel Williams, Professor at the Dept. of Exercise Science, Physical Education and Recreation at Old Dominion University, USA, advises 500–1000 mg vitamin C, 400–800 IU vitamin E and 50–100 μg selenium.

Food or supplements?

The best advice is to get as many antioxidants as possible from food. It is not possible to replicate what you get from food in a pill. Food contains hundreds of phytochemicals, all of which have slightly different anti-oxidant actions. Taking a selected few in the form of a supplement will not give you the best protection.

The Department of Health and the World Health Organisation advise a minimum of 400 g or five portions of fruit and vegetables a day. Aim to consume at least 2–3 portions of fruit and 3–4 portions of vegetables – the more intensely coloured the better. (Table 16.7 shows the healthiest fruit and vegetables, ranked by researchers at Tuft's University for their ability to soak up free radicals.)

	ORAC Score*
Fruit	
Prunes	5770
Raisins	2830
Blueberries	2400
Blackberries	2036
Strawberries	1540
Raspberries	1220
Plums	949
Oranges	750
Red grapes	739
Cherries	670
Vegetable	
Kale	1770
Spinach	1260
Brussel sprouts	980
Broccoli	890
Beetroot	840
Red peppers	710
Onion	450
Sweetcorn	400

Table 16.7 The healthiest fruit and vegetables

*Oxygen Radical Absorbance Capacity – i.e. the ability to combat harmful free radicals per 100 g.

A number of experts have recommended optimal doses of selected antioxidants, which are considerably higher than the intakes you could hope to get from a normal diet (*see below*). For example, to get 80 mg vitamin E you would need to consume 162 g (about 15 tbsp) sunflower oil (one of the richest sources of vitamin E) daily. To obtain 25 mg beta-carotene you would need to eat 333 g carrots (that's six carrots) daily. Therefore, it makes sense to take a daily antioxidant supplement.

♦ Supplements ♦

Numerous supplements claim to increase muscle size and strength or help burn body fat, but do they really work? Here is the low-down on six of the most popular supplements aimed at strength trainers.

♦ Creatine ♦

What is it?

Creatine is a protein made naturally in the body from three amino acids (glycine, arginine and methionine). You can also obtain it from fish, beef and pork, although you would need to eat at least 2 kg/day to get a performance-boosting effect. In the muscle cells, it combines with phosphate to make phosphocreatine (PC). PC is an energy-producing compound that regenerates adenosine triphosphate (ATP, a compound which provides energy) extremely rapidly during high-intensity activity. The idea with creatine supplementation is to increase your muscles' PC content. In theory, the more PC you have, the longer you will be able to sustain high-intensity activity.

Does it work?

Creatine supplementation typically raises PC stores in the muscle by around 20%.[31] In terms of performance, most – although not all – studies have found that creatine supplements increase your strength (as measured by the 1RM), allow you to perform more repetitions (at 70% 1RM) before reaching failure, and enable you to recover faster between sets.[32] This would allow you to increase your training volume (i.e. lift heavier weights; perform more repetitions) and therefore gain a greater training effect. In terms of muscle growth, studies have also found that creatine supplements promote muscle hypertrophy and produce significant gains in total body weight, muscle size and muscle mass.[33] For example, researchers at Pennsylvania State University measured a total body weight gain of 1.7 kg and muscle mass gain of 1.5 kg after seven days of creatine supplementation in a group of 19 weight trainers.[34] After 12 weeks, total weight gain averaged 4.8 kg and muscle mass gain averaged 4.3 kg.

Weight gain is partly due to increased cell water content and partly due to increased protein content.[35] Creatine draws water into the muscle cells and this increased cell volume becomes an anabolic signal for muscle growth. Protein breakdown is reduced and protein manufacture is increased.

How much?

The original creatine-loading strategy used in the studies of the 1990s was a five-day course. This involved taking 20 g/day in four divided doses of 5 g each. More recent research suggests that lower daily doses over a longer period is just as effective and results in less water retention. You could take 3 g creatine/day for 30 days[30] or 6 g/day (in 6 x 1 g doses) for six days.[36]

Creatine appears to be more effective when taken with carbohydrate. That's because carbohydrate stimulates insulin release, which increases creatine uptake by the muscles. The ideal amount of carbohydrate is debatable. Studies at Creighton University in Omaha, Nebraska, have found 34 g carbohydrate to be just as effective as the higher doses (80–100 g) used in previous research.[37] Don't be persuaded by supplement manufacturers to buy expensive creatine–carbohydrate supplements – you could end up consuming far too much carbohydrate if you take them on top of your usual meals! Take creatine at your usual meal or snack times (provided they contain at least 34 g carbohydrate). In fact, since protein and carbohydrate taken together stimulate insulin more than carbohydrate alone, this is by far the most effective and cheapest strategy. Drink an extra glass or two of water when loading with creatine to compensate for the increased uptake of water by your muscle cells.

Are there any side effects?

Reports of side effects such as muscle cramps, stomach discomfort, dehydration and muscle and kidney damage have not been proven. In fact, a team of researchers at the School of Biomedical Sciences at Nottingham University analysed blood samples of volunteers after taking a standard five-day loading dose of creatine followed by a 3 g maintenance dose for nine weeks. They found no evidence of liver, muscle or kidney damage and concluded that creatine has no health risks in healthy people when taken in the recommended doses.[38] The only 'side effect' appears to be water-retention-related weight gain. However, this is associated mainly with the high creatine loading doses (20–30 g/day), and lower loading doses of 6 g/day or less result in very little water retention.

◆ HMB (beta-hydroxy ◆ beta-methylbutyrate)

What is it?

HMB is a metabolite of the BCAA leucine. Your body breaks down leucine into HMB, and you can also get it from grapefruit, catfish and alfalfa. HMB is a precursor to a component of cell membranes which helps with the growth and repair of muscle tissue. Its role is not yet clear but scientists believe it either helps protect the muscle from excessive breakdown during intense exercise or it accelerates muscle repair after training. The idea behind supplementation is to increase muscle mass and speed up recovery.

Does it work?

HMB is a relatively new supplement and has only been researched since the late 1990s, so it's early days to make strong recommendations. Studies at Iowa State University have measured greater gains in muscle mass and strength after taking HMB supplements for 3–7 weeks, compared with a placebo,[39] and this may be due to HMB's ability to prevent muscle breakdown during intense training. The same researchers also found that HMB helps to reduce body-fat levels and improve body composition, although the exact mechanism is not clear.[40] Several researchers believe that HMB may work even better when combined with creatine and protein–carbohydrate supplements.[41]

How much?

If you decide to use HMB, stick to the doses used in the studies: 3 g/day for men and 2 g/day for women. This works out at about

38.1 mg/kg body weight/day. Higher doses of 6 g/day have been used but give no further benefit. It would also be better to take HMB with a MRP or at meal times. Studies at Iowa State University found that muscle mass gains were greater when HMB was taken with a carbohydrate–protein supplement.[41]

Are there any side effects?

No side effects have been found in athletes nor in animals tested using higher-than-recommended doses. As HMB is a water-soluble substance, any excess is excreted in the urine.

♦ Glutamine ♦

What is it?

Glutamine is a non-essential amino acid – i.e. it can be made from other amino acids in your body. It makes up more than half of your body's amino acid pool and 5–7% of its muscle protein, and it can be broken down to supply energy during intense training. It also fuels your immune system: when your immune system is stressed or during periods of intense training, your body's glutamine needs increase. Under these circumstances, the rate of production cannot keep up with requirements and so blood levels of glutamine fall. Extra glutamine is then released from the muscles, so your muscles become catabolic, despite continued training. Glutamine release and muscle breakdown increase when muscle glycogen levels are low – for instance, if you are on a calorie-restricted diet or if you over train. Glutamine supplementation may therefore offset muscle breakdown and conserve muscle tissue during periods of intense training or dieting, and also boost the immune system.

Does it work?

It is possible that glutamine supplements may help preserve muscle mass and bolster your immune system during periods of particularly intense training. Studies at Oxford University have found that taking glutamine supplements immediately after hard training reduced the risk of upper respiratory tract infection.[42] However, glutamine won't increase your strength, muscle size or performance. Don't bother taking it if you are eating normally – it's only likely to benefit you if you are dieting and undergoing intense training.

How much?

Doses of 5–7 g have been used in the studies – equivalent to 100 mg glutamine/kg body weight. Take glutamine within two hours after training, either in your post-workout drink or as a separate supplement. In fact, many reputable brands of MRPs and protein supplements contain added glutamine, making a separate supplementation unnecessary.

Are there any side effects?

No side effects have been found. Since glutamine is made in your body, high doses of supplements would simply cause your body to make less of it.

♦ 'Andro' supplements ♦

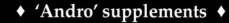

What are they?

'Andro' supplements include androstenedione and androstenediol. They are precursors to testosterone – and, although you produce them naturally in the adrenal glands, they are also available as supplements. The 'andro' hormones have very little muscle-building activity themselves, but the theory is that 'andro' supplements will convert into testosterone in your body and increase your testosterone levels. As testosterone – a powerful anabolic hormone which increases your strength, muscle mass and athletic performance – is classed as a banned substance and is illegal to buy, they could therefore be viewed as a legal alternative for strength and power athletes.

Do they work?

Despite extravagant claims made by the manufacturers, the 'andro' supplements do not enhance strength, muscle mass or athletic performance when taken in the dosages recommended by the manu-facturers. In 'The Andro Project', researchers at East Tennessee State University carried out a major study of the effects of 'andro' supplements in 50 men aged 35–65 and found no evidence to back up the manufacturers' claims.[43] The men took part in a 12-week weight-training programme and were given either 200 mg androste-nedione, 200 mg androstenediol or a placebo (dummy pill). Although testosterone levels increased by 16% after one month in those taking the androstenedione, by the end of 12 weeks they went back to normal. That's because their bodies shut down their own production of testosterone. All the men got stronger during the 12-week programme but there was no difference between those taking the 'andro' supplements and those taking the placebo. What's more, levels of the female hormone oestrogen rose in those using supplements! This could lead to feminisation over a period of time, the opposite of what male strength trainers want to achieve.

What dose?

Clearly, the doses of 200 mg recommended by manufacturers of 'andro' supplements do not raise testosterone levels nor change your body composition. Androstenedione may raise testosterone levels when taken in higher doses (300 mg), according to researchers at Massachusetts General Hospital/University of Massachesetts Medical School, but they still fail to increase stength or muscle mass.[44]

Are there any side effects?

The 'andro' supplements raise levels of female sex hormones, including oestrogen and its related compounds. This could lead to gynecomastia (breast development) and lowered libido in men. Some manufacturers recommended taking an oestrogen blocker, chrysin, to counteract this side effect. How-ever, there is no evidence that it works. Another serious side effect of 'andro' use is lowered levels of high-density liporotein or the 'good' cholesterol, increasing the risk of heart disease.

Two more good reasons not to take 'andro' supplements are the danger of contamination and the risk of failing a drugs test. In a study carried out at the University of California, Los Angeles, all those taking androstenedione were found to have high levels of 19-norandrosterone (the standard marker for nandrolone use) in their urine.[45] The levels were high enough to 'test positive' in a drugs test for steroids. 'Andro' itself does not produce 19-norandrosterone, so researchers concluded that the 'andro' supplements were contaminated with it. When researchers then analysed seven brands of androstenedione, they found that five did not contain the amount stated on the label while one actually contained testosterone!

Should 'andro' supplements be banned?

At the time of publication, androstenedione is banned at the Olympics but is still legal to buy and readily available from manufacturers of nutritional supplements. It is not yet classed as an illegal anabolic steroid but a number of scientists are seeking justification to ban it. The fact that it is chemically very similar to testosterone makes it a likely candidate. However, scientists would also need to prove to drug-enforcement agencies that androstenedione builds muscle. As there is mounting evidence that it doesn't promote muscle growth, it may not receive a ban in the end and could continue to be sold under misleading claims.

♦ Conjugated linoleic acid ♦

What is it?

Conjugated linoleic acid (CLA) is the collective term for a number of variants of linoleic acid, one of the essential fatty acids (*see* p. 177). It differs from linoleic acid only in the placement of two double bonds in the fatty-acid chain. CLA is found in foods normally associated with being high in saturated fat such as full-fat milk, meat and cheese. It was first discovered by Professor Michael Pariza at the University of Wisconsin, Madison, in 1987 when he was researching the potential cancer-causing effect of fried hamburgers. During this research he discovered that hamburgers contained CLA and that this was, in fact, anti-carcinogenic. Since then, scientists have established that CLA protects against several cancers. A major discovery for athletes is that CLA may also play a big part in regulating body composition and metabolism. However, it is impracti-

cal to get enough CLA from food alone to get a beneficial effect, so supplementation may be important. Supplements are made from sunflower and safflower oils. The CLA content of various foods is shown in Table 16.8.

Does it work?

Research shows that CLA can reduce fat storage and increase fat burning. It does this by increasing the activity of an enzyme called hormone sensitive lipase that releases the fat from fat cells into the blood. At the same time it reduces the activity of another enzyme called lipoprotein lipase that transports fat into the fat cells. The net result is that more fat is burned as fuel and less fat is stored. Research conducted in Norway found that those taking 3,000 mg CLA daily for three months reduced their body fat by 20%.[46] When CLA is combined with strength training, it can reduce muscle breakdown, enhance muscle growth and increase strength. University of Memphis researchers gave 27 experienced weight trainers either 5.6 g CLA/day or an olive oil placebo, and found that CLA improved their strength in the bench press and leg press by 13.6 kg compared with the placebo group's 4.3 kg.[47] Kent State University researchers gave 24 novice bodybuilders either 7.2 g CLA/day or a placebo vegetable oil.[48] After six weeks of training the CLA weight trainers had greater gains in arm size (circumference), total muscle mass and enhanced stength – around twice the gains of the placebo group.

How much?

Researchers estimate that the average diet probably provides around 100–300 mg CLA/ day. In studies, beneficial effects of CLA – such as reduced body fat and increased muscle – have been shown at intakes of 3 g

(3000 mg) or more. This is the amount most researchers recommend. Some researchers also believe the reduction in CLA intake in the typical Western diet accounts for some of the rise in obesity in this country. We get less from our food because we eat less animal fat and also because the CLA content of milk and meat has dropped due to changes in cattle feed.

Are there any side effects?

So far, researchers haven't found any negative side effects from excess CLA. There have been reports of stomach irritation but the newer forms of CLA (micellar CLA) eliminates this side effect.

Food	Portion	CLA (mg per portion)
Butter	1 tsp (7 g)	76
Yoghurt	1 carton (150 g)	1050
Processed cheese	1 slice (28 g)	169
Cheese	1 slice (28 g)	108
T-bone steak (cooked)	1 small (100 g)	730
Vegetable oil	1 tsp (5 g)	1

Table 16.8 The CLA content of various foods[49]

♦ Caffeine ♦

What is it?

Caffeine is a substance that has a pharmacological (drug-like) effect on the body. It is classed as a drug rather than a nutrient but is still considered a 'nutritional supplement' because it is found in many everyday drinks. The caffeine content of coffee varies between 50 and 100 mg/cup, tea contains 30–60 mg/cup, cola 50 mg/330 ml can and caffeinated 'energy' drinks roughly 100 mg/250 ml can.

It has long been used in sport to mask fatigue and increase endurance. The amount needed to get a performance-enhancing effect varies depending on your individual metabolism but studies have used amounts ranging from 3–15 mg/kg body weight (210–1050 mg for a 70 kg athlete). There are three main theories to explain caffeine's action on athletic performance:

1. In doses above 5 mg/kg body weight (350 mg for a 70 kg athlete), caffeine increases fat burning during exercise while sparing glycogen. It does this by stimulating adrenaline production, which in turn speeds up the release of fatty acids from fat cells into the blood stream. Therefore, taking caffeine before exercise may encourage the muscles to use more fat and less glycogen, and hence postpone fatigue.
2. Caffeine is a stimulant and has a direct effect on muscle contraction. It does this by stimulating the release of calcium from its storage sites in the muscle cells, enabling calcium to stimulate muscle contraction more effectively. This could increase strength and power output.
3. Caffeine stimulates the central nervous system and therefore works at a psychological level. It may increase concentration, mask your perception of fatigue and increase your motivation to train hard.

Does it work?

Caffeine supplementation above 3 mg/kg body weight has proved beneficial for many types of exercise: endurance events lasting more than 90 minutes, high-intensity events lasting about 20 minutes and short-term high-intensity activities lasting about 5 minutes.[50] This is particularly true for aerobic-based events but caffeine also benefits power and strength activities. Although the studies to date have measured performance improvements during activities such as high-intensity running, cycling, rowing and swimming, it is likely that caffeine would improve your performance during weight training. For example, researchers at RMIT University, Australia, found that caffeine improved performance and enhanced power output during 2000 m time trials on a rowing ergometer, a power event lasting approximately 7 minutes.[51] Caffeine probably works via theories 2 and 3 (p. 192) – i.e. increasing muscle contraction and masking feelings of fatigue.

How much?

Doses between 3–5 mg/kg/body weight taken 30–60 minutes before training should produce a performance-boosting effect in most people. That would be equivalent to about three cups of coffee or three cans of caffeinated energy drink. However, as the sensitivity to caffeine varies, you may need to adjust the exact dose. Exceeding 5 mg/kg body weight will not give you further benefit and would probably increase the caffeine concentration of your urine to levels above 12 micrograms/ml. This is the upper limit permitted in drug-tested sports.

Are there any side effects?

Up to a certain level, caffeine can make you feel more alert and wide awake. Excessive amounts can increase restlessness, nervousness, trembling, irritability and cause diarrhoea or even heart palpitations. If you are susceptible to caffeine's side effects, it probably isn't worth taking as you won't get a performance-boosting effect. Caffeine is also a diuretic, causing you to excrete more fluid. If you do decide to use caffeine, drink extra water before and during exercise to counteract this effect.

♦ Summary of key points ♦

- The general guideline for carbohydrate intake is 5–7 g/kg body weight/day.
- Pre-workout carbohydrate may help those training for maximum size (it may help you train for longer) but is best avoided by those wishing to lose fat.
- Carbohydrate during training may help delay fatigue, reduce muscle breakdown and encourage faster muscle growth.
- Carbohydrate plus protein, in a ratio of approximately 2:1, promotes the fastest post-exercise recovery of glycogen and creates a more favourable anabolic environment for muscle growth.
- It is recommended that strength trainers consume 1.4–1.8 g protein/kg body weight/ day. Higher intakes provide no further benefits.
- Meal replacement or protein supplements may benefit those with high-protein requirements, those on a calorie-restricted plan and vegetarians.
- Fat should contribute 15–30% of calories, with an emphasis on obtaining sufficient essential fatty acids.
- The omega-3 sub-group of fats are particularly important as they can help recovery after heavy training, reduce joint stiffness and inflammation, and enhance aerobic metabolism.
- Keeping well hydrated before, during and after training will help your performance and promote recovery.
- Aim to consume at least 1–2 litres/day plus an additional 125–250 ml every 10–20 minutes during training. Water is the best choice for workouts lasting less than one hour; sports drinks containing carbohydrate are beneficial for longer workouts.
- Vitamin and mineral needs are likely to be higher than those of the general population and the published RDAs.
- A multivitamin and mineral supplement can act as a good insurance policy if you aren't getting enough from food but avoid megadoses; they will not improve performance and may cause imbalances.
- Taking extra antioxidants may be helpful in reducing free radical damage caused by exercise.
- Creatine can increase bodyweight, muscle mass, strength and total training volume.
- HMB may help increase muscle mass, strength and body composition.
- Glutamine may preserve muscle mass and boost immunity during periods of hard training and calorie restriction.
- 'Andro' supplements do not live up to their claims of enhancing strength or muscle mass and may produce undesirable side effects.
- CLA may prove to be useful for reducing fat and building muscle.
- Caffeine taken before training can increase power output and endurance, and mask fatigue.

Chapter 17

The Weight-gain Eating Plan

When it comes to gaining solid muscle mass, most people find it a struggle. Gains are often slow or you find yourself taking two steps forwards and one step back as you lose muscle mass the moment you let up on your training. But with a good eating programme and the right intake of calories and nutrients, it is possible for everyone, whatever your body type, to achieve consistent gains in muscle size and stop the gain–loss cycle. Use the nutritional advice in Chapter 16 as the basis of your eating plan. In addition, this chapter helps you set realistic weight-gain goals and explains why some people find it harder to gain weight than others. It gives you sound weight-gain guidance and features a unique step-by-step guide to work out your nutritional needs. Finally, it provides three balanced eating plans that you can use as a basis for developing your own personal weight-gain eating plan.

◆ How much muscle mass can ◆ I expect to gain?

The amount of muscle mass you can expect to gain will be determined partly by your genetic make-up and partly by the quality of your training and diet. Naturally, there's nothing you can do to change your genetic background, but by understanding your personal limitations you can work out your real strengths and weaknesses and set realistic goals. The follow-ing four factors will help you to decide your natural potential for muscle growth.

Four factors affecting muscle growth

1. Body type

You need to be aware of your natural body type, as this to a large extent dictates your genetic potential to add muscle or fat (*see* pp. 151–2). If you have a naturally slender frame with a small musculature (ectomorphic body type), your muscle gains will be slower and, ultimately, smaller than someone with a natur-ally athletic frame (mesomorphic body type). Chances are you will never closely resemble a heavyweight bodybuilder but, with hard work in the gym, you could achieve more of a life-guard's physique. If you have a naturally large, stocky frame with a fair amount of body fat (endomorphic body type), you will gain muscle readily but will need to work harder with your cardio-vascular training and cut back your calorie intake in order for your muscles to show. You may not achieve the sharp definition of a world-class 100 m sprinter but you could achieve the impressive muscle bulk and athleticism of a rugby player. If you are fortunate enough to be blessed with broad shoulders, narrow waist and hips and low body fat (mesomorph), you could achieve the perfect symmetry of a champion bodybuilder!

2. Muscle fibre mix

You probably have a rough idea of your mix of fast-twitch (FT) and slow-twitch (ST) muscle fibres (*see* pp. 21–2) simply from your sporting experience. If you tend to do well at sports requiring a lot of strength, speed and power, you probably have a high ratio of FT to ST fibres and will tend to gain muscle size relatively fast. On the other hand, if you tend to perform better in endurance activities, you probably have a higher proportion of ST fibres and will make slower muscle size gains. Since FT muscle fibres have the highest capacity for hypertrophy, you will experience greater gains if you have a high proportion of these.

3. Motor units

The arrangement of your motor units – i.e. the number of muscle fibres activated by each motor nerve (*see* pp. 18–19) – determines your rate of progress too. People who tend to gain strength and size very rapidly probably have an above-average number of muscle fibres in each motor unit. For the same effort, they generate a higher force output than the average person. This creates a bigger stimulus for muscle growth.

4. Hormonal balance

Your natural hormonal balance will affect your degree of muscularity and how fast you can add muscle. If you have naturally high levels of anabolic hormones such as testosterone and growth hormone (GH), you will respond to a strength-training programme more readily, and achieve greater gains in muscle mass and strength than more average people. This explains why women generally never achieve the muscle bulk and strength of men, despite heavy training, as they have only one-tenth of the testosterone levels. Only by taking anabolic steroids can they achieve more masculine proportions.

The bottom line...

Even if you have few of these genetically determined factors on your side, you can still make great gains by paying extra attention to the quality of your training and your eating plan. Regardless of your body type, muscle fibre-type mix, motor unit make-up and hormonal level, you can improve your physique beyond measure by following a well-planned training and nutrition programme.

♦ Realistic expectations ♦

Most men can expect to gain 0.5–1 kg/month on an established programme.[1] Women usually experience about 50–75% of the gains of men – i.e. 0.25–0.75 kg/month – partly due to their smaller initial body weight and smaller muscle mass, and partly due to lower levels of anabolic hormones.

Your weight gain may be as much as 2 kg/month during the first few months of starting strength training. In fact, lean mass gains of 20% of your starting body weight are common after the first year of training. But, after a few years, you may struggle to gain 0.5 kg/month. For example, if you weigh 70 kg at the start of your training programme, you could weigh as much as 76 kg after the first three months. This would then probably drop to about 1 kg/month, so after the first year you may weigh 85 kg – that's a gain of 15 kg. Don't expect to continue adding 6–12 kg a year every year, though. Your rate of weight gain will gradually drop off over the years as you approach your genetic potential. Also, the chances are you will have temporary and unavoidable breaks from your training programme – when you go on holiday or stop training due to illness, for example. Remember, your exact rate of weight gain will be influenced by your genetic potential. That's why two people can gain very different amounts of weight despite following the same training and eating programme. If you are putting on more than 3–4 kg/month, you are probably adding body fat, so you will need to cut down on your calorie intake.

♦ What should I eat? ♦

The most important part of your weight-gain nutrition plan is to eat the right number of calories. If you are a hard gainer and normally struggle to put on weight, you must concentrate first and foremost on increasing calories. It takes a lot of energy to fuel a heavy training programme and to support muscle growth, so you must eat enough calories to allow you to train sufficiently hard and recover fully. Most scientists recommend increasing calories by 20%. In practice, that amounts to 500–750 kcal for men and 250–500 kcal for women. If you find you still do not gain weight, increase your calories by a further 10%.

These calories should come from a balanced ratio of carbohydrate, protein and fat if you want to achieve optimal muscle gains. It is important to get these basics right before you even consider taking muscle-building supplements such as creatine. Such supplements will be a waste of money if you are not eating the right amount of calories, carbohydrate, protein and fat.

Do weight training and aerobic training mix?

Include 2–3 cardio workouts per week in your weight-gain plan to keep body-fat levels low and reap the immune-boosting benefits of aerobic exercise. But do not go overboard. Too much cardio vascular exercise could backfire on you. It can take those valuable calories away from muscle growth and cause you to break down muscle tissue – the reverse of what you are trying to achieve! If you continue to experience strength and mass increases, you are probably doing just the right amount of aerobic activity. But if you start losing strength or size, you may be doing too much cardio training and/or failing to eat enough calories. For these reasons, cardio should be done in moderation, as per the general guidelines for cardio training detailed in Chapter 18.

♦ How to design your weight-gain plan ♦

To achieve the greatest gains in strength and muscle mass, use the following guidelines when designing your diet.

Step 1. estimate your calorie needs

1. Estimate your resting metabolic rate (RMR) using the appropriate equation in Table 17.1. This is the number of calories you burn at rest over 24 hours maintaining essential functions such as respiration, digestion and brain function.

Example
For a 28-year-old 70 kg man:
RMR = (70 x 15.3) + 679
= 1750 kcal

Age (years)	Men	Women
10–18	(body weight in kg x 17.5) + 651	(body weight in kg x 12.2) + 746
19–30	(body weight in kg x 15.3) + 679	(body weight in kg x 14.7) + 496
31–60	(body weight in kg x 11.6) + 879	(body weight in kg x 8.7) + 829

Table 17.1 Resting metabolic rate in athletes[2]

2. Calculate your daily energy expenditure (without exercise) by multiplying your RMR by one of the numbers below

- if you are mostly sedentary (mostly seated or standing activities during the day):
  RMR x 1.4

- if you are moderately active (regular brisk walking or equivalent during the day):
  RMR x 1.7

- If you are very active (generally physically active during the day)
  RMR x 2.0

Example
For a 28-year-old 70 kg man who is mostly sedentary:

Daily energy needs (without exercise)
= 1750 x 1.4
= 2450 kcal

3. Add on the number of calories expended during exercise (*see* Table 17.2). It's best to estimate your exercise calorie expenditure over a week, then divide this by seven to get a daily average. This final figure gives you an idea of how many calories you expend on an average day and therefore how many calories you would need to consume to maintain your weight.

Example
For a 28-year-old 70 kg man, mostly sedentary, who spends 3 hours/week weight training and 1 hour/week running:

No. of calories burned during exercise/ week = (3 x 492) + 840
= 2316 kcal
Daily energy needs (with exercise)
= 2450 + (2316 ÷ 7)
= 2781 kcal

4. To gain weight, increase your calorie intake by 20% – i.e. multiply your maintenance calories by 1.2 (120%).

Sport	Kcal per hour	
	Men	Women
Cycling (11.2 kph)	300	234
Cycling (16 kph)	450	354
Rowing machine	480	377
Running (12 kph)	840	660
Running (16 kph)	1092	858
Swimming (crawl, 4.8 kph)	1200	942
Tennis (singles)	426	330
Weight training	492	384

Table 17.2 Calories expended during exercise

Note: figures are for a 70 kg man and a 55 kg woman. Values will be greater for heavier body weights; lower for smaller body weights

Example
For a 28-year-old 70 kg man, mostly sedentary, who spends 3 hours/week weight training and 1 hour/week running:

Daily energy needs to gain weight
= 2781 x 1.2
= 3337 kcal

Step 2: calculate your carbohydrate needs

The general guideline for strength training is 5–7 g carbohydrate/kg body weight/day (*see* p. xx). For optimal weight gain, you should also increase your carbohydrate intake by 20%, bringing it up to 6–8 g/kg body weight/day.

Example
For a 28-year-old 70 kg man, mostly sedentary, who spends 3 hours/week weight training and 1 hour/week running, and who wants optimal weight gains:

Carbohydrate needs = 8 x 70
= 560 g/day

Step 3: calculate your protein intake

The general guideline on protein requirements for strength training is 1.4–1.8 g/kg body weight/day (*see* p. 175). For weight gain, an intake at the upper end of this range – i.e. roughly 1.8 g/kg body weight/day – is most appropriate. Higher intakes will not produce further gains in muscle mass and offer no performance benefit (*see* p. 175).

Example
For a 28-year-old 70 kg man, mostly sedentary, who spends 3 hours/week weight training and 1 hour/week running, and who wants optimal weight gain:

    Protein needs = 1.8 x 70
                  = 126 g per day

Step 4: calculate your fat needs

Fat should contribute 15–30% of your calorie intake. In effect, your fat calories are the balance remaining after you have subtracted your carbohydate and protein calories from your total calorie intake.

Kcal per gram

- To calculate carbohydrate calories, multiply g carbohydrate by 4: 1 g carbohydrate yields 4 kcal.
- To calculate protein calories, multiply g protein by 4: 1 g protein yields 4 kcal.
- To calculate fat g, divide fat calories by 9: 1 g fat yields 9 kcal.

Example
For a 28-year-old 70 kg man, mostly sedentary, who spends 3 hours/week weight training and 1 hour/week running, and who wants optimal weight gain:

    Carbohydrate calories = 560 x 4
                          = 2240 kcal
    Protein calories   = 126 x 4
                          = 504 kcal
    Fat calories = total calorie intake – calories from carbohydrate and protein
                          = 3337 – 2240 – 504
                          = 593 kcal
    Daily fat intake   = 593 ÷ 9
                          = 66 g

♦ Weight-gain meal plan ♦ providing 3000 kcal

Meal	Food
1	4 slices (160 g) wholegrain toast 4 tsp (20 g) olive oil spread 4 tsp (60 g) honey 1 scoop whey protein powder
2	2 portions of fruit 1 carton (150 g) yoghurt
3	1 medium (225 g) baked potato 1 small (70 g) chicken breast 3 tbsp (125 g) sweetcorn Salad 1 tbsp (11 g) oil/vinegar dressing*
4	2 portions of fruit 1 carton (112 g) cottage cheese
5 (post-workout)	1 serving (70 g) meal replacement shake
6	6 tbsp (350 g cooked weight) pasta 2 tbsp (60 g) pasta sauce 1 portion (175 g) cod/haddock/plaice 2 portions (200 g) vegetables or salad 1 large bowl (300 g) low-fat rice pudding 2 portions of fruit
Analysis	**Total: 3000 kcal 374 g carbohydrate (60%) 190 g protein (25%) 49 g fat (15%)**

♦ Weight-gain meal plan ♦ providing 3500 kcal

Meal	Food
1	100 g porridge oats 500 ml skimmed milk 2 tbsp (60 g) raisins
2	1 protein/energy bar (70 g)
3	Sandwiches made with 4 slices wholemeal bread (160 g) 4 tsp (20 g) olive oil spread 100 g tuna in water/brine (drained) Salad 1 tbsp (11 g) oil/vinegar dressing*
4	5 ready-to-eat apricots (200 g) 2 cartons (2 x 150 g) fruit yoghurt
5 (post-workout)	1 serving (70 g) meal replacement shake
6	6 tbsp (400 g cooked weight) noodles 1 tbsp (11 g) olive oil 1 breast (125 g) turkey 2 portions (200 g) vegetables or salad 1 serving (70 g) meal replacement shake 2 portions of fruit
Analysis	**Total: 3500 kcal 521 g carbohydrate (57%) 239 g protein (27%) 61 g fat (16%)**

*Using an omega-3-rich oil, e.g. rapeseed, walnut or flaxseed.

◆ Weight-gain meal plan ◆ providing 4000 kcal

Meal	Food
1	4 slices (160 g) wholegrain toast 4 tsp (20 g) olive oil spread 3 poached eggs 1 scoop whey protein powder
2	2 portions of fruit 1 serving meal replacement shake 1 wholemeal roll 2 tbsp (100 g) cottage cheese
3	1 large bowl (450 g cooked weight) pasta 1 small tin (100 g) tuna in water/ brine (drained) Chopped peppers, tomatoes 1 tbsp (11 g) oil/vinegar dressing* 1 portion of fruit
4	1 protein/energy bar (70 g)
5 (post-workout)	1 serving (70 g) meal replacement shake
6	2 baked potatoes (450 g) 2 tbsp (20 g) olive oil spread 1 portion (175 g) cod/haddock/ plaice 2 portions (200 g) vegetables or salad 4 small (Scotch) pancakes
Analysis	**Total: 4000 kcal** **587 g carbohydrate (55%)** **254 g protein (25%)** **89 g fat (20%)**

*Using an omega-3-rich oil, e.g. rapeseed, walnut or flaxseed.

Practical weight-gain tips

- Put more total eating time into your daily routine. This may mean rescheduling other activities. Plan your meal and snack times in advance and never skip or rush them, no matter how busy you are.
- Increase your meal frequency – eat at least three meals and three snacks daily.
- Eat regularly – every 2–3 hours – and avoid gaps longer than three hours.
- Plan nutritious high-calorie low-bulk snacks – e.g. meal replacement shakes, smoothies, yoghurt, nuts, dried fruit, energy/protein bars.
- Eat larger meals but avoid overfilling!
- If you are finding it hard to eat enough food, have more drinks such as meal replacement or protein supplements once or twice a day to help bring up your calorie, carbohydrate and protein intake.
- Boost the calorie and nutritional content of your meals – e.g. add dried fruit, bananas, honey, chopped nuts or seeds to breakfast cereal or yoghurt. This is more nutritious than the common practice of adding sugar or jam ('empty calories').

◆ Summary of key points ◆

- The amount of lean weight you can gain depends on your genetic make-up as well as the quality of your training and diet.
- Your genetic make-up influences your natural body type, your mix of FT and ST muscle fibres, the arrangement of the motor units in your muscles and your hormonal balance.
- As a guideline, most men can expect to gain 0.5–1 kg body weight/month on an established programme. Women can expect to gain 0.25–0.75 kg/month.
- Gains in the first year of training may be up to 20% of starting body weight, then gradually slow down over the years.
- A slightly positive calorie balance results in the fastest lean weight gain. Increase your maintenance calorie intake by 20%.
- Carbohydrate intake should also increase by 20%. Aim to consume 6–8 g/kg body weight/day.
- The general guideline for protein intake is 1.4–1.8 g/kg body weight/day. For weight gain, an intake at the upper end of this range – i.e. 1.8g/kg body weight/day, is appropriate. Higher intakes provide no additional benefit.
- Hard-gainers should focus on increasing meal frequency, eating at regular intervals and consuming more high-calorie low-bulk nutritious foods.

Chapter 18

The Fat-burning Eating Plan

You may have good muscle size but your muscles won't look very impressive if they are hidden under a thick layer of fat. Developing well-defined muscles requires paying as much attention to your eating plan as to your training programme. No amount of training in the gym will give you a rippling six-pack unless you combine it with the right sort of eating programme. That does not mean 'dieting' though. The term 'dieting' is often laden with negative advice and creates a negative mind-set, setting you up for failure rather than success. Use the nutritional advice in Chapter 16 as the basis of your eating plan. In addition, this chapter helps you decide on your body-fat goal and make a plan of action to achieve it. It gives you a clear fat-burning strategy to shedding body fat without losing muscle. To help you devise your fat-burning eating plan, this chapter also provides step-by-step guidance – based on cutting-edge science – to calculate your calorie, carbohydrate, protein and fat requirements. Finally, it gives three nutritionally balanced eating plans that you can use as the basis for your personal diet plan.

♦ What is my optimal ♦ body-fat percentage

It is impossible to set an optimal body-fat percentage that applies to everyone. The body-fat level that your body comfortably reaches without strict dieting is dependent on your genetic make-up as well as your diet and activity. Your natural body type (*see* pp. 151–2) dictates to some extent how much fat you carry and how readily you store it. For example, if you are an ectomorph (narrow frame, long limbs) or mesomorph (athletic frame, well muscled), you are naturally lean and will be able to achieve a lower body-fat percentage than an endomorph (stocky frame, rounded build) who stores fat easily. But, whatever your natural body type, you can still achieve a lower body-fat level and more defined physique through consistent hard training and healthy eating. The important point is to decide on a level that is realistic for your build and shape.

How low can I go?

Healthy ranges for the general population are 18%–25% for women and 13%–18% for men.[1] But if you are a strength trainer or bodybuilder, you may desire lower levels. Between 10 and 20% for women and between 6 and 15% for men are common among well-trained athletes – levels that are generally associated with peak performance – but these percentages should be regarded with some caution. If you try to attain a low body-fat percentage that is unnatural for your genetic make-up, you may encounter problems.

For women, a body-fat percentage that is under their individual threshold for menstruation (14–20%) can be risky. Below this, a deficiency of oestrogen and progesterone similar to those levels experienced during and after the menopause can result in amenorrhoea (cessation of menstruation). This can lead to infertility, a loss of bone density, stress fractures and premature osteoporosis. Most experts therefore recommend a lower limit of 14% body fat for women.[2]

If a man's body-fat percentage dips too low, there are health risks too. Studies have shown that when men reach a body-fat level of 4–6%, their bodies start to feed on muscle tissue as a source of energy and to allow them to maintain their fat stores at a minimal level.[3] It is definitely unwise, if not impossible, to reduce your body fat below this level. Other studies have found that testosterone levels plummet below 5% body fat, causing reduced sexual drive and fertility![4]

♦ Fat-burning strategy ♦

To lose body fat, adopt the following eight-step fat-burning plan in conjunction with your strength-training programme and the fat-burning cardio programme detailed in Chapter 13.

Step 1: cut your calories by 15%

This small calorie drop may surprise you, as it is almost certainly a lot smaller than most diets you have tried before. However, this method will produce lasting success because it minimises any drop in your metabolic rate and allows you to retain your hard-earned muscle.

The problem with drastically restricting your calorie intake is that you cause your metabolic rate to slow down – the last thing you want to happen. This is called the 'starvation adaptation response' and means that your body stockpiles fat and calories rather than burning them for energy so that it becomes harder and harder for your body to burn fat. Your glycogen stores also quickly deplete, causing fatigue, a drop in performance, low energy levels and mounting hunger. Worse still, you end up breaking down muscle tissue as well as fat to provide fuel and – let's face it – muscle loss is the worst thing any strength trainer wants! On the other hand, cutting your calories by a modest 15% will produce steady fat loss without sacrificing muscle. You won't get instant results, of course, but you can expect to lose roughly 0.5 kg fat/week, perhaps slightly more when combined with the cardio training programme described in Chapter 13.

Step 2: eat several meals a day

Eating at least four or, ideally, six meals a day will help you lose body fat and maintain muscle size, although you will still consume the same number of calories. When you eat more frequently throughout the day, you encourage your body to use the calories more efficiently rather than storing them as body fat. You also help to keep your metabolic rate high, because every time you eat a meal, extra calories are burned to digest and metabolise the food. This is called the 'thermic effect of food'. A mixed meal – protein, carbohydrates and fats blended together – uses about 10% of the calories for this purpose. Eating more frequent meals increases this effect and, along with it, your metabolic rate. You also avoid hunger pangs and keep your blood glucose levels more even. When you feed your body regularly throughout the day you are providing it with a continual supply of nutrients for muscle growth and repair.

Step 3: eat more protein

Increasing your protein intake while cutting your calories helps protect against muscle loss. Researchers recommend 1.8–2.0 g/kg body weight/day to maintain muscle mass.[5] For example, if you weigh 80 kg, you will need to eat 144–160 g protein each day.

Divide this amount of protein evenly throughout the day. If you eat six meals a day, you should consume around 23 g protein at each meal. Protein also has the highest thermic effect of all the nutrients. When you consume protein, about 20–25% of calories are lost to its own metabolism and the rise in body temperature it causes. Carbohydrate and fat do the same thing but to a lesser extent; for carbohydrate, only 12–15% of its calories are lost as heat, while fat loses only 3% – another good reason to keep your protein intake high and your fat intake low. Protein also has the ability to curb the appetite. High-protein meals (e.g. fish) switch off hunger and produce longer-lasting feelings of meal-satisfaction than high-carbohydrate, high-fat meals (e.g. croissants). So, increasing your protein intake will help to control hunger pangs as well.

Step 4: time your meals and exercise for greater fat burning

If you want to burn more body fat during training, don't eat a high-carbohydrate meal within three hours of your workout. If you consume pre-workout carbohydrate, your muscles will burn more carbohydrate and less fat.

Carbohydrate can inhibit fat burning because it raises insulin levels, which encourage fat storage rather than fat burning. By working out without pre-workout carbohydrate you force your body to dip into its fat stores. After your workout, wait one hour before eating. This increases the residual fat-burning effect of exercise (*see* p. 171).

Step 5: don't cut out the carbs

Reducing your carbohydrate intake too much will leave you feeling drained and tired and unable to train hard in the gym. Low muscle glycogen levels can trigger muscle breakdown, as protein is then used to fuel your muscles. For fat loss, aim to consume 4–5 g carbohydrate/kg body weight/day, which is slightly lower than the 5–7 g range recommended for regular training in Chapter 16 (*see* pp. 167–8). For example, if you weigh 80 kg, you will need to eat 360–400 g carbohydrate daily. This will still allow you to train hard and lose body fat.

Consume most of your carbohydrate early in the day, spread over your first three or four meals. If you train in the evening, however, make sure you save some of your carbohydrate allowance for your post-workout recovery meal as this speeds glycogen storage and enhances muscle protein manufacture (*see* p. 171). Plan low GI meals (*see* p. 168), and combine carbohydrate with protein to lower the GI and help maintain your blood glucose for several hours.

Step 6: not all fats are bad

Do not cut fat out completely. Certain fats – the omega-3 and omega-6 fatty acids – are vital for health and peak performance. The omega-3 fatty acids can even help you burn fat more efficiently (*see* p. 179). Include foods such as oily fish, avocados, nuts and olives in moderation, and supplement your diet with a tablespoon of omega-3-rich oil (e.g. flaxseed, rapeseed or walnut) each day.

Keep your fat intake between 15 and 20% of total calories – which is at the lower end of the 15–30% range recommended on p. 177 – by cutting down on the fats your body doesn't need. Avoid sources of saturated fat – meat (except very lean), full-fat dairy products, cakes, biscuits and chocolate – and hydrogenated vegetable fat (margarine, spreads, biscuits, bars, cakes and pastries made with hydrogenated oil).

Fat calories can be converted into body fat

far more easily than any other nutrient. You need very little energy to metabolise fat compared with carbohydrate or protein. For every 100 kcal of fat you eat, 3 kcal are used to convert them into body fat, in contrast to 12–15 kcal for carbohydrate and 20–25 kcal for protein. In other words, your body would rather store fat as fat than convert carbohydrate and protein to fat.

Step 7: bulk up

Make your diet filling and satisfying by selecting foods with a high content of water and fibre. That means you get maximum volume of food per calorie. Eat plenty of vegetables and fruit. They are low in calories, yet give you numerous health benefits: vitamins, minerals, phytochemicals and fibre. Include other fibre-rich foods such as beans, lentils, and whole grains. Fibre slows down stomach emptying, making you feel full for longer, and slows the absorption of carbohydrate, giving a slower blood glucose rise.

Step 8: indulge yourself once a week

Allow yourself to eat anything you like one day a week. Many people find that this helps to satisfy their desire for less healthy foods and keeps them on track the rest of the time. Provided you do not go overboard, eating a few extra calories once a week may prevent the metabolic slowdown associated with calorie restriction. The psychological benefits of indulging in your favourite foods outweigh any risks of extra calories. It relieves feelings of deprivation and means that you won't get caught in the diet–binge spiral that defeats many dieters.

◆ How to design your ◆ fat-burning eating plan

The following steps show you how to calculate your calorie, carbohydrate, protein and fat needs to lose body fat.

Step 1: estimate your calorie needs

1. Estimate your daily energy needs for weight maintenance by following the formulae on pp. 197–8 in Chapter 16.
2. To lose body fat, reduce your maintenance intake by 15%. Simply multiply the figure from 1. by 85%.

Example
For a 28-year-old 80 kg man, mostly sedentary, who spends 3 hours/week weight training and 1 hour/week running:

RMR = (80 x 15.3) + 679
  = 1903 kcal

Daily energy needs (without exercise)
  = 1903 x 1.4
  = 2664 kcal

No. of calories burned during exercise per week = (3 x 492) + 840
  = 2316 kcal

Daily energy needs (with exercise) for weight maintenance
  = 2664 + (2316 ÷ 7)
  = 2995 kcal

Daily energy needs to lose fat
  = 2995 x 0.85
  = 2546 kcal

Step 2: calculate your carbohydrate needs

For moderate-intensity training lasting up to one hour, you should aim to consume 4–5 g carbohydrate/kg body weight/day (*see* above).

Example

For a 28-year-old 80 kg man, mostly sedentary, who spends 3 hours/week weight training and 1 hour/week running:

Carbohydrate needs = (4 x 80)–(5 x 80)
= 320–400 g/day
Average = 360 g/day

Step 3: calculate your protein intake

The protein requirement for strength training during weight loss is 1.8–2.0 g/kg body weight/day.

Example

For a 28-year-old 80 kg man, mostly sedentary, who spends 3 hours/week weight training and 1 hour/week running:

Protein needs = 2.0 x 80
= 160 g/day

Kcal per gram

- To calculate carbohydrate calories, multiply g carbohydrate by 4: 1 g carbohydrate yields 4 kcal
- To calculate protein calories, multiply g protein by 4: 1 g protein yields 4 kcal
- To calculate fat g, divide fat calories by 9: 1 g fat yields 9 kcal

Step 4: calculate your fat needs

Fat should contribute 15–20% of your calorie intake. In effect, your fat calories are the balance remaining after you have subtracted your carbohydrate and protein calories from your total calorie intake.

Example

For a 28-year-old 80 kg man, mostly sedentary, who spends 3 hours/week weight training and 1 hour/week running:

Carbohydrate calories = 360 x 4
= 1440 kcal
Protein calories = 160 x 4
= 640 kcal
Fat calories = total calories – calories from carbohydrate and protein
= 2546 – 1440 – 640
= 466 kcal
Daily fat intake = 466 ÷ 9
= 52 g

◆ Fat-burning meal plan ◆ providing 1750 kcal

Meal	Food
1	60 g porridge oats 300 ml skimmed milk 1 tbsp (30 g) raisins
2	1 portion of fruit
3	1 medium (225 g) baked potato 1 tsp (5 g) olive oil spread 1 small tin (100 g) tuna (in water/brine) Salad 1 tbsp (11 g) oil/vinegar dressing* 1 portion of fruit
4	½ carton (150 g) fruit yoghurt
5 (post-workout)	1 standard serving (35 g) meal replacement shake
6	1 turkey breast (150 g), grilled or baked 4 tbsp (180 g cooked weight) brown rice 2 portions (200 g) vegetables or salad
Analysis	**Total: 1750 kcal** **272 g carbohydrate (58%)** **121 g protein (27%)** **28 g fat (15%)**

◆ Fat-burning meal plan ◆ providing 2000 kcal

Meal	Food
1	1 large bowl (85 g) whole grain cereal (e.g. muesli, bran flakes) 300 ml skimmed milk 1 portion of fruit
2	1 protein/energy bar (35 g)
3	2 small rolls (90 g) 2 tsp (10 g) olive oil spread 4 slices (70 g) cooked chicken Tomatoes (150 g) 1 portion of fruit
4	½ carton (150 g) fruit yoghurt
5 (post-workout)	1 standard serving (35 g) meal replacement shake
6	1 portion (175 g) cod/plaice/haddock, grilled or baked 1 medium (250 g) baked potato 2 tsp (10 g) olive oil spread 2 portions (200 g) vegetables or salad 1 tbsp (11 g) oil/vinegar dressing*
Analysis	**Total: 2000 kcal** **290 g carbohydrate (57%)** **136 g protein (27%)** **31 g fat (16%)**

*Using an omega-3-rich oil, e.g. rapeseed, walnut or flaxseed.

♦ Fat-burning meal plan ♦ providing 2500 kcal

Meal	Food
1	2 slices (80 g) wholegrain toast 2 tsp (10 g) olive oil spread 2 poached eggs
2	2 portions of fruit 1 carton (150 g) yoghurt
3	1 medium (300 g) baked potato 1 small (100 g) turkey breast Salad 1 tbsp (11 g) oil/vinegar dressing* 1 portion of fruit
4	1 protein/energy bar (70 g)
5 (post-workout)	1 standard serving (70 g) meal replacement shake
6	6 tbsp (450 g cooked weight) pasta 1 small portion (85 g) salmon 3 tbsp (90 g) white sauce Broccoli 1 portion (100 g) vegetables or salad
Analysis	**Total: 2500 kcal** **344 g carbohydrate (54%)** **160 g protein (26%)** **57 g fat (20%)**

*Using an omega-3-rich oil, e.g. rapeseed, walnut or flaxseed.

♦ Summary of key points ♦

- Your body-fat level depends on your genetic make-up, including your natural body type, as well as diet and activity.
- A body-fat percentage of 6–15% for men and 10–20% for women is generally associated with peak performance.
- A lower limit of 5% for men and 14% for women is recommended. Attaining lower body-fat percentages is associated with oestrogen deficiency in women and testosterone deficiency in men, as well as other health risks.
- To reduce body fat and maintain muscle, reduce calories by no more than 15%.
- Larger calorie reductions or weight losses greater than 0.5 kg body weight/week result in a loss of muscle and a drop in the metabolic rate.
- Key fat-loss strategies include eating more frequently (but the same number of calories) during the day, slightly increasing protein intake (to protect against muscle loss) and consuming more fibre-rich, bulky foods.
- To promote greater fat burning, avoid pre-workout carbohydrate, exercise on a near-empty stomach and wait for one hour after training before eating.
- Allow yourself to eat anything you like one day a week. This has psychological benefits.
- Most of your calorie reduction should come from saturated fats, the remainder from carbohydrate. Fat should contribute 15–20% of your calorie needs; carbohydrate should be 4–5 g/kg body weight/day and protein 1.8–2.0 g/kg body weight/day.

Quick Reference for the Major Muscle Groups, their Locations, Main Functions and Exercises

Muscle	Location	Main function	Exercises
Legs Quadriceps • Rectus femoris • Vastus lateralis • Vastus medialis • Vastus intermedialus	Front of thigh	Collectively extend the knee. Rectus femoris also flexes the hip	• Barbell squat • Dead lift • Leg press • Leg extension • Front lunge • Reverse lunge
Adductors • Adductor brevis • Adductor longus • Adductor magnus	Inner thigh	Pull the legs together	• Barbell squat • Dead lift
Abductors • Gluteus minimus • Gluteus medius	Outer thigh	Pull the legs sideways	• Barbell squat • Dead lift
Hamstrings • Biceps femoris • Semiteninosus • Semimembranosus	Back of thigh	Bend the knee and pull the hip back	• Barbell squat • Dead lift • Leg press • Front lunge • Reverse lunge • Lying leg curl • Seated leg curl • Straight-leg dead lift
Gastrocnemius	Calf	Bends the knee and straightens the ankle	• Standing calf raise • One-leg dumbbell calf raise • Leg press machine calf press • *Seated leg curl*

Muscle	Location	Main function	Exercises
Legs cont. Soleus	Calf	Straightens the ankle	• Standing calf raise • One-leg dumbbell calf raise • Leg press machine calf press
Gluteals Gluteus maximus	Backside	Extends the hip and rotates it outwards	• Barbell squat • Dead lifts • Leg press • Front lunge • Reverse lunge • Straight-leg dead lift • Back extension
Gluteus medius	Backside	Abducts and rotates the hip inwards	• Barbell squat • Dead lift • Leg press • Front lunge • Reverse lunge • Straight-leg dead lift • Back extension
Gluteus minimus	Backside	Stabilises the hip, and abducts and rotates it inwards	• Barbell squat • Dead lift • Leg press • Front lunge • Reverse lunge • Straight-leg dead lift • Back extension
Back Latissimus dorsi	Upper back	Draws the arms backwards	• Dead lift • Lat pull-down • Chin • One-arm row • Seated cable row • Bent-over barbell row • Straight-arm pull-down

Muscle	Location	Main function	Exercises
Back cont. Trapezius	Upper and mid-back	Draws the shoulder blades backwards	• Dead lift • Chin • One-arm row • Seated cable row • Bent-over barbell row • Straight-arm pull-down • Dumbbell shrug • *Dumbell press* • *Lateral raise* • Upright row • *Bent-over lateral raise*
Rhomboids	Deep central upper back	Draws the shoulder blades backwards	• Lat pull-down • Chin • One-arm row • Seated cable row • Bent-over barbell row • Straight-arm pull-down • *Dumbell press*
Infraspinatus	Shoulder blades	Rotates the arm outwards	• Chin • One-arm row
Teres major	Shoulder blades	Rotates the arm outwards	• Chin • One-arm row • Seated cable row • Bent-over barbell row • Straight-arm pull-down
Teres minor	Shoulder blades	Rotates the arm outwards	• Chin • One-arm row • Seated cable row • Bent-over barbell row • Straight-arm pull-down

Muscle	Location	Main function	Exercises
Back cont. Erector spinae	Lower back	Flexes the spine and keeps you upright when standing	• Barbell squat • Dead lift • Straight-leg dead lift • Back extension • Back extension, Swiss ball • *Seated cable row*
Chest Pectoralis major	Chest	Pulls the arm in front of the chest from any position, flexes the shoulder to allow pushing and lifts the arm forwards	• Barbell bench press • Dumbbell bench press • Dumbbell flye • Pec dec flye • Cable cross-over • *Seated cable row* • *Dumbell press*
Pectoralis minor	Chest	Lowers the shoulder blade	• Incline barbell bench press • Incline dumbbell bench press
Shoulders Anterior deltoids	Shoulder	Lifts arm forwards and upwards	• Dumbbell press • Upright row • *Barbell bench press* • *Dumbbell bench press* • *Incline barbell bench press* • *Incline dumbell bench press* • *Dumbbell flye* • *Pec dec flye* • *Cable cross-over* • *Lateral raise*
Medial deltoid	Shoulder	Lifts arm to the side	• Dumbbell press • Lateral raise • Upright row

Muscle	Location	Main function	Exercises
Shoulders cont. Posterior deltoid	Shoulder	Lifts arm to the rear and draws the elbow backwards	• Bent-over lateral raise • *Lat pull-down* • *Chins* • *One-arm row*
Arms Triceps	Outside of the upper arm	Partially or fully straightens the arm from a bent position	• Lying tricep extension • Triceps kickback • Triceps push-down • *Barbell bench press* • *Dumbbell bench press* • *Incline barbell bench press* • *Incline dumbbell bench press* • *Dumbell press* • Bench dip
Biceps brachii	Front of the upper arm	Bends the elbow, rotates the forearm and assists in raising the shoulder forwards	• Barbell curl • Preacher curl • Dumbbell curl • Incline dumbbell curl • Concentration curl • *Lat pull-down* • *Chins* • *One-arm row* • *Bent-over barbell row* • *Upright row*
Brachialis	Front of the upper arm beneath the biceps	Bends the elbow	• Barbell curl • Preacher curl
Brachioradialis	Top side of forearm	Bends the elbow, rotates the forearm	• *Lat pull-down* • *Chins* • *Seated cable row* • *Bent-over barbell row* • *Upright row* • *Barbell curl* • *Preacher curl* • *Dumbbell curl* • *Incline dumbbell curl*

Muscle	Location	Main function	Exercises
Arms cont. Brachioradialis cont.			• *Concentration curl* • *Triceps push-down*
Abdominals Obliques – internal and external	Waist	Rotates and flexes the trunk to the side	• Oblique crunch • Side crunch
Rectus abdominis	Centre of the abdomen	Flexes the spine	• Crunch • Swiss ball crunch • Reverse crunch • Hanging leg raise
Transversus abdominis	Sheathing the abdomen	Supports the abdomen	• All the abdominal exercise performed with a Swiss ball

Note: Exercises in italics indicate those in which the muscles are not the target muscles being developed.

References

♦ Chapter 1 ♦

1. Campbell, W. et al. (1994), 'Increased energy requirements and changes in body composition with resistence training in older adults', *Am. J. Clin Nutr.*, vol. 60, pp. 167–175.
2. Forbes, G. B. (1976), 'The adult decline in lean body mass', *Human Biology*, vol. 48, pp. 161–73.
3. Evans, W. and Rosenberg, I. (1992), *Biomarkers* (New York: Simon & Schuster) p. xx.
4. Hurley B. (1994), 'Does strength training improve health status?', *Strength & Cond. J.*, vol. 16, pp. 7–13.
5. Taafe, D. R. et al. (1997), 'High impact exercise promotes bone gain in well-trained female athletes', *J. Bone Miner. Res.*, vol. 12 (2), pp. 255–60.
6. Menkes, A. et al. (1993), 'Strength training increases regional bone mineral density and bone remodelling in middle-aged and older men', *J. Appl. Physiol.*, vol. 74, pp. 2478–84.
7. Keyes, A. et al. (1973), 'Basal metabolism and age of adult man', *Metabolism*, vol. 22, pp. 579–87.
8. Westcott, W. (1995), *Strength Fitness: Physiological Principles and Training Techniques*, 4th ed. (Dubuque, Iowa: Wm C. Brown Publishers).
9. Stone, M. et al. (1982), 'Physiological effects of a short-term resistence training programme on middle-aged untrained men', *Nat. Strength & Cond. Assoc. J.*, vol. 4, pp. 16–20.
10. Risch, S. et al. (1993), 'Lumbar strengthening in low back pain patients', *Spine*, vol. 18, pp. 232–8.

♦ Chapter 2 ♦

1. Roberts, G. et al. (1992), *Motivation in Sport and Exercise* (Champaign. IL: Human Kinetics).

♦ Chapter 3 ♦

1. Goldberg, A. L. et al. (1975), 'Mechanism of work-induced hypertrophy of skeletal muscle', *Med. Sci. Sports Exerc.*, vol. 7, pp. 248–61.
2. MacDougall, J. D. et al. (1994), 'Muscle fibre number in biceps brachii in bodybuilders and control subjects', *J. Appl. Physiol.*, vol. 57, pp. 1399–1403.
3. Sale, D. G. et al. (1987), 'Voluntary strength and muscle characteristics in untrained men and women and bodybuilders', *J. Appl. Physiol.*, vol. 62, pp. 1786–93.
4. Macdougall, J. D. et al. (1979), 'Mitochondrial volume density in human skeletal muscle following heavy resistance training', *Med. Sci. Sports Exerc.*, vol. 11 (20), pp. 164–6.
5. Macdougall, J. D. et al. (1980), 'Muscle ultrastructure characteristics of elite powerlifters and bodybuilders', *Med. Sci. Sports. Exerc.*, vol. 2, pp. 131.
6. Schmidtbleicher, D. and Haralambie, G.

(1981), 'Changes in contractile proteins of muscle after strength training in man', *Eur. J. Appl. Physiol.*, vol. 46, pp. 221–8.

7. Dons, B. K. et al. (1979), 'The effect of weight lifting exercise related to muscle fibre composition and muscle cross-sectional area in humans', *Eur. J. Appl. Physiol.*, vol. 40, pp. 95–106.

♦ Chapter 4 ♦

1. Raastad, T. et al. (2000), 'Hormonal responses to high- and moderate-intensity strength exercise', *Eur. J. Physiol.*, vol. 82, pp. 121–8.

♦ Chapter 11 ♦

1. Bompa. T. O. and Cornacchia, L. J. (1998), *Serious Strength Training* (Champaign, IL: Human Kinetics).
2. Baechle, T. R. and Earle, R. W. (eds) (2000), *Essentials of Strength Training and Conditioning* (Champaign, IL: Human Kinetics).
3. Fleck, S. J. and Kraemer, W. J. (1997). *Designing Resistance Training Programmes* (Champaign, IL: Human Kinetics).
4. Westcott, W. L. (1986), 'Four key factors in building a strength program', *Schol. Coach.*, vol. 55., pp. 104–5.
5. Hass, C. J., et al. (2000), 'Single v. multiple sets in long-term recreational weightlifters', *Med. Sci. Sports & Exerc.* vol. 32 (I), pp. 235–42.
6. Stowers, T. et al. (1983), 'The short-term effects of three different strength-power training methods', *NSCA J.*, vol. 5 (3), pp. 24–7.
7. Tan, B. (1999), 'Manipulating resistance training program variables to optimise maximum strength in men', *J. Strength Cond. Res.*, vol. 13 (3), pp. 280–304.

8. Baechle, T. R. and Groves, B. R. (1998), *Weight training: Steps to Success* (2nd ed.) (Champaign, IL: Human Kinetics).
9. Herrick, A. R. and Stone, M. H. (1996), 'The effects of periodisation versus progressive resistance exercise on upper and lower body strength in women', *J. Strength Cond. Res.*, vol. 10 (2), pp. 72–6.
10. Garhammer J. and McLaughlin, T. (1980), 'Power output as a function of load variation in Olympic and power lifting', *Abstract J. Biomech.*, vol. 13 (2), p. 198.
11. Hedrick, A. (1995), 'Training for hypertrophy', *Strength Cond.*, vol. 17 (3), pp. 22–9.
12. Bompa. T. O. (1996), *Periodisation of training* (Toronto, Canada: Veritas Publishing Incs.).

♦ Chapter 12 ♦

1. Shrier, I. and Gossal K. (2000), 'Myths and truths of stretching', *Phys. Sportsmed.*, vol. 28.
2. Kokkonen, J. et al. (1998), 'Acute muscle stretching inhibits maximal strength performance', *Res. Quarterly Exerc. Sport*, vol. 69 (4), pp. 411–5.
3. Johansson, P. H. et al. (1999), 'The effects of pre-exercise stretching on muscle soreness, tenderness and force loss following heavy eccentric exercise', *Scand. J. Med. Sci. Sports*, vol. 9 (4), pp. 219–25.
4. Check author & title (2000) *J. Strength Cond. Res.*, vol. 14 (3), pp. 332–7.

♦ Chapter 13 ♦

1. American College of Sports Medicine (1995), *Guidelines for Exercise Testing and Prescription*, 4th ed. (Baltimore: Williams and Wilkins).
2. Wilmore, J. H. and Costill, D. L. (1994), *Physiology of Sport and Exercise* (Champaign, IL: Human Kinetics).

3. Phillips, S. M. (1996), 'Effect of training duration on substrate turnover and oxidation during exercise', *J. Appl. Physiol.*, Vol. 81 (5), pp. 2182–91.

4. Tremblay, A. et al. (1994), 'Impact of exercise intensity on body fatness and skeletal muscle metabolism', *Metabolism*, vol. 43, pp. 814–18.

5. Smith J. and McNaughton L. (1993), 'The effects of intensity of exercise and excess post-exercise oxygen consumption and energy expenditure in moderately trained men and women', *Eur. J. Appl. Physiol.*, vol. 67, pp. 420–5.

6. Kraemer, W. J. et al. (1995), 'Compatibility of high-intensity strength and endurance training on hormonal and skeletal muscle adaptations', *J. Appl. Physiol.*, vol. 78 (3), pp. 976–89.

7. Coyle, E. F. (2000), 'Physical activity as a metabolic stressor', *Am. J. Clin. Nutr.*, vol. 72(2), pp. 512S – 520S.

8. 'Weights or cardio first', *Int. J Sports Med.*, vol. 21, pp. 275–80.

9. Osterberg, K. L. and Melby, C. L. (2000), 'Effect of acute resistance exercise on post-exercise oxygen consumption and resting metabolic rate in young women', *Int. J. Sport Nutr. Exerc. Metab.*, vol. 10(1), pp. 71–81.

♦ Chapter 16 ♦

1. Williams, C. and Devlin J. T. (eds) (1992), *Foods, Nutrition and Performance: an International Scientific Consensus* (London: Chapman & Hall).

2. Hawley, J. and Burke L. (1998), 'The training diet', in *Peak Performance*, Chap. 10 (St Leonards, NSW: Allen & Unwin), pp. 211–32.

3. Leeds A., et al. (2000), *The Glucose Revolution* (London: Hodder & Stoughton), pp. 215–23.

4. Burke, L.M. et al. (1993), 'Muscle glycogen storage after prolonged exercise: effect of glycaemic index of carbohydrate feedings', *J. Appl. Physiol.*, vol. 75, pp. 1019–23.

5. Haff, G. G. et al. (2000), 'The effect of carbohydrate supplementation on glycogenolysis during acute performance of resistance training exercise', *Med. Sci. Sports Exerc.*, Supplement 32 (5), no. 135.

6. Langfort, J. et al. (1997), 'The effect of a low-carbohydrate diet on performance, hormonal and metabolic responses to a 30-s bout of supra-maximal exercise', *Eur. J. Appl. Physiol.*, vol. 76(2), pp. 128–33.

7. Tsintzas, O. K. et al. (1996), 'Influence of carbohydrate supplementation early in exercise on endurance running capacity', *Med. Sci. Sports Exerc.*, vol. 28, pp. 1373–79.

8. Fahey, T. D. et al. (1993), 'The effects of intermittent liquid meal feeding on selected hormones and substrates during intense weight training', *Int. J. Sport Nutr.*, vol. 3, pp. 67–75.

9. Jeukendrup, A. E. et al (1997), 'Carbohydrate-electrolyte feedings improve 1-h time trial cycling performance', *Int. J. Sports Med.*, vol. 18, pp. 125–9.

10. Ivy, J. L. et al. (1988), 'Muscle glycogen syhthesis after exercise: effect of time on carbohydrate ingestion', *J Appl. Physiol.* vol. 64; pp. 1480–5.

11. Baker, S. K. et al. (1994), 'Immediate post-training carbohydrate supplementation improves subsequent performance in trained cyclists', *Sports Med. Training Rehab.*, vol. 5, pp. 131–5.

12. Rasmussen, B. B. et al. (1999), 'Effect of timing of an essential amino acid/carbohydrate supplement on muscle protein metabolism following resistance exercise', presented at Experimental Biology 99, Washington, D.C.

13. Zawadski, K. M. et al. (1992), 'Carbohydrate–protein complex increases the rate of muscle glycogen storage after exercise', *J. Appl. Physiol.*, vol. 72(5), pp. 1854–9.

14. Ready, S. L. et al. (1999) 'The effect of two sports drink formulations on muscle stress

and performance', *Med. Sci. Sports Exerc.* Vol. 31(5), pp. S119.

15. Tarnopolsky, M. A. et al. (1997) 'Post exercise protein–carbohydrate and carbohydrate supplements increase muscle glycogen in males and females', *J. Appl. Physiol.* abstracts, vol. 4, pp. 332A.

16. Chandler, R. M. et al. (1994), 'Dietary supplements affect the anabolic hormones after weight-training exercise', *J. Appl. Physiol.*, vol. 76(2), pp. 834–9.

17. Bloomer, R. J. et al. (2000), 'Alterations in mood following acute post-exercise feeding with variance in macronutrient mix', *Med. Sci. Sports Exerc.*, Supplement, vol. 32 (5), no. 121.

18. Balon, T. W. et al. (1992), 'Effects of carbohydrate loading and weight lifting on muscle girth', *Int. J. Sport Nutr.*, vol. 2, pp. 328–4.

19. Kraemer W. J. et al. (1996) 'Physiological mechanisms of adaptation', *Exerc. Sports Sci. Rev.*, vol. 24, pp. 363–97.

20. Tarnopolsky, M. A. et al. (1992) 'Evaluation of protein requirements for trained strength athletes', *J. Appl. Physiol.*, vol. 73, pp. 1986–95.

21. Lemon, P. W .R. (1998), 'Effects of exercise on dietary protein requirements', *Int. J. Sport Nutr.*, vol. 8, pp. 426–47.

22. Simopoulos, A. P. and Robinson, J. (1998), *The Omega Plan* (New York: HarperCollins).

23. Kremer, J. M. (1996), 'Effects of modulation of inflammatory and immune parameters in patients with rheumatis and inflammatory disease receiving dietary supplements of n-3 and n-6 fatty acids', *Lipids*, vol. 31, pp. S243–7.

24. ACSM (1996), 'Position stand on exercise and fluid replacement', *Med. Sci. Sports Exerc.*, vol. 28, pp. i–vii.

25. Kleiner, S. M. et al. (1994), 'Nutritional status of nationally ranked elite bodybuilders'. *Int. J. Sport Nutr.*, vol. 4, pp. 54–69.

26. Newton, L. E. at al. (1993), 'Changes in psychological state and self-reported diet during various phases of training in competitive bodybuilders', *J. Strength Cond.*

Res., vol. 7(3), pp. 153–8.

27. Telford, R. et al. (1992) 'The effect of 7–8 months of vitamin/mineral supplementation on athletic performance', *Int. J. Sport Nutr.*, vol. 2, pp. 135–53.

28. Singh, A. et al. (1992), 'Chronic multivitamin–mineral supplementation does not enhance physical performance', *Med. Sci. Sport Exerc.*, vol. 24, pp. 726–32.

29. Goldfarb A. H. (1999), 'Nutritional antioxidants as therapeutic and preventative modalities in exercise-induced muscle damage', *Can. J. Appl. Physiol.*, vol. 24(3), pp. 249–66.

30. Krotkiewski, M. et al (1994), 'Prevention of muscle soreness by pre-treatment with antioxidants', *Scand. J. Med. Sci. Sports*, vol. 4, pp. 191–9.

31. Hultman, E. et al. (1996), 'Muscle creatine loading in man', *J. Appl. Physiol.*, vol. 81, pp. 232–9.

32. Volek, J. S. and Kraemer, W. J. (1996), 'Creatine supplementation: its effect on human muscular performance and body composition', *J. Strength Cond. Res.* vol. 10(3), pp. 200–10.

33. Volek J. S. et al. (1996), 'Creatine supplementation enhances muscular performance during high intensity resistance exercise', *J. Amer. Diet. Assoc.*, vol. 97, pp. 765–70.

34. Volek, J. S. et al. (1999), 'Performance and muscle fibre adaptations to creatine supplementation and heavy resistance training', *Med. Sci. Sports Exerc.*, vol. 31(8), pp. 1147–56.

35. Kreider R. et al. (1996), 'Effects of ingesting supplements designed to promote lean tissue accretion on body composition during resistance training', *Int. J. Sport Nutr.*, vol. 63, pp. 234–46.

36. Harris, R. (1998), 'Ergogenics 1', *Peak Performance*, vol. 112 (Dec.), pp. 2–6.

37. Stout, J. et al. (1997), 'The effects of a supplement designed to augment creatine uptake on exercise performance and fat-free mass in football players', *Med. Sci. Sports. Exerc.*, vol. 29(5), pp. S251.

38. Robinson, T. M. et al. (2000), 'Dietary creatine supplementation does not affect some haematological indices, or indices of muscle damage and hepatic and renal function', *Brit. J. Sports. Med.*, vol. 34(9), pp. 284–8.
39. Nissan, S. et al. (1996), ' Effect of leucine metabolite HMB on muscle metabolism during resistance exercise training', *J. Appl. Physiol.*, vol. 81, pp. 2095–104.
40. Nissen, S. L. et al. (1997), 'Effect of feeding HMB on body composition and strength in women', *FASEB J.*, vol. 11, A150.
41. Kreider, R. B. (1999), 'Dietary supplements and the promotion of muscle growth with resistance exercise', *Sports Med.*, vol. 27(2), pp. 97–109.
42. Castell, L. M. and Newsholme, E. A. (1997), 'The effects of oral glutamine supplementation on athletes after prolonged exhaustive exercise', *Nutrition*, vol. 13(7), pp. 738–42.
43. Broeder, C. E. et al. (2000), 'The Andro Project: Physiological and hormonal influences of androstenedione supplementation in men 35 to 65 years old participating in a high-intensity resistance training program', *Arch. Int. Med.*, vol. 160(20), pp. 3093–104.
44. Leder, B. Z. et al. (2000), 'Oral androstenedione administration and serum testosterone concentrations in young men', *J.A.M.A*, vol. 283(6), pp. 779–82.
45. Catlin, D. H. et al. (2000), 'Trace contamination of over the counter androstenedione and positive urine test results for a nandrolone metabolite', *J.A.M.A.*, vol. 284(20), pp. 2618–21.
46. Thom, E. (1997), 'Efficacy and tolerability of Tonalin CLA on body composition in humans', Medstat Research Ltd, presented at the 19997 Federation for Applied Science and Experimental Biology (FASEB) national meeting in New Orleans.
47. Ferreira, M. et al. (1998), 'Effects of CLA supplementation during resistance training on body composition and strength', *J. Strength Cond. Res.*, vol. 11(4), pp. 280.
48. Lowery, L.M. et al. (1998), 'Conjugated linoleic acid enhances muscle size and strength gains in novice bodybuilders', *Med. Sci. Sports Exerc.*, vol. 30(5), pp. S182.
49. Sebedio, J. L. et al. (1999), 'Recent advances in CLA research', *Curr. Opin. Clin. Nutr. Metab. Care*, vol. 2(6), pp. 499–506.
50. Spriet, L. (1995), 'Caffeine and performance', *Int. J. Sport Nutr.*, vol. 5, pp. S84–S99.
51. Anderson, M. E. et al. (2000), 'Improved 2000-meter rowing performance in competitive oarswomen after caffeine ingestion.', *Int. J. Sport Nutr. Exerc. Metab.*, vol. 10, pp. 464–75.

♦ Chapter 17 ♦

1. Gatorade Sports Science Institute (1995), 'Roundtable on methods of weight gain in athletes', *Sports Science Exchange*, vol. 6(3), pp. 1–4.
2. Williams, M. H. (1999), *Nutrition for Health, Fitness and Sport*, 5th ed. (New York: McGraw-Hill).

♦ Chapter 18 ♦

1. Williams, M. H. (1992), *Nutrition for Fitness and Sport* (Dubuque, IO: William C. Brown).
2. Gatorade Sports Science Exchange Roundtable (1998), 'Methods and strategies for weight loss in athletes', *Sports Science Exchange*, vol. 9(1), pp. 1–5.
3. Friedl, K. E. et al. (1994), 'Lower limit of body fat in healthy active men', *J. Appl. Physiol.*, vol. 77, pp. 933–40.
4. Strauss, R. H. et al. (1993), 'Decreased testosterone and libido with severe weight loss', *Phys. Sportsmed.*, vol. 21(12), pp. 64–71.
5. Walberg-Rankin, J. (1995), 'A review of nutritional practices and needs of bodybuilders', *J Strength Cond. Res.*, vol. 9(2), pp.116–24.

Recommended Reading

Bompa. T. O. & Cornacchia, L. J. (1998), *Serious Strength Training* (Champaign, IL: Human Kinetics)

Baechle, T. R. & Earle, R. W. (eds) (2000), *Essentials of Strength Training and Conditioning* (Champaign, IL: Human Kinetics)

Fleck, S. J. & Kraemer, W .J. (1997), *Designing Resistance Training Programmes* (Champaign, IL: Human Kinetics)

Baechle, T. R. & B. R. Groves (1998), *Weight Training – 2nd ed: Steps to Success* (Champaign, IL: Human Kinetics)

Wilmore, J. H. and Costill, D. L. (1994), *Physiology of Sport and Exercise* (Champaign, IL: Human Kinetics)

McArdle, W. D., Katch, F. I. and Katch, V. L. (1986), *Exercise Physiology* (Led & Febiger)

Glossary of Key Terms

Aerobic In the presence of oxygen.

Actin A muscle protein that acts with myosin to produce muscular activity.

Agonist (prime mover) A muscle that is primarily responsible for bringing about a movement.

Alpha-linolenic acid An essential fatty acid, belonging to the omega-3 series.

Anabolic The building of body tissue.

Anaerobic In the absence of oxygen.

Antagonist The muscle that acts in opposition to the agonist, opposing the movement.

Atrophy The gradual wasting of a muscle.

Calorie A unit of energy measurement, defined as the amount of heat required to increase the temperature of 1 g of water by 1°C. The common unit used in food labelling is known as a kilocalorie (kcal) and has the value of 1000 calories.

Cardiovascular exercise ('cardio') Exercise that improves the efficiency of the cardiovascular (heart, blood and blood vessels) system.

Catabolic The breaking down of body tissue.

Compound or multi-joint exercise Involves one or more large muscle groups and works across two or more main joints.

Concentric The shortening of a muscle during contraction.

Descending (drop) sets A training method that involves performing repetitions to muscle failure followed immediately by further repetitions using a lighter weight until muscle failure is reached again.

Eccentric The lengthening of a muscle under controlled tension.

Eccentric (negative) training Training that involves eccentric action.

Endurance The ability to resist fatigue.

Fast-twitch fibre A type of muscle fibre with a low aerobic capacity and high anaerobic capacity; best suited to speed and power activities.

Forced, or **assisted rep training** A method of training that allows you to train past the point of muscular failure; a spotter provides assistance for the last 1 or 2 repetitions of a set.

Hypertrophy An increase in muscle size due to increased cell size.

Interval training Repeated brief high-intensity work interspersed with short periods of recovery.

Isolation or single-joint exercise Involves smaller groups of muscles and only one main joint.

Isometric A contraction in which tension develops but there is no change in muscle length.

Ligament A strong band of fibrous tissue that connects bones to other bones.

Linoleic acid An essential fatty acid, belonging to the omega-6 series.

Macrocycle A period of training including several mesocycles, usually one season in duration.

Mesocycle A period of training usually 2–6 weeks long.

Microcycle Period of training, usually one week.

Motor unit   The motor nerve and the group of muscles it innervates.

Muscle fibre   An individual muscle cell.

Muscle spindles   A sensory receptor in the muscle that senses how much the muscle is stretched.

Muscular failure   An inability of the muscle to complete another repetition.

Myosin   A muscle protein that acts together with actin to produce muscular contraction.

One-repetition maximum   The maximum weight that can be lifted for one repetition.

Overload   A training load that challenges the body's current level of fitness (e.g. strength) and has the scope to bring about improvements in fitness (e.g. strength).

Periodisation (training cycles)   A process of structuring training into periods.

Power   The ability to produce both force and speed.

Pre-exhaustion training   A method of training that involves performing an isolation exercise prior to the compound exercise to pre-exhaust the target muscle.

Prime mover (agonist)   A muscle that is primarily responsible for bringing about a movement.

Progression   A gradual increase of work load over a period of time.

Rating of perceived exertion   A subjective assessment of hard you are working.

Repetition   One complete movement from the starting position to a position of maximum contraction and back to the starting position.

Set   A group of repetitions.

Slow-twitch muscle   A type of muscle fibre with a high aerobic capacity, low anaerobic capacity; best suited to endurance activities.

Strength   The ability of a muscle to produce force.

Supersets   Two or more sets of different exercises performed consecutively with no rest period.

Synergist   A muscle that assists the agonists (prime movers) in bringing about a movement.

Tendons   Bundles of collagen fibres that connect muscle to bone.

Toning   A non-technical term that refers to a relative increase in strength, producing a firmer appearance and feel in the relaxed state.

Training intensity   The quantitative element of training such as speed, strength or power.

Training volume   The number of sets multiplied by the number of repetitions.

VO$_2$max (or maximum aerobic capacity)   The maximum capacity for oxygen consumption by the body during maximal exertion.

Index